SUN SIGNS

JANE STRUTHERS

Magpie Books, London

To my godchildren, Beth Cameron, Maggie Genthner, Holly Granville-Edge, Isabella Struthers, Jack Struthers and Misty Struthers, with much love

Constable & Robinson Ltd
3 The Lanchesters
162 Fulham Palace Road
London W6 9ER

This edition published by Magpie Books,
an imprint of Constable & Robinson Ltd 2005

A copy of the British Library Cataloguing in Publication Data
is available from the British Library

ISBN 1 84529 333 9

Printed and bound in the European Union

3 5 7 9 10 8 6 4 2

Contents

Each sign is divided into the following sections:
- The [sign] Adult
- The [sign] Child
- Health
- Money
- Career
- Love and Friendships
- Family Relationships
- Creativity and Potential
- Holidays
- Home
- Clothes and Image
- Famous Members of the Sign
- Top Ten Characteristics
- Quick Quiz

Acknowledgements

Many people helped in the writing of this book, whether they assisted in its actual production or they inspired me when I was writing about their Sun sign. I'd like to thank everyone at Constable Robinson and Magpie Books who helped to publish this book, but especially Nova Jayne Heath who first suggested it, Hugh Barker and Duncan Proudfoot. And love and thanks as ever to Chelsey Fox and Bill Martin.

Aries

21 March–20 April

The Aries Adult

Everyone needs at least one Arien in their lives. That's because Ariens are so enthusiastic and lively. They consider life to be one long adventure, and they're always looking for the next thrill. And if you'll go along with them for the ride, so much the better because you'll both enjoy the company.

The most important thing to know about Aries is that it's the first sign of the zodiac. This explains a lot about Ariens! They spend their lives wanting to be first in everything they do, which makes them fiercely competitive. They aren't interested in being a sporting runner-up because they can't see the point of that. It's first or nothing, for an Arien. Forget that old saying about it not being the winning that's important but the taking part. As far as Ariens are concerned, the winning is everything. This gives them a very determined streak, because they aren't going to give up without a fight. If you combine this determination to be first with the Fire element to which Ariens belong, you get a very feisty and spirited sign indeed.

So Ariens like to accomplish things, especially if they're breaking the mould in some way or blazing a trail that everyone else can follow. But they won't wear themselves out flogging a dead horse, so they can give up quite quickly if they don't succeed at the first or second attempt. Ariens are not known for their sticking power, unlike Taureans who will plod away for years if necessary before they achieve their goals. Ariens haven't got time for all that dogged determination. They want instant results so they can move on to the next project. Life's too short to hang around hoping that they'll finally get something right. As a result, catching up on an Arien's news can be quite bewildering, as they repeatedly tell you that they gave up on this or that venture long ago and are now busily working on something else. And you know that they'll probably have abandoned that one as well by the time you see them again.

This Arien desire for quick results inevitably leads us on to the famous Arien temper. Ariens are hot-blooded creatures who aren't renowned for holding back their feelings. If they're angry, they're going to let you know all about it. Probably at 120 decibels. After all, they are ruled by Mars, the god of war. In fact, Arien temper tantrums are quite something to behold, especially if you belong to a more muted and restrained sign. Ariens of all ages think nothing of yelling at the tops of their voices when they're angry about something, and some even stamp their feet or throw the china around. But the good thing about all this is that they get rid of their anger very quickly and then they return to their normal, cheerful selves. This is very different from the smouldering anger of Scorpios, which is often followed by the sulks, or the slow-burning fuse of Taureans, who can be quite terrifying when they finally let rip. So the plaster may still be falling from the ceiling after an Arien has calmed down, but at least they are smiling again. And you may even get up the courage to crawl out from behind the sofa after a while, which will be a relief. Ariens who can't let off steam in this way need some other physical or emotional outlet, otherwise all that smothered anger won't do them any good at all.

One of the most endearing Arien qualities is their trusting, affectionate natures. Unfortunately, they can be terrible judges of character. They imagine that everyone they meet is as nice as they are themselves, which means they leave themselves wide open to being manipulated, exploited, bullied and hurt. And they rarely learn from their mistakes, either, so they're quite capable of extricating themselves from one disastrous relationship and going straight into another one. The phrase 'jumping out of the frying pan into the fire' must have been invented for Ariens because it's something they're always doing.

Ariens, being Fire signs, have no hang-ups about being demonstrative and showing their feelings. If they love you, they want to show it, whether that involves whisking you off to bed for some passionate, lusty Arien sex or giving you a rib-cracking bear hug. They're also extremely generous, not only with their affections but also with their money. They simply don't understand people who are stingy, whether emotionally or financially, because it's an attitude that's light years away from their own.

Mind you, there are times when Ariens can be extremely ungenerous, especially when it comes to getting their own way. Being the first sign of the zodiac means they really do want their own preferences and needs to be considered above everyone else's, and they'll come up with all sorts of ruses to make sure this happens. Then, when their partners or friends complain about being expected to go with the Arien to a football match instead of to the cinema, the Arien becomes bewildered and hurt. This may be partly play-acting but it's also partly genuine, because the Arien really can't understand why anyone would want to go to the cinema instead of watching the Arien's favourite football team in action. This Arien tendency of wanting their own needs to take preference over everyone else's can be a problem if they don't learn to be more adaptable.

The Arien's need to be first means that members of this sign are born pioneers. Some of the great inventors have been Ariens, including Joseph Lister who discovered antiseptics, Sir William

Harvey who discovered the circulation of the blood, Samuel Hannemann who developed homeopathy and James Watson who was one of the men who discovered DNA. They love to be in the vanguard of things and, like Geminis, enjoy owning the latest gadgets and any other examples of technical wizardry. They'll soon get bored with them, of course, but by then there will probably be a new electronic toy on the market that they can buy. And so it goes on. Canny Ariens will sell off their old equipment. Sentimental ones will shove it all in the attic, discover it twenty years later and be able to sell it to a museum.

The Aries Child

It's easy to spot an Aries child. This will be the small bundle of energy running around in several directions at once, falling over, getting up again, laughing, crying, hitting their sister over the head just for the fun of it, chasing the dog and then asking their mother for an ice cream in tones that suggest butter wouldn't melt in their mouth.

Aries children have so much energy that you'd be able to power an entire city if you could connect five of them to the National Grid. Although you'd have to catch them first. They're on the go from the minute they get up in the morning to when they've finally been persuaded to go to bed at night. They need to keep active and entertained, otherwise they start to get bored, which is when the trouble starts. When tedium sets in they can become boisterous, loud, aggressive, argumentative and a complete handful. They'll pick fights just for the sake of having something to do, tunnel through your neighbour's prized vegetable patch while trying to find the centre of the earth or dress up the cat in the baby's clothes and then deny all knowledge of why Tiddles is sitting on the top branch of the apple tree in a bonnet and refusing to come down.

Arien boys are classic naughty boys, and Arien girls are typical tomboys. They often have cuts and scratches on all the exposed parts of their bodies because they lead such active lives, and their clothes are permanently covered in grass stains and smears of mud. Ideally, Arien children should live in the countryside, where they can romp about to their hearts' content, fording streams and climbing trees. If they live in towns, they need plenty of open spaces in which to play, preferably without a concerned parent looking on anxiously. Arien children aren't happy if they're confined indoors for long stretches at a time. It simply doesn't suit them. If they are restricted in this way, they need very energetic and physical hobbies, such as judo, football or running.

You can expect plenty of displays of that famous Arien temper from the children of this sign. Their moods change quickly like the weather, from squalls to showers to storms and back again. They haven't yet learnt to hide or moderate their feelings, so these tumble out in a great rush of emotion.

Speaking of emotion, Arien children are wonderfully cuddly and affectionate. As babies, they will happily blow bubbles, wave their podgy arms about and give you beaming, gummy smiles. They can melt grandparents' hearts at fifty paces. They look sweet in little knitted hats and then go red in the face with rage when their food is late in arriving or their nappies need changing. The moment their needs have been satisfied, they're happy again. But they do need a lot of love. It makes them feel secure and special, and it teaches them to be equally loving and demonstrative in return.

The Arien pioneering streak means that Arien babies learn to crawl and then walk as soon as they can possibly manage it. They aren't going to lie around on their backs when there's a whole world out there waiting to be explored! But as soon as they've discovered they can get around under their own steam, even if it's on their hands and legs, everyone should watch out. The Arien need for adventure means that an Arien toddler will have to be supervised throughout their waking hours. These are the children who will shove anything into their mouths, from lumps of coal to the contents of your whisky bottle. They'll stick knitting needles into electrical sockets and jam their fingers in the kitchen cabinets. You certainly need a massive first aid kit for a small Arien because there will inevitably be lots of falls and tumbles. When I was growing up, my Arien brother was always in the wars. He fell in a rose bush on one occasion, nearly bit his tongue in half going down a slide, ate a bar of soap which made him foam at the mouth, and conducted a scientific experiment to find out if my mother was telling the truth when she said that milk combined with orange juice would make him sick. It did. His most celebrated exploit was giving my mother a karate chop on the backs of her knees while she was carrying a loaded tea tray. She dropped the lot but he managed to get away with it because he'd made the rest of the family laugh.

Arien children benefit from having siblings around. Brothers and sisters rarely stand for any nonsense, so they'll teach their little Arien that they can't always have their own way. This is important because it will make them less selfish and self-centred, and therefore much more popular with their friends. Arien children aren't very good at sharing their toys, either, so they need to be encouraged to do this as well in the hope that they'll gradually become less territorial.

The one thing they can't bear, and which they continue to hate throughout their lives, is being ridiculed and criticized. They simply can't cope, and won't understand why someone is being so horrible to them. Despite that boisterous and exuberant exterior, the Aries child needs to be handled with great care and consideration.

Health

It's important for every sign to look after their health, but some are better at it than others. Ariens, it must be said, aren't very bothered about their health. They mostly believe that, provided they can still stand up without having to hang on to the furniture, they're doing OK. This means there's little danger of them turning into hypochondriacs, as some Virgos are prone to do, but it also means they can overlook ailments that really ought to be treated.

Having said that, Ariens are notoriously bad patients when something does go wrong. If they've got to lie in bed, they want the experience to be as satisfying as possible so they'll expect everyone else to run up and down stairs looking after them. They can also get quite tetchy, partly as a result of enforced inactivity and partly because they want you to bring them their soup or cup of tea right this minute. Don't ever hit on the bright idea of giving your ailing Arien a stick to thump or a bell to ring so they can summon you when necessary. They'll either get RSI from repeatedly ringing the bell or they'll bash a hole in the ceiling with the stick because you haven't responded to their summons quickly enough.

Each sign of the zodiac rules a particular part of the body, and in Aries' case it's the head. This means that some Ariens have a tendency to get headaches and possibly even migraines whenever they become tense or het up. They can also suffer from sinus problems or hayfever, as well as earaches and eyestrain. What's more, they have a tendency to bash or bump their heads more often than other signs, especially when they're young.

Some Ariens can have problems with their kidneys, such as kidney stones or infections. That's because the kidneys are the area of the body ruled by Aries' opposite sign of Libra, so they are connected to them by the law of opposites. Equally, you'll find some Librans who get lots of headaches. They need to keep their systems flushed through with plenty of liquids, preferably fresh water. However, many Ariens enjoy alcoholic liquids much more, which can add to the problem. They particularly enjoy rather unusual drinks, such as vodkas with strange things such as chillies in the bottles, although they're equally enthusiastic about spirits, wines and beers. Almost anything, in fact!

Most Arien health problems are caused by stress and tension, so it's very important for Ariens to keep active as much as possible. Aries is ruled by Mars, the planet of war and action, which means that Ariens are not cut out to be couch potatoes. They need to keep on the go whenever they can, otherwise they get rather agitated, nervy and, dare I say it, irritable. And all these personality traits are made worse when an Arien is confined to one place for too long, whether by circumstance or illness. Ideally, every Arien should go on a brisk walk every day, take off on a bike ride or get their money's worth out of all the equipment in their local gym. However, whatever they choose to do they should try not to go at it hammer and tongs. Ariens set themselves high goals and then expect to achieve them in no time at all, so it's not unusual for an Arien to go from being virtually sedentary to wearing themselves out by taking too much exercise too soon. They're at risk of getting muscle strains, aching joints and blisters, so they need to build up their exercise routine gradually. It's no surprise that Roger Banister, the first man to run the four-minute mile, was an Arien. What else could he be?

A canny Arien will take a portable first-aid kit with them on their exercise trips, because they belong to a remarkably accident-prone sign. They often get cuts and scalds because they're distracted when handling sharp or hot implements, especially if they're secretly fuming about something. It doesn't help that they're usually in too much of a hurry to do things safely. They also collect an above-average number of scars over the years.

Usually, Ariens are slim and wiry when young, but they have an unfortunate tendency to pile on the pounds as they get older. Whether it's because their metabolisms slow down slightly or their lives become more sedentary for some reason, it's another compelling reason why they need to keep fit and active for as long as possible.

Money

Money may be the be-all and end-all for some signs of the zodiac but that isn't true for Ariens. They need money, of course, in order to survive, but they don't give it as much importance as some of the other signs. Having said that, Ariens truly believe that money is energy, and they can be very enterprising about getting their hands on it. And they certainly enjoy spending it, too.

Don't get the idea that this is a sign that believes in giving away every last penny to charity. Oh, no. Ariens will gladly hand over a generous amount of cash to a good cause, sometimes even parting with more money than they can comfortably afford, but they always know when to stop and put their wallets back in their pockets. They aren't fools, and they usually have some expensive habits to support, such as a love of good food and wine or a thirsty sports car. Most Ariens also have a hobby that can swallow up lots of cash, especially if it's connected with speed and transport, such as a motorbike or taking flying lessons.

Despite all these drains on their purses, Ariens can be extremely generous. They take genuine delight in pleasing their friends and relatives, whether that means picking up the bill for delicious meals in their favourite restaurants, buying them special treats or spending money on other things that will make them happy. They'll devote a lot of time to picking out exactly the right gift for someone, and often spend more money than is strictly necessary on buying Christmas and birthday presents.

Ariens are also very impetuous when it comes to parting with their hard-earned money. An Arien is the sort of person who goes out for a pint of milk and comes back with a new motorbike or having booked an expensive holiday. They love doing things on the spur of the moment, even if they're slightly reckless. Who cares if they can't really afford that new bike or holiday? They'll find a way to pay for it somehow. They love impulse buys because they're so exciting. As a result, many Ariens have credit card bills that would make a careful Capricorn keel over in a dead faint (which is one of the reasons why there can be a lot of friction between these two signs).

'Enterprise' is an Arien's middle name, and many of them come up with some very clever ways to make money. They enjoy the cut and thrust of competing against others and they aren't afraid to work hard for what they want. Sometimes, Ariens find more exciting ways to accumulate money, such as stealing it. Clyde Barrow, of Bonnie and Clyde fame, and Butch Cassidy, of Butch Cassidy and the Sundance Kid fame, are two examples of Ariens who decided to help themselves to money rather than wait for it to come to them. However, most Ariens are too honest to consider such chicanery.

Saving money for a rainy day isn't really a concept that appeals to Ariens. They're usually far too busy living for today to worry about tomorrow, so generally speaking they need a partner or friend who can help them to cultivate some financial prudence. They might enjoy playing the stock market, but they won't be very keen on buying shares that will take years to develop in value. Ariens are looking for instant results, and that goes for their savings, too.

'Budget' isn't a word in most Arien's vocabularies. They simply don't understand the concept, because it strikes them as being so boring and, well, sensible. If they've got the money they've got it, and if they haven't they can always borrow it. Life's too short to worry about such things.

Career

You can't keep a good Arien down. Aries is a Cardinal sign, which means it's a sign that's always looking for results. The Cardinal signs are great achievers, and in Aries' case this is emphasized because it's the first sign of the zodiac. So Ariens always want to come first, and they want to achieve more things than anyone else. Competitive? You bet! An Arien is never going to sit around watching other people stealing a march on them.

Ariens enjoy making a name for themselves because it's a good opportunity to get involved in some cut and thrust jockeying for position. They like to be leaders, not followers, and can be very successful innovators. They also like to be pioneers, and love the idea of being the first person to do something. There are plenty of examples of this, too. For instance, the great Victorian engineer, Isambard Kingdom Brunel, was an Arien, as was Wilbur Wright, who with his brother was one of aviation's pioneers. This may be the sign of the Ram but it's certainly not the sign of the sheep, and no Arien worth his salt will be content to meekly follow in other people's footsteps.

When it comes to choosing a suitable career, an Arien needs something that will offer them plenty of challenges and versatility. They're easily bored and quickly lose interest in things, so they've got to have a job that is always changing and is rarely predictable. And it's even better if it involves lots of short journeys and changes of scene. A few minor battles and skirmishes won't go amiss, either, because they help to keep the Arien amused. However, most Ariens are much better at starting projects than they are at finishing them, so ideally they need a back-up team to tidy up all the loose ends they leaves trailing along in their wake.

Typical Arien careers involve anything connected with engineering, mining or metalwork. Ariens love driving fast cars, so being a racing driver is a secret dream of many of them. It certainly worked for Arien Ayrton Senna. They might enjoy working in the car industry, whether as a designer, a member of the sales team or a mechanic, or they might prefer to work with motorbikes. Two Ariens whose names are synonymous with the cars they designed are Sir Henry Royce and W. P. Chrysler. Alternatively, an Arien might consider becoming a driving instructor, although they probably won't be known for their patience! Many Ariens are very sporty, so might be good enough to have a career as an athlete, footballer or rugby-player. Other sports, such as martial arts or boxing, would also suit many Ariens, although they should make sure they take care of their delicate heads.

Another possibility for Ariens is to enter politics. They adore the cut and thrust of it, the sense of competition that's stirred up by running for election and the belief that they're doing something to make the world a better place. Of course, one person's brilliant politician is another's complete scoundrel, so here's a selection of a few Arien politicians so you can make up your own mind about them: John Major, Helmut Kohl, Al Gore, Colin Powell, Kim Il-Sung, Thomas Jefferson, François 'Papa Doc' Duvalier and Nikita Kruschev.

Whatever an Arien does for a living, it's essential that it captures their interest and enthusiasm. Ideally, it should also keep them active. Bored or sedentary Ariens are troubled Ariens, because they start to get agitated and irritable, and they hate feeling that they're stuck in a rut. If they have dreary, nine-to-five jobs, they need to release all that pent-up adrenalin in their spare time, otherwise it will soon turn to aggression and frustration.

Ariens are great at being part of a team, provided that their input is always valued and they get the chance to call the shots every now and then. They're endearing colleagues because they take an interest in everyone else's lives, without being nosy, and they're always the first one to buy a round of drinks in the pub or to suggest everyone goes out for a meal to cheer themselves up. They can also be pretty hot stuff at office parties, too, which can land them in deep trouble if they aren't careful.

Love and Friendships

Before we go any further, here's some interesting information. Giovanni Casanova, the celebrated eighteenth-century lover, was – yes, you've guessed it, an Arien. In typical Aries style, he loved the thrill of the chase, and managed to make it his life's work. And Hugh Hefner, the founder of Playboy, is also an Arien.

Not every Arien has the energy or inclination to be another Casanova, of course, but this is still a very sexy sign. In astrology, Mars rules sex, among other things, and it just happens to be the planetary ruler of Aries. This means that many Ariens are highly-sexed and enjoy proving it to willing volunteers. They can also be quite promiscuous, given the chance, especially when young, and some of them adore adding to the notches already on their bedposts.

However, this isn't the end of the story by any means because Ariens have the potential to be extremely faithful and loving. When you meet an Arien who's sleeping around, they're usually doing it because deep down they are trying to find the love of their life. Ariens have a wonderfully romantic and idealistic streak, which means they never give up on the idea of finding true love, even if they are continuously disappointed. They'll simply keep moving on from one romance to the next, convinced that one day they'll find their very own Mr or Ms Right. When they do, it's got to be a partner who will keep them on their toes in order to keep them interested. The last thing they want is a boring, stuck-in-a-rut relationship that's lost all its sparkle and zest. That's when they'll start to stray, purely to keep life interesting and to boost their confidence again.

Even if they're full of bravado on the outside, Ariens are easily hurt. They have a rather naïve and innocent quality that makes them vulnerable to people who want to take advantage of them or who will end up breaking their hearts. Their friends may see it coming and warn them, but will they listen? No! They have to find out for themselves, and the shock of having their hearts broken leaves them bewildered and dejected. Ariens always take people at face value, believing that what they see is what they get, so they're sometimes taken for a ride by people who turn out to be very different from the image they present to the world. Sadly, Ariens can find it very difficult to learn from their mistakes, so are quite likely to repeat them all over again with the next person who comes along. That's because Ariens are always ready to think the best of people, and to give them the benefit of the doubt. And they never lose their idealism, which is one of their most charming characteristics. Like one of those rubber children's toys, an Arien will always bounce back after a hard knock.

When it comes to friendship, Ariens have got it taped. They're warm, affectionate and enthusiastic, and they truly love their friends. In return, their friends adore them, because they're so lively and such good fun to be around.

However, there is a big snag in all this and that's the Arien tendency to be self-centred. This is the first sign of the zodiac, don't forget, and Ariens naturally expect to come first. It's literally part of their birthright. Which means they can be rather selfish partners or friends unless their birth charts are balanced by planets in much more selfless signs. For instance, they may always want to call the shots, rather than let their partner have a say in making decisions. When they go out for a meal it might always be to the Arien's choice of restaurant, so everyone else has to like it or lump it. When this happens, the Arien needs to be told some gentle home truths, because they're usually horrified to hear how they've been behaving and are keen to make amends. Although how long this change of heart lasts is another matter!

Family Relationships

Aries isn't the most family-minded sign of the zodiac but, even so, Ariens set a lot of store by their family relationships. Mind you, they aren't the most patient sign of the zodiac either (far from it, in fact), so they won't want to spare much time for any members of the family that they aren't very keen on. They can even be surprisingly sharp-tongued about them, and if possible will give them little more than a passing hallo at family gatherings. But if you're related to an Arien and they like you, then you're laughing. Probably literally, actually, as Ariens can be very funny and enjoy playing the fool.

Ariens love being around children but they aren't so keen on newborn babies. That's because babies don't do much except sleep, eat and make a horrible mess. Ariens get much more interested in children when they start to walk and talk, because by then they've developed personalities of their own. Besides, the Arien in question can then start playing with the child's toys, especially if they happen to be train sets or toy cars. Sometimes you'll find the child looking fed up in the corner while the Arien crawls around on the floor, making zooming noises as the toy cars rush back and forth across the carpet or Thomas the Tank Engine crashes into the sofa. Pow, smash, bang! Will the child get a look-in? No, unless they happen to be an Arien as well, in which case there will probably be a lot of competitive grabbing of toys and cries of 'It's not fair! It's my turn!' from the adult Arien, countered by hair-pulling and kicking from the Arien child. Although it could just as easily be the other way round. Better put away any fragile ornaments if this is taking place in your house. It's so easy (and so irritating) to be wise after the event, when all your precious china ornaments are lying smashed in the hearth because the Ariens got carried away.

As you will have realized by now, adult Ariens are still children at heart, which makes them great parents because they understand how children feel and behave. They are also wonderfully affectionate with their children, finding nothing embarrassing in telling them how much they're loved. As a result, their children feel emotionally secure from the cradle onwards. However, if the Aries parent has a very volatile personality and is always losing their temper, this can be rather alarming for more sensitive children, even if the outbursts are over quickly.

Arien parents believe in educating their children, but they like to do it in fun, interesting ways. For instance, a family day out might involve visiting a small farm or going to a paint-your-own-pottery place, so the children can be active while learning something at the same time. What's more, it won't matter if the children get completely covered in cow pats, fall in puddles or decorate themselves with the pottery paints, because their Arien parent will simply laugh, clean them up and carry on as if nothing had happened. If they're clever, they will probably have a change of the child's clothes in the car ready for exactly that sort of eventuality. If the family goes to a museum, the children will be encouraged to try every exhibit possible, from making their hair stand on end with static electricity to standing in front of a blue screen and pretending to be Superman saving the citizens of Metropolis. Their Arien parent will probably join in, and then there will be competitions to see who can make the loudest (or rudest) noises or who gets the most right answers in the museum quiz. There's never a dull moment when an Aries is around.

Creativity and Potential
Ariens have a tremendous amount to offer the world and they need as many opportunities to express their potential as possible. This isn't a sign that can be content with one triumph

followed by a life spent doing nothing. Ariens are always looking for new challenges, and no sooner have they got one project under their belt than they're looking around for the next thing to tackle. They certainly don't want to rest on their laurels, and they also hate the thought of becoming complacent or lazy.

Ariens have an enormous capacity for hard work, and will happily slog away all night on something if that's what's needed to get it done in time. However, they won't be pleased if all their efforts go unnoticed by everyone else, because then they'll feel unappreciated and overlooked.

To make the most of their potential, Ariens need to tackle activities that fire their enthusiasm and get their adrenalin pumping. And if some sort of competition is involved, then so much the better, even if they're only competing with themselves. Many Ariens excel at DIY projects, and they adore the thought of wielding a sledgehammer to knock down walls or ripping down flimsy shelving with their bare hands. Such activities are fantastic outlets for their natural aggression and boundless energy. But they need to keep a first-aid kit standing by for the cuts and bruises that will inevitably follow.

Any sporty activity is also good for Ariens, because it's another way for them to release any pent-up anger. Ariens love speed, so will get a real thrill out of dashing round an athletics track or beating their partner hollow at squash. They might even find that they're really good at it, so it becomes an important and rewarding part of their lives. Even if they don't have the time or aptitude for such things, they still need to keep active. Ambling from the kitchen table to the sofa and back again is not the life for any Arien who is fit and healthy. Riding a mountain bike to work and back is a good option, as it will help to keep their weight down while also giving them a burst of speed. And they'll love being the first to get away at the traffic lights.

Other spare-time activities that would suit Ariens include bungee-jumping, which offers them a much-needed taste of danger, hang-gliding and rock climbing. Anything, in fact, that allows them to get out into the great outdoors and do something daring. Something else that would appeal is breaking records, and I don't mean the sort made from vinyl. There are all sorts of world records waiting to be broken, from the daft to the serious, so there's bound to be something that might appeal to the Arien. Or they might enjoy working hard to achieve their personal best in a favourite sport, such as football, athletics or golf.

And, of course, there is always the prospect of inventing something. The Arien may not be able to become an inventor by profession, but they might enjoy working quietly on an invention in their spare time, even if it's something very simple and they're the only one who'll ever know about it.

Ariens love doing things that are big and bold, so they might enjoy slapping great blobs of paint on to huge canvases. They won't have much patience with anything on a miniature scale, though, so should forget all about painting delicate water-colours or getting entire landscapes on to the back of postage stamps. Vincent van Gogh was an Arien who demonstrated a typical love for fiery colours.

If an Arien wants to test out their musical abilities they'll want to make a dramatic impact at the same time. If they fancy learning to sing, they'll be more interested in belting out songs at the top of their voice than in quietly warbling something gently melodic. Aretha Franklin, Billie Holiday, Diana Ross, Celine Dion and Elton John are all typically Arien singers, so the Arien would be following in some excellent footsteps.

Holidays
In an ideal world, an Arien would never visit the same holiday destination twice because they'd hate thinking 'been there, done that'. Besides, there's a whole world out there waiting to be explored, so why should they waste their valuable holiday time going back to the same old resort year after year? That sort of behaviour is strictly for the more conservative members of the zodiac, such as Taureans, Cancerians and Capricorns. An Arien is much more

interested in exploring new destinations each time, especially if they're off the beaten track and no one else has discovered them yet. This is a sign that likes to be first, after all.

Some Ariens really enjoy expressing their sense of adventure on holiday. They might choose an activity holiday in which they can relax by keeping busy (a concept not understood by Taureans, so let's hope they don't go along to keep any Ariens company). You'll even find some Ariens risking life and limb while on holiday, perhaps by hacking their way through a jungle or having to cross a mosquito-infested swamp to reach their destination. 'What fun!' the Arien will cry, while their companions madly flap their arms in the air and try not to swallow any nasty-looking insects.

If exploring jungles is going a bit far (perhaps literally), a typical member of this sign will still consider excitement, heat and plenty of action to be the prime ingredients for the perfect holiday. If a little courage is required, then so much the better. When they get home again they'll enjoy regaling their friends and family with eye-popping tales of their bravery as they mastered white-water rafting, braved huge rollers on their surfboard, went on safari, trekked up a mountain or endured the baking heat of a desert. They may have the scars to prove it but they'll have had a fantastic time.

If an Arien has to settle for something that they consider to be more tame, perhaps because everyone refuses to go with them on their own choice of holiday, they'll enjoy a fly-drive holiday because there will be little chance to get bored by being stuck in one place for too long. At a pinch, an Arien might be persuaded to lie on a beach but they won't want to do it for long because they'll soon get bored, so they'll have to take off on some day trips every now and then. Mind you, when they are spending the day on the beach or by the hotel pool they'll be assiduous about being one of the first people to grab a sun-lounger in the mornings. It will bring out their competitive spirit and they'll get a big thrill out of lying in the sun in comfort while people who didn't get up early enough have to make do with gritty towels on the sandy beach.

Ariens are very generous souls so part of the fun of the holiday will lie in choosing suitable souvenirs for everyone back home. These will probably be rather jokey and light-hearted. They'll also send lots of postcards but, as they will probably all carry the same message to save time having to dream up lots of different messages, the Arien will hope that the recipients don't get together to compare them. That would be too embarrassing for words.

Home

Home means many things to many people, but what does it mean to an Arien? For young Ariens, it's probably little more than a place to sleep, eat and drop their clothes on the floor before disappearing out of the front door again with a cheery wave and a deliberately mumbled response to questions about where they think they're going. To say that they aren't very sentimental about their homes would be rather like saying that sharks can have quite sharp teeth.

When Ariens get older and have homes of their own, they can still be surprisingly unsentimental about them. A house is a house, as far as they're concerned, so what's all the fuss about? As long as it's got a roof and four walls, all is well. If an Arien buys a house that's more like a derelict tip, they'll have a field day getting covered from head to foot in plaster dust while they sort out all the problems themselves rather than hiring a builder. Bashing holes in walls and knocking down ceilings are perfect ways to spend the Arien's weekends, even if they secretly haven't got a clue what they're doing. "It can't be that difficult, can it?" they ask as they stand knee-deep in rubble and wonder why they can suddenly see daylight through the sitting room wall. If it all becomes a disaster, they'll turn it into a funny story to tell their friends. Although they'll have to do that in a bar or restaurant, of course, because their home won't be fit for habitation.

When it comes to decorating their house, an Arien prefers plain, modern items. They like antiques but they don't have to be surrounded by them, and they're quite happy to choose contemporary pieces of furniture that can withstand a few knocks and spills. If they can afford it, the Arien will buy modern classics that will make interesting talking points, such as items by their fellow Arien, Mies van der Rohe. But an Arien's home is unlikely to be very cosy. That's not their style at all, and they much prefer a more minimal look. If they live with a partner who loves creating a cosy atmosphere there will be flaming rows about all the clutter that keeps being left lying about.

Everything in the kitchen must be functional, and if the Arien enjoys cooking they'll have fun buying all the latest gadgets and cooking appliances they can get their hands on. The cupboards will be crammed with rice steamers, ice-cream makers and woks, even if the Arien has only used them once. But pride of place will go to the cooker, which will be the biggest and most expensive one they can afford. It will also be in the latest fashionable finish, whatever that happens to be. Many Ariens are excellent cooks, and have the enviable ability of being able to juggle lots of pots and saucepans at once so they can whip up a delicious meal in no time at all.

It must be said that some Ariens' houses would never win any design awards because they have other things to think about besides choosing the perfect colour for the sofa. Their furniture can be quite tatty, or they might have bought the first thing they saw, regardless of whether it's comfortable or suits its surroundings.

However, one item will be very important in an Arien's home and that's the television. Ariens like their televisions, especially if they're really big, and they enjoy having DVD- and video-players to go with them. There will probably be about ten different remote controls lying around, making it difficult to remember which one does what, but somehow the Arien will manage.

Clothes and Image

No matter how old Ariens are, they still want to look young and stylish. This isn't a sign that will happily let themselves go, so that they slide into a frumpish middle age followed by an even more dreary old age. Instead, they will do their best to wear youthful and flattering clothes for as long as possible.

Aries don't like to be smartly dressed in the way that Virgos and Capricorns do. They much prefer to be casually dressed whenever they can get away with it. For some Arien men, wearing a clean T-shirt is their idea of being smart, and they're usually happiest in jeans. They're also keen on sports gear, such as football strips and trainers. Anything else is too much trouble, unless it's an important occasion and it would be rude not to put on a suit and tie. Aries is a military sign and many Arien men enjoy wearing combat trousers, flak jackets, old army greatcoats and anything else that makes them look as though they've just come off the battlefield.

Arien women enjoy getting dressed up, but even then they won't want to look as though their steam-iron is their best friend. They really want to wear clothes that look good but which will cope with their active lifestyles, because they haven't got time to worry about getting their high heels caught in the hems of their skirts or creasing their new linen suits. They love wearing trousers and jeans, whatever their age, and feel uncomfortable in the sort of dainty, ultra-feminine clothes that suit so many Libran and Piscean women. Actually, many Arien women are really tomboys at heart, so frilly clothes and tight waistbands restrict their movements.

Aries is such a casual sign that it goes without saying that Ariens won't want to spend hours looking after their hair. They simply can't be bothered with it. They'll comb it first thing in the morning, if it's lucky, and then forget about it for the rest of the day. But something they do like is to wear hats. Aries rules the head, so it makes sense that Ariens enjoy wearing all sorts of headgear, from Panama hats to baseball caps, plus everything in between. Hats can serve another purpose as well, because many Arien men start to lose their hair at a relatively early age. So hats can disguise their bald spots, as well as protect them from fierce sunshine or winter gales. For both sexes, their planetary ruler, Mars, gives their hair a reddish tint, and some of them have very red hair indeed.

When it comes to physique, many Arien men have the sort of muscular but streamlined look that makes other signs gnash their teeth in envy. Arien men usually have wide shoulders, narrow hips and long legs, which can be a pretty devastating combination. And they know all about how to put it to good use! The young Marlon Brando who appeared in *On The Waterfront* embodied the classic Aries look, complete with leather jacket and motorbike. Other Arien actors who look the part include Jean-Paul Belmondo, Robert Downey Jr, Steve McQueen, Rod Steiger, Warren Beatty and Eddie Murphy.

Arien women are usually much shorter than their male counterparts, and they have much more rounded, softer bodies, too. Many Arien women battle with their weight, much to their disappointment, especially as they get older. Typical Arien women include Bette Davis, Joan Crawford, Elizabeth Montgomery, Doris Day and Debbie Reynolds.

There's one other typical Arien characteristic, and that's their eyebrows. Many Ariens have arched eyebrows that dip down towards the bridge of their noses, conjuring up images of a ram's horns. They're an easy way to spot an Arien.

Famous Ariens

J. S Bach. (21 March 1685); Marcel Marceau (22 March 1923); Joan Crawford (23 March 1904); Steve McQueen (24 March 1930); Elton John (25 March 1947); Aretha Franklin (26 March 1942); Quentin Tarrantino (27 March 1963); Mariah Carey (27 March 1970); St Teresa of Avila (28 March 1515); Jennifer Capriati (29 March 1976); Eric Clapton (30 March 1945); Franz Joseph Haydn (31 March 1732); Sergei Rachmaninov (1 April 1873); Marvin Gaye (2 April 1939); Eddie Murphy (3 April 1961); Maya Angelou (4 April 1928); Bette Davis (5 April 1908); Jackie Chan (6 April 1954); Russell Crowe (7 April 1964); Patricia Arquette (8April 1968); Severiano Ballesteros (9 April 1957); Omar Shariff (10 April 1932); Sir Charles Hallé (11 April 1819); Ann Miller (12 April 1923); Seamus Heaney (13 April 1939); Loretta Lynn (14 April 1935); Guru Nanak (15 April 1469); Charlie Chaplin (16 April 1889); Nikita Khruschev (17 April 1894); Lucrezia Borgia (18 April 1480); Jayne Mansfield (19 April 1933); Ryan O'Neal (20 April 1941).

The Top Ten Arien Characteristics

Impulsive; Enthusiastic; Rash; Impatient; Loving; Romantic; Idealistic; Naïve; Generous; Sporty.

Are You a Typical Arien?

Try this quiz on the Ariens you know to find out whether they're typical members of their sign.

1 Can you wait patiently for things and people?
2 Do you learn from your mistakes?
3 Do you believe it's always important to take your time over things and not be hurried?
4 Do you usually finish the projects that you start?
5 Do you always keep to the speed limit when you're driving?
6 Do you like to take your time over everything?
7 Do you have a horror of taking risks?
8 Do you like to play safe?
9 Do you always think before taking action?
10 Can you keep your temper?

Scores

Score one point for every "yes" and zero points for every "no".

0–3   You're such a typical Aries! You're a textbook case! But maybe you would benefit from taking life at less of a headlong rush sometimes.

4–6   You have a strong Aries streak but it's tempered by the influence of other signs. Read the Top Ten Characteristics of the other signs to see which ones ring a bell with you.

7–10   Although you were born under the sign of Aries you don't have many Arien characteristics. Look through the Top Ten Characteristics of Pisces and Taurus to see if either of these sounds more like you.

Taurus

21 April–20 May

The Taurus Adult

It's often said that Taureans are the salt of the earth, and it's absolutely true. These people are solid, practical, dependable and reliable. You know where you stand with them. It's difficult for them to disguise their emotions, so you know when they're feeling angry and when they're feeling happy. They can't see the point of pretending to be something they're not. It's all too much trouble.

Taurus is the sign of the Bull, and Taureans are very similar to their animal namesakes in many ways. Like bulls, Taureans are perfectly happy being allowed to mooch about in the open air, eating whenever they get the urge. They like the simple life and enjoy being left to get on with it.

If you've ever walked past a field with a bull in it, you'll know that he looks pretty placid on the surface. But you will probably notice a sign saying 'Danger, beware of the bull' and keep well clear, just in case. It's the same story with Taureans, who appear to be completely calm and controlled. It takes a lot to make them angry, but when you've succeeded you need to run for cover because they can be quite terrifying when they're roaring their heads off.

Taureans are the first of the Earth signs, which is what gives them their stable, down-to-earth natures. They're strongly grounded in reality, even if they sometimes wish they weren't, and they're also very strong-minded. When a Taurean makes up their mind about something, it will practically take an earthquake to make them change it. On the plus side, this means they're extremely determined, with the ability to plod on regardless until they achieve whatever they've set out to do. On the minus side, they can be stubborn and obstinate, and hell-bent on standing their ground even when it's crazy to do so. They get these traits from being a Fixed sign, which means they like stability and dislike change. They stick to their guns.

Material security is immensely important to Taureans, who have a real fear of not having enough to go round. They can get by on very little money but it worries them, and they need to know that they'll get regular injections of cash. Thanks to their planetary ruler, Venus, they also need the emotional security of being surrounded by people who love them and whom they can love in return. Without such security, they feel lost and out of their depth.

Taureans find security in doing things in a tried and tested way. They like their habits and show a distinct reluctance to change them. These are the people who believe "If it ain't broke, don't fix it." And if it is "broke," they'd rather mend it than replace it. As a result of this need for stability in their lives, whether it concerns their career or their kettle, Taureans can get awfully bogged down in routine. They'll do things in a certain way because that's how they've always done them and they're darned if they're going to change now. To the Taurean in question, this is simply common sense, but to any onlookers it's yet another example of the Taurean's exasperating ability to get themselves stuck in dreary ruts. It can cause a lot of friction with the Taurean's loved ones, especially if they belong to signs that need more variety in their lives.

Taureans like to take things slowly and can see no benefit in rushing. You might overlook something important or make a silly mistake if you rush, and then where will you be? But don't imagine that this makes them lazy, because they're among the most hard-working signs of the zodiac.

As you will have guessed by now, Taurus is one of the most conservative signs of the zodiac. Taureans want to fit in with everyone else, and it usually isn't in their natures to do anything that makes them stand out from the crowd. It's a rare Taurean who wants to be seen as eccentric or weird. Powerful, yes. Weird, no. You'll find lots of Taureans in politics, and the roll call includes Tony Blair, Harry S. Truman (the US president who gave the order to bomb Hiroshima and Nagasaki in 1945), Robespierre, Eva Perón, Adolf Hitler, Joachim von Ribbentrop, Saddam Hussein, Malcolm X and Karl Marx. You couldn't call any of these people lightweights. The Taurean desire for power comes from their opposite sign of Scorpio, and they'll wield their power somehow or other, even if it means refusing to eat a different brand of breakfast cereal and thereby calling the shots around the kitchen table.

Values and possessions are very important to Taureans. They place a lot of importance on what they own, and also on what they believe in. If a Taurean really has to do something revolutionary, it's because they don't think they have any other choice. Charlotte Brontë, who wrote several novels, including *Jane Eyre*, while living in the repressive atmosphere of her father's parsonage with her sisters, flew in the face of Victorian morals that said women shouldn't write books. But even she disguised her identity by writing under a pseudonym.

Generally speaking, Taureans aren't keen on taking risks. They've got too much to lose and they think that the signs with a daredevil streak, such as Aries and Sagittarius, are high-spirited at best and crazy at worst. You wouldn't catch a Taurean behaving like that! But what Taureans may lack in spontaneity and recklessness, they more than make up for in their generosity, affection and charm. They're kind-hearted souls who help to make life run smoothly for everyone else, and we all benefit from knowing and loving them.

The Taurus Child

Taurean children need plenty of hugs. It's essential that they know they're loved and cherished, even when they've done something wrong. That Taurean need for emotional stability and material security starts in the womb, so even tiny Taurean babies will feel it. Not that hugging a Taurean baby will be a chore, because they're usually very responsive. They smile at you, producing lots of sweet dimples for the camera, and will sleep peacefully while looking cherubic. They have the sort of soft, curly hair that their doting parents are reluctant to cut, and chubby feet that it's a shame to cover up with bootees. And, speaking of chubby, they are often slightly plump babies, too.

The Taurean love of food begins in the cradle and goes on till the grave. Taurean babies rarely need to be encouraged to suckle because they know exactly what to do, and they'll carry on doing it until they fall asleep. When they're weaned on to solids, their parents should try to introduce them to as wide a variety of foods as possible. This will help to counteract the Taurean tendency to stick to a limited diet of foods that are considered safe to eat, while everything else is rejected without even being tasted. "I don't like it," the Taurean child will say on seeing a strange food for the first time. So it's a good idea to encourage a Taurean child to be an adventurous eater, yet without making a big deal of it. The baby Taurean should also be steered clear of too much sugar, especially in cakes, sweets and chocolate, otherwise they'll develop a life-long sugar addiction that won't do them any good and might even lead to serious health problems.

The Taurean child should also be encouraged to be flexible, rather than to become stubborn and obstinate at an early age. It will help if there are some brothers and sisters around to encourage the small Taurean to be more adaptable and less determined to dig their heels in at every opportunity.

Taureans like to take things slowly, even as children, so young members of this sign shouldn't be rushed. They need to be allowed to do things at their own pace, even if it's frustrating for everyone else, because that's simply the way they are. Their minds may also work more slowly than those of their brothers and sisters or classmates, but that doesn't mean they're stupid in any way. It simply means that they take longer than others to process information, but with the great benefit that once they've understood it they're able to remember it.

Something else that needs to be encouraged in a Taurean child is a love of exercise. Many Taureans think of exercise as a chore rather than as something to be enjoyed, so junior members of this sign should be shown what fun it can be. Even something as simple as running a three-legged race in the garden with their friends or going for a swim once a week will help to set up good habits that can last for life and will help to keep the Taurean healthy. Another good option is to take a Taurean child to dance lessons. These will not only keep them active but will also help to encourage their innate musical ability and sense of rhythm. After all, both Martha Graham and Dame Margot Fonteyn were Taureans, which is a pretty good recommendation in itself.

Music lessons won't go amiss, either, although the Taurean child may have to be nagged into doing their practice at home instead of flopping in front of the television set or computer. They'll probably enjoy learning how to play a traditional instrument rather than anything too unusual, and may even follow in the footsteps of a relative by playing the same instrument as them.

A Taurean child should also be introduced to creative and artistic activities at an early age. They'll love being given a set of crayons or paints and some paper, and being able to do exactly what they want with them. Their parents shouldn't push them, though, by hoping that they've got a budding Van Gogh on their hands, and nor should they stifle their imaginations by asking them exactly what that strange blob is and why they've painted the trees bright pink. Other tactile hobbies, such as pottery and needlework, are very good for them, and will help them to develop better hand and eye co-ordination. To encourage their love of outdoors, they could be given a few seed packets, a child's fork and trowel, and a small patch of garden that they can call their own. Those Taurean green fingers should be nurtured from an early age.

Finally, all Taurean children should learn to cook. With food such an important priority in their lives, they really ought to know how to prepare it. They'll enjoy making delicious treats, such as cakes and fudge, but they'll also get a kick out of helping to make the Sunday lunch or being in charge of the roast potatoes when they're old enough. It's a skill that will stand them in good stead throughout their lives.

Health

Above all else, Taureans need plenty of fresh air. These people belong to the earth element, which means they thrive when they have plenty of contact with nature. Taureans are not happy if they're stuck at the top of a high-rise block of flats without a blade of grass in sight. If a Taurean doesn't have their own garden to enjoy, they should try to cultivate some herbs or salad leaves in window boxes or fill their home with plenty of house plants. These will help the Taurean to feel more rooted and grounded, and as a result their life will be more balanced and satisfying. Ideally, a Taurean should have their own garden to stroll around in, even if all they do is lie on a sun-lounger while their more energetic partner mows the grass and weeds the flowerbeds.

Note the phrase "more energetic". Taureans, it has to be said, aren't known for their desire to rush around and work themselves up into sweaty heaps. They can't see the point of it. Which means that they really have to force themselves to take any sort of physical exercise, otherwise they're in danger of becoming complete couch potatoes or the sort of people who consider a long walk to be the four tottering steps they take from their car to the front door.

One ideal form of exercise for Taureans is long country walks, where they can distract themselves by enjoying the scenery. Of course, they may reward themselves at the end of the walk with a slap-up meal in a favourite pub or restaurant, but they've got to have some incentive for setting foot outside the house. Have a heart!

Many Taureans have a great sense of rhythm and appreciation for music, thanks to their planetary ruler, Venus, so they might enjoy dancing. This could be anything from stately ballroom dancing, which is a lot more energetic than it looks and uses muscles you didn't even knew you had, to tap dancing, ballet or the latest dance steps. Probably the most famous Taurean dancer of all time is Fred Astaire, who used to practise his routines until his feet bled (showing classic Taurean determination and strength of will) and who looked effortlessly elegant and lighter than air.

Taureans really shouldn't be in any doubt about the need for them to take plenty of exercise. That's because one of their favourite hobbies is eating, with inevitable consequences unless they can keep a watchful eye on their weight. They enjoy eating rich foods and most of them would be thrilled to have a dispenser of double cream always at the ready in their fridge. They also have a terrible weakness for traditional dishes, which are often laden with calories and fat, and can't resist puddings either. Most Taureans have a sweet tooth, so they're suckers for cakes and biscuits, and often find that once they start eating them they can't stop. And nor do they want to!

Each sign of the zodiac rules a particular part of the body, and Taurus governs the neck and throat. This means that many Taureans suffer from throat ailments, such as sore throats, hoarseness and stiff necks, whenever they become run down. It's as though their throats are their early-warning signals telling them that they need to take more care of themselves. Alternatively, Taureans can get stiff necks, especially if they're feeling tense about something.

Most Taureans have slow metabolisms, which may help to account for their tendency to put on weight, and this condition is made worse if they start to develop underactive thyroid glands. The thyroid gland is also ruled by Taurus because it's located in the throat.

The opposite sign to Taurus is Scorpio, which rules the

reproductive organs, so sometimes Taureans can have problems with this area of their bodies, either instead of or in addition to their throats.

Money

Taureans may not be very clued up when it comes to taking exercise but they know all about how to make (and keep) money. Money is an essential part of life for them because it offers them the one thing they need more than any other: material security. When a Taurean has money in the bank, they can hold their head up high and know that they're doing well in life. When they're broke, they feel a failure and they worry about how they're going to manage.

Some signs can live quite happily not knowing where the next penny is coming from and watching the unpaid bills pile up on the mantelpiece, but this is a Taurean's idea of hell. A Taurean needs plenty of certainty in their life and that most definitely includes regular infusions of cash. They also need to know that their money is being spent in practical and sensible ways, so they're far more likely to own their own home than to rent one which, they reason, simply makes someone else rich. If they've got the money they'll want to invest it in other things besides property, such as stock and shares. Mind you, it will be a very rare Taurean who wants to buy risky stocks that might lose them more money than they stand to gain. They aren't interested in such things unless they have so much money that they can afford to gamble with some of it, but even that tends to go against the Taurean grain.

Taureans are very clever when it comes to making their money go far, and they can be extremely good at business, too. George Lucas, the writer and director of the *Star Wars* films, is one example of a Taurean with his head screwed on financially. When he signed the contract to make the original Star Wars film, he persuaded the film company to give him the rights to all the film's merchandise. They agreed, thinking that no one would want to buy any Star Wars toys anyway, and in doing so signed away millions of dollars in royalties. It's the sort of move that makes other Taureans feel faint with envy and admiration. Liberace is another Taurean who made a lot of money from his career, and he loved to flaunt it with massive limousines, outrageous outfits and so many rings it was amazing he could move his fingers enough to play the piano.

When it comes to spending money, once again there are no flies on Taureans. But there might be a few moths, which will flutter out of a typical Taurean's wallet whenever they reluctantly have to open it. It's not that they're stingy, exactly, more that they're very, very careful about what they spend their money on. If they can save it rather than spend it, they will. In extreme cases, this might mean the whole family has to put on more clothes in the winter rather than turn up the thermostat on the central heating when there's thick snow on the ground, or the Taurean may drive a rickety old car that's really only fit for the scrap heap rather than go to the monstrous expense of buying a new one. Sometimes, you'll come across Taureans who have plenty of money stashed away in savings but who are so reluctant to spend it that they will make do with tatty old furniture and threadbare carpets rather than buy anything new. I've known Taureans who keep the central heating thermostat on low even when there's thick snow on the ground. Brrrr!

When they do spend money, a Taurean wants to know that they've spent their money wisely. They'll enjoy hunting out bargains in the supermarket but are far more likely to buy the supermarket's own range of products than fork out for the more expensive big-name brands. These may be small savings but they mount up, you know! They will also enjoy buying items that they think are beautiful and which are made to last.

With so much emphasis on financial security, it's hardly surprising that some Taureans can take this to extremes and become very materialistic. They become too concerned with amassing possessions and acquiring status symbols, and start to believe that they are what they own. This will inevitably make them miserable in the long run, so they need to guard against adopting such a materialistic attitude.

Career

Taurus is the first of the Earth signs, which means exactly what it suggests – Taureans are very down-to-earth and sensible. They like to take life at a measured and steady pace, and are slightly suspicious of anyone who has a meteoric rise to the top. They believe they should work hard to achieve success and aren't comfortable with the idea of being given an easy ride. They are particularly suspicious of people who get to the top because of who they are rather than what they are, so they frown on nepotism or having influential contacts.

Taureans certainly put a lot of effort into whatever they do for a living. Like their fellow Earth signs of Virgo and Capricorn, they aren't afraid of hard work and will slog away round the clock to complete a job if that's what's needed. Colleagues and superiors appreciate the Taurean brand of patience, perseverance and practicality. Taureans are rarely flustered in a crisis and other people know they can depend on them. In fact, reliability and steadfastness are two of the greatest Taurean traits, so it's always good to know that you've got a Taurean on your team. They usually don't mind doing their fair share of the donkey work, either, because this isn't a sign that puts on airs and graces or expects everyone else to be at their beck and call. But that doesn't mean they like being taken for granted, because they have a high sense of their own worth and will want you to share it.

One potential problem for Taureans in their careers is their tendency to err on the side of caution. As far as a Taurean is concerned, if a particular strategy has worked in the past then there's no reason why it shouldn't continue to work in the future, even if everyone else says it's out of date or that technology has improved dramatically since then. This means the Taurean can be highly reluctant to make radical changes (or even minor changes, sometimes) or to get involved in anything that is ephemeral or led by fashion. They can dig their heels in and refuse to budge. This can be the sort of person who still uses a typewriter because they always have, and who dismisses computers and word processors as flash-in-the-pan gimmicks. Email? Nonsense! What's wrong with sending letters in envelopes, just as before? It's a system that's worked well for over a hundred years, hasn't it? So why change it?

Jobs that fit a Taurean like a glove are anything connected with the beauty or fashion businesses, horticulture, agriculture, floristry, finance and property. A Taurean may also enjoy working in a government department, especially if they think they can work their way to the top. It may not be the most exciting job in the world but they'll be attracted by the benefits it offers, such as a good pension (which is a consideration for Taureans even when they're in their twenties) and a steady income. You will also find many Taureans in the catering industry, whether working as chefs, waiters or hotel managers, because they have a healthy enjoyment of food and understand the importance of good service.

The one thing Taureans don't like is to be self-employed. You'll find a few of them, of course, but they'll always be worried about having enough work and they'll take every job they're offered because they're frightened to turn it down. They're much happier working in an office with colleagues and superiors, because then they've got people to chat to and they have the reassurance of knowing they'll receive regular pay cheques. But having cash-flow problems or a sudden dearth of work when they're self-employed? No, thank you!

Love and Friendship

Let's get one thing clear straightaway. Taureans belong to one of the two most attractive signs in the zodiac, an accolade they share with Librans. This means most Taureans are never short of admirers and probably even have to beat them off with a stick every now and then. Combine this with their natural modesty, charm and shyness, and it's an irresistible combination.

Taureans and Librans have their ruler, Venus, to thank for this. You only have to look at a list of some famous Taureans to appreciate that yes, members of this sign really can be very attractive indeed. Rudolph Valentino was an early cinematic Taurean heart-throb who caused untold grief and despair when he died tragically young. Other Taurean film stars whose faces have made millions of hearts start fluttering include Audrey Hepburn, Stewart Granger, James Stewart, Gary Cooper, Cher, Harvey Keitel, Jean-Pierre Léaud, George Clooney, Jack Nicholson, Michelle Pfeiffer, Pierce Brosnan and Al Pacino. Not a bad line-up, you must admit.

Yet despite belonging to such a good-looking sign, most Taureans aren't interested in playing the field and breaking hearts left, right and centre. They're far too faithful and loyal for that. They're happiest if they can pair up with someone at an early age and stick to them like glue for the rest of their lives. Infidelity is a massive no-no for them. They'd rather be accused of cheating at cards than of being unfaithful.

Emotional security is so important to a Taurean that occasionally they may try to help it along by keeping a watchful eye on their partner, just in case they might be doing something that will make the Taurean feel threatened. Unfortunately, this can sometimes spill over into possessiveness or jealousy, both of which can cause severe problems for many Taureans and their loved ones. Some Taureans definitely behave as though their loved ones are their personal property, not wanting to let them out of their sight and feeling miffed if they want to spend time with other people. None of this will do a relationship much good, and the Taurean's partner will inevitably end up feeling as though they're trapped and being suffocated by the heavy weight of the Taurean's neediness and emotional dependence. This can have the very effect that the Taurean has been dreading by driving the partner into the arms of someone else, purely to escape from the Taurean's emotional stranglehold. Even their friends can feel swamped if their Taurean chum is very possessive.

We've dealt with the bad news about Taureans and love. So what's the good news? Taureans have tremendous powers of affection and are very demonstrative. If they love someone, they want to show it. This means that sex is a vital part of life for a Taurean, and they need a partner who shares their enthusiasm for it. They aren't the most sexually inventive sign in the zodiac because they usually like to find a winning formula and then stick with it, even between the sheets, but they can be very earthy and sensual. Ideally, they should have a partner who's willing to take the lead sometimes and who encourages them to experiment so their sex life doesn't get stuck in a dreary and predictable rut.

Taureans love the idea of growing old gracefully with their partner and of being surrounded by a huge family, whether it consists of children and grandchildren, close friends or beloved pets. They need to be part of a loving and happy gang.

When it comes to friendship, Taureans make staunch friends. They're dependable, affectionate and trustworthy. They're also very good at keeping in touch, and are often the ones to do all the running. They will even stay in touch with people they don't really like any longer, especially if they've known them for a long time. After all, it's so important for them to preserve the status quo.

Family Relationships

Family is everything to a Taurean. Members of this sign place nearly as much importance on their family ties as Cancerians, who are the most family-minded members of the zodiac. A Taurean's family means the world to them, and they'll do everything they can to support them. Part of this support means providing for the family's daily needs, so the Taurean is perfectly prepared to work round the clock if that's what it takes to feed, clothe and educate their children. They'll also do what they can to give their family a stable, secure and loving background, in which material security plays a massive role, as does the importance of tradition and not letting others down. As you might expect, this will be a very conventional home in which the children are brought up to be polite and well-behaved, to learn the importance of family values, to understand the need for discipline and to respect their elders. Their Taurean parents will be very strict with them when necessary, even to the point of bringing up their children to be slightly intimidated by or frightened of them. But the children will grow up knowing that they're part of a loving, united family, even if they don't have the most carefree childhoods.

Taureans are extremely loyal and steadfast, so loved ones know they can count on them to be there when they need them. In return, Taureans need to be loved and appreciated. Sometimes, an element of possessiveness may creep into the equation, making the Taurean treat their loved ones like personal belongings. For instance, the Taurean may secretly feel neglected if the children spend too much time with their friends or may feel as though they've been supplanted when their children are old enough to fall in love. If the Taurean relaxes, they'll realize that there's more than enough love to go round. They also need to work hard to bridge what can become a yawning generation gap between the Taurean parent and their growing children, especially if there's a big age difference between them, otherwise there can be misunderstandings and a lack of communication that will hurt the Taurean's feelings and make life difficult for their offspring.

Unless a Taurean's relatives live on the other side of the world or are so ghastly that the Taurean wishes they did, they'll spend a lot of time with their nearest and dearest. Taureans understand the importance of being part of an extended family, where grandparents, cousins, uncles and aunts all mix together. It gives them a sense of family history and of continuity among the different generations. They may not approve of all the members of their family, or even like them very much in some cases, but a Taurean will always believe that blood is thicker than water. The family always comes first for a Taurean, and they expect the same sort of treatment in return. Taureans have massive family holidays, even when that involves peeling enough potatoes to feed a small army or having to listen to Uncle Fred's war reminiscences yet again.

As you will have no doubt gathered by now, Taureans aren't very good at living by themselves. It doesn't suit them because they need someone to come home to at night and to say hello to in the morning, even if it's only the budgie.

Creativity and Potential

Taureans have oodles of talent and potential, especially if they play to the strengths conferred on them by their ruling planet, Venus, and their Earth element. In fact, they can't lose.

For a start, Venus gives Taureans a tremendous amount of artistic ability. They might translate this into painting or drawing, in which case they'll be following in some very famous Taurean footsteps. The French painter, Georges Braque, was a Taurean, as was the Dutch abstract impressionist, Willem de Kooning, and the two Spanish Surrealists, Salvador Dalí and Joan Miró. It's difficult to equate surrealism and abstract art with the convention and solidity usually loved by Taureans, but all these painters had the sort of sensual relationship with paint and canvas that is so typical of Taureans.

Alternatively, Taureans can make the most of their magnificent voices. Many Taureans have beautiful speaking or singing voices, or both if they're really lucky. Think of the rich, deep voices of Orson Welles (who also suffered from the Taurean problem of weight gain) and James Mason, and the vulnerable-sounding Audrey Hepburn. There are many famous Taurean singers, including Bono, Stevie Wonder, Glen Campbell, Barbra Streisand and Ella Fitzgerald, too. The Taurean may never reach such dizzy heights but there's no harm in trying, and they might be perfectly content to have a wonderful time as a member of a choir or playing the lead in their local operatic society. Even if the Taurean doesn't think they can sing a note, they might enjoy finding their natural voice and developing their self-expression. Even learning how to project their voice and speak better might give them a huge boost of confidence. After all, the throat is ruled by Taurus so it's a very important part of the body for members of this sign.

You'll find lots of Taurean composers, too, so a Taurean might like to write music. After all, it worked for such Taureans as Brahms, Tchaikovsky, Irving Berlin and Burt Bacharach. And if that doesn't appeal, they could try their hand (literally) at conducting. They'll be following in some illustrious Taurean footsteps, including those of Sir Malcolm Sargent, Sir Thomas Beecham, Zubin Mehta and Otto Klemperer.

Anything that brings a Taurean into contact with the great outdoors is another way of helping them to express their creativity. They might enjoy designing or working on a garden, and therefore making the most of those Taurean green fingers, or may be perfectly content to visit some of the famous gardens created by other people. Something else that could appeal is teaching themselves about the flora and fauna, such as wild flowers and insects, that are found where they live. For instance, they might develop a passion for feeding wild birds and noting how many visit their garden, or become an expert on trees.

Many Taureans have a sweet tooth, so they might enjoy combining it with their love of nature by keeping bees and eating the honey. If that is out of the question for some reason, a Taurean could have a wonderful time making their own cakes and chocolates. They'll never be short of volunteers to taste them, either, and might even turn it into a money-making hobby. Never underestimate that practical Taurean streak.

Other hobbies that could suit a Taurean include learning about aromatherapy. Scented oils are strongly Taurean, so any member of this sign would enjoy using them, whether in very simple ways or as a trained aromatherapist. Taureans make wonderful masseurs because they are powerfully connected to their own bodies and therefore understand the importance of bodywork and massage. And, finally, with their need for physical security and a roof over their head, a Taurean might enjoy developing their interior design skills, whether purely for their own benefit or in order to advise other people.

Holidays

As the great hedonists of the zodiac, the Taurean idea of a blissful holiday is one in which they do as little as possible while other people attend to their every need. Even though they're usually so practical and sensible, they're sure they could learn to be waited on hand and foot, if the opportunity ever arose. After all, how difficult is it to lie around relaxing all day, so that eating the maraschino cherry garnishing their drink becomes the most strenuous thing they have to do? They're sure they could get used to it, and they usually like to practise while they're on holiday.

If money is no object the Taurean will be in seventh heaven staying in a luxury hotel that serves delectable drinks, sumptuous food and has the finest cotton sheets. Some signs are completely incapable of sitting around doing nothing but Taureans could turn it into an art form, given half a chance. Even if they can only afford a package holiday and they have to carry their own luggage, rather than have 24 suitcases transported in a separate stretch limo by their chauffeur, they'll do their best to spend hours relaxing on a sun-lounger by the pool or snoozing on the beach. They might fit in a bit of sight-seeing every now and then, but they won't want to go crazy or wear themselves out. As far as a Taurean is concerned, holidays are for taking life easy.

If a Taurean has to lower their holiday sights because of a lack of cash, they would enjoy staying in a self-catering cottage in beautiful surroundings. The cottage must have all mod cons, of course, because the charm of pumping their own water from a tumble-down well would pall after the first ten minutes. The accommodation should also be free of spiders and other creepy-crawlies. Many Taureans enjoy the natural world when they can watch it on television but draw the line at getting too involved with it on a one-to-one basis, such as having to evict several woodlice from their face flannel each morning or seeing a spider waving its legs at them on the pillow when they're getting ready for bed.

Wherever a Taurean goes on holiday, they'll want to know that they've got a good deal and aren't being ripped off. This is the sign with an eye for a bargain, and they'll soon smell a rat (sometimes literally) if their accommodation doesn't live up to what was promised in the holiday brochure. And it's got to be pretty comfortable. Taureans don't like roughing it, so you can forget all about persuading them to join you in a tent under the stars. Unless, of course, it comes complete with proper beds and running water.

Food is another important consideration. Taureans love eating and they want to do lots of it on holiday. They won't even entertain the idea of staying anywhere that offers the sort of unappetizing food that they worry about shoving in their mouths. This can mean several parts of the world are off-limits to them for culinary reasons. And it's no good trying to persuade them that it will be OK when they get there, because they won't believe you. If you're going on holiday with a Taurean it will be far better to choose a destination in which they'll be happy than to select somewhere that makes them uncomfortable or where they're even afraid to drink the water in case it has a disastrous effect on them.

So which destinations should a Taurean choose? They feel revived and rejuvenated when they're surrounded by nature and beauty, so they might enjoy a holiday tour of famous gardens, especially if they're proud of their own green fingers. Alternatively, they might love a visit to a country renowned for its autumn colours or a trip to an unspoilt island paradise.

Home

Home is where a Taurean's heart is. It's the centre of their life and one of the reasons why they work as hard as they do. When a Taurean puts their key in the door they always get a big thrill out of entering their own little empire, whether it's a one-bedroom flat or the biggest mansion money can buy.

And the Taurean will buy their home as soon as they possibly can. They don't like the idea of living in rented accommodation because it's not only a poor financial investment but it carries a certain amount of insecurity with it. What if the lease runs out or the landlord evicts them? These are the sorts of worries a Taurean can do without, so they'll solve them by owning their own home. They'll also do their best to pay off the mortgage as quickly as they can manage as well, because they hate having huge debts.

So what does a typical Taurean home look like? Ideally, it should have a garden that's big enough for the children or pets to play in, and where the Taurean can develop their green fingers and satisfy their need to be surrounded by nature. It doesn't have to be a massive garden because, as the ever-practical Taurean will point out to you, that involves a lot of upkeep and responsibility, from mowing the grass to weeding the flowerbeds and trimming the hedges. If time and space permit, there is bound to be a highly productive vegetable patch so the Taurean can provide at least some of the family's food. They'll want some fruit trees as well, so they can make plenty of pies. Taureans have a love of farm animals, too, so there could even be a few chickens running around or a couple of goats to keep the grass down. It will all feel gentle, safe, rustic and timeless.

Indoors, don't expect a Taurean house to be a monument to the latest design crazes or wacky features such as Louis XIV chairs upholstered with fake zebra skin. The furniture and décor in a Taurean's home are always conventional, solid and built to last. They believe that big is best, so have massive sofas and armchairs that will give you a hernia if you try to move them, as well as huge televisions and king-sized beds. They like traditional styles in uncontroversial colours, and everything will be as hard-wearing and practical as possible. Although this sign is ruled by Venus, the planet of beauty, it must be said that beauty is definitely in the eye of the beholder for some Taureans who like their rooms to be full of so many different patterns and designs that your eyes start to cross when you look at them all. They might also have lots of fussy knick-knacks and ornaments dotted around, making you nervous about knocking them over and breaking them, as well as many other possessions that the style police would confiscate in five seconds flat.

A typical Taurean spends a lot of money on two rooms in particular – the kitchen and the bedroom. The kitchen must be well-equipped because otherwise how is the Taurean going to be able to eat properly? If they can afford it and there's enough room, they might have an Aga or some other form of range on which they can cook plenty of their favourite meals while also keeping the house warm. There will be lots of saucepans and cooking utensils, even if these are rather old because they belonged to the Taurean's mother, and some well-thumbed cookery books. The Taurean bedroom will be as cosy and welcoming as possible, with plenty of soft pillows on the comfortable bed. Well-heeled Taureans may even choose a bed that goes up and down at the touch of a button or which has a control panel on the headboard so they can open and close the curtains without having to get out of bed. They like anything that increases their sense of luxury and comfort.

Clothes and Image
As you might expect from a sign ruled by Venus, Taureans place a lot of importance on the way they look. And they like to look good whenever possible, which means most of them have sizeable wardrobes.

The Taurean idea of looking good doesn't necessarily correspond to what other signs like. Taureans tend to go for classic, fairly simple clothes in styles and fabrics that are made to last. They're wary of very outrageous or highly fashionable clothes because they know these will date quickly and therefore it isn't worth spending a lot of money on them. What's the point, they think, of buying something that will only last for one season before it looks ridiculous? In fact, they tend to turn up their noses at people they consider to be fashion victims. Instead, they like to choose clothes that they can wear year after year, and which will become comfortable old friends. Clever Taureans enjoy jazzing up their old faithfuls with fashionable accessories to make them look new or more interesting, but even then they refuse to spend good money on items that won't earn their keep.

Taureans have a tendency to go back to the same clothes shops time after time. They like to know that they can rely on a particular department store, shop or designer label to give them what they want, even if it isn't very adventurous. And that's one potential problem with Taureans: they can get stuck in fashion ruts. These are the people who continue to wear the style of clothes they favoured when they were teenagers, even if they've slightly altered them over the years. Look around you and you'll see Taurean men who still go for the Teddy Boy look they had in the 1950s or the long feather-cut hairstyle they first discovered as schoolboys in the 1970s. It's as if they're afraid to try something different. Taurean women can also get trapped in a fashion time-warp, whether by wearing the same make-up styles and colours that they first experimented with more years ago than they care to remember, or by continuing to wear the padded shoulders and big hair that make them look like extras from *Dynasty*.

The Taurean's tendency to put on weight as they get older is another reason for them wanting to blend tastefully into the background rather than stand out in the latest fashions. They need to choose their clothes carefully so they can disguise any lumpy bits rather than accentuate them. One way to do this is to draw attention to their necks, which is the area of the body ruled by Taurus, with scarves, ties, necklaces or interesting collars. Taureans are often shorter than average, too, so should avoid clothes that emphasize their lack of inches.

Taureans are very interested in the tactile quality of clothes, so they prefer to buy fabrics that feel and look good. If they can afford it, or if they care enough about their clothes (and some Taureans don't, dismissing them as too frivolous to make much effort with), they'll always choose natural fabrics such as wool, silk, cotton and linen over synthetics.

Scent is important to members of this sign, because it's another way for them to express the sensual side of their personalities. Taurean men like to smell masculine and slightly macho, so they avoid unisex colognes and aftershaves. They may even still be wearing the first aftershave they were ever given, purely because it smells OK and they've never seen any reason to change it. They're always devastated if it's discontinued. Taurean women love floral and very feminine scents, but can be rather heavy-handed when spraying them on. They also like to stick to old favourites rather than to experiment with lighter and more contemporary perfumes. Only ever spraying on one scent is another way of ensuring that the Taurean feels safe in what can often be a hostile world.

Famous Taureans

HM Queen Elizabeth II (21 April 1926); Jack Nicholson (22 April 1937); Roy Orbison (23 April 1936); Shirley MacLaine (24 April 1934); Renée Zellweger (25 April 1969); Rudolph Hess (26 April 1894); Cecil Day Lewis (27 April 1904); Saddam Hussein (28 April 1937); Michelle Pfeiffer (29 April 1958); Queen Juliana of the Netherlands (30 April 1909); Joanna Lumley (1 May 1946); Satyajit Ray (2 May 1921); Golda Meir (3 May 1898); Audrey Hepburn (4 May 1929); Karl Marx (5 May 1818); George Clooney (6 May 1961); Eva Perón (7 May 1919); Candice Bergen (8 May 1946); J. M. Barrie (9 May 1860); Bono (10 May 1960); Salvador Dalí (11 May 1904); J. Krishnamurti (12 May 1895); Stevie Wonder (13 May 1950); George Lucas (14 May 1944); Pierre Curie (15 May 1859); Liberace (16 May 1919); Dennis Hopper (17 May 1936); Tsar Nicholas II (18 May 1868); Malcolm X (19 May 1925); Honoré de Balzac (20 May 1799).

The Top Ten Taurean Characteristics

Affectionate; Security-loving; Loyal; Sensuous; Conservative; Possessive; Practical; Stubborn; Strong-willed; Resistant to change.

Are You A Typical Taurean?

Try this quiz on the Taureans you know to find out whether they're typical members of their sign.

1 Do you think that strenuous exercise is overrated?
2 Does food ease most of your ills?
3 Do you save money on a regular basis?
4 Do you enjoy tradition?
5 Are you scared of being abandoned?
6 Does your family come first?
7 Do you like things that are built to last?
8 Do people accuse you of being obstinate?
9 Does the prospect of change make you nervous?
10 Do you love being surrounded by nature?

Taurus

Score one point for every "no" and zero points for every "yes".

0–3 You couldn't be more Taurean if you tried. People love you for your warm character but can find your inflexibility hard to deal with.

4–6 You have a strong Taurean streak but it's tempered by the influence of other signs. Read the Top Ten Characteristics of the other signs to see which ones ring a bell with you.

7–10 Although you were born under the sign of Taurus you don't have many Taurean characteristics. Look through the Top Ten Characteristics of Aries and Gemini to see if either of these sounds more like you.

Gemini

21 May–21 June

The Gemini Adult

The Gemini's quicksilver mind and high levels of nervous energy make them one of the liveliest members of the zodiac. They're bright, vivacious, bubbly, intelligent, witty and entertaining. They're also very popular, thanks to their brainpower, charm and sense of humour. A Gemini is unlikely to be one of those people who sit quietly in the corner, barely saying a word. If they are, you can bet that they're doing it for a very good reason. Maybe they're taking note of what's going on in the interests of gossip or so they can put it all into their next novel. Alternatively, they may have a sore throat from having done too much chatting, so they're giving their voice a short rest.

Gemini is the first of the three Air signs, so members of this sign have an innate ability to communicate with others. They also spend a lot of time in their heads, thinking things through. They can be rational and objective, too, when the occasion demands it.

All these characteristics are emphasized by Gemini's planetary ruler, Mercury. This little planet is named after the winged messenger of the gods, thereby increasing Gemini's ability to communicate with others. In fact, Geminis must communicate, in whichever form they choose, otherwise they aren't fulfilling themselves.

Mercury is responsible for the Gemini's well-known mental agility and their seeming ability to be in several places at once. They certainly know what's going on around them! They seem to absorb information through the ether, almost as though they can tune into sound waves They are also good at noticing things that pass other people by. It can be quite scary for other signs who are less quick on the uptake, because they wonder how on earth the Gemini knows so much about them without being told. But in fact Geminis are endlessly curious about life and really enjoy talking to people so they can discover what makes them tick.

Mind you, Geminis aren't always listening because they also enjoy chattering away. I've met some Geminis who enjoy a good chat but who also know when to shut up and listen, and others who like to indulge in a stream of consciousness, mostly about the most trivial topics you can imagine. This is one of the Gemini pitfalls – a tendency to go on, and on, and on, without letting anyone else get a word in edgeways. Happily, most Geminis are entertaining conversationalists, so even if they never draw breath you'll enjoy listening to what they've got to say. When it comes to gossip, Geminis are past masters. They absolutely love it! I'm a Gemini, and once worked as an editor for a small publishing company. The office was open-plan, which meant I could see almost everything that was going on, and I answered the phone quite a lot, too, so I was always up to date with the latest gossip. It was endlessly fascinating.

Speaking of phones, these could have been invented for Geminis. There was even a British phone company called Mercury during the 1990s. Geminis enjoy using telephones and they now also have the internet to play with, which makes life even better for them.

One of the greatest Gemini qualities is versatility. Geminis can turn their hands to almost anything, and usually know a little about a lot. They are adaptable and enjoy change, provided that it isn't too drastic or unpleasant, because it makes life interesting. In fact, they are happiest when life offers them plenty of variety and diversions, and they can quickly become fed up when events take on a rather monotonous and predictable flavour. The sort of easy-going, largely uneventful life that can appeal to the more unadventurous members of the Earth signs is a Gemini's idea of hell. It's the kind of mundane existence that can drive them round the bend or send them in search of the nearest bottle. Geminis thrive in what other people think of as stressful situations; it's the boring times that get them down.

However, a Gemini needs to keep a watchful eye on their boredom threshold and learn to tolerate a little ennui every now and then. If they're so flighty that they're constantly searching for stimulation and new experiences, they will find it increasingly hard to cope with everyday life and will be endlessly looking for distractions. As a result, they'll get bored very quickly and will struggle to settle down to anything for long. This is the sort of Gemini who's like a butterfly, flitting from one occupation or activity to the next as the fancy takes them, starting projects but never finishing them, and feeling increasingly discontented and restless at the same time. This is the Jack of all trades, master of none, and you can meet Geminis who have tried a string of different jobs or hobbies but have never stuck with anything for long.

Gemini is a dual sign because it's symbolized by the Twins, which means that Geminis like to do things in twos. You can conduct a little research of your own about this by talking to the Geminis in your life. There are Geminis who like to have two books on the go at any one time, so they can switch between them as the fancy takes them. Many Geminis are able to do two things at once, such as doing the crossword and watching television at the same time, or carrying on one conversation while listening to another. Some Geminis (including me) are known by two different names, others have had two major relationships or marriages, and some have two jobs running at the same time or have two careers within their lifetime. Such duality comes completely naturally to them, and they may not even have paid much attention to it until you point it out. And, it must be said, it's equally natural for some Geminis to practise this duality in their love lives as well by juggling two partners at the same time.

The Gemini Child

Endlessly inquisitive, a little Gemini will be taking an interest in their surroundings almost as soon as they've popped out of their mother's womb, and they won't stop throughout the rest of their lives. They're completely fascinated by life and want to immerse themselves in it as much as possible. While other babies are snoozing the day away, a Gemini baby will be awake and watchful for much of the time. In fact, getting a Gemini baby to go to sleep can be quite difficult because they're so easily stimulated by what's going on around them. They'll play with the mobile hanging above their cot, try eating their covers or fiddle with their fingers, rather than close their eyes and drift off to dreamland.

Small Geminis should be encouraged to eat healthily and regularly right from the start. Although some of them love food, other Gemini babies aren't so keen on eating and must be coaxed into doing so. Most children go through a stage of not eating much or being very fussy about their food, but it's especially important for Gemini children to break this habit. Even as toddlers they tend to live on their nerves, and they must learn to counter this by eating plentiful amounts of healthy food. However, their parents shouldn't make a big song and dance about it, because that might be counterproductive. Although I eat like the proverbial horse these days, as a toddler I went on hunger strike and my mother was worried about how I was going to keep body and soul together. We went for walks in the park each afternoon, when I would feed the ducks, and in her perceptive Piscean way she soon noticed that I was eating the bread intended for my little feathered friends. Ingeniously, she quietly substituted tiny Marmite sandwiches for the stale bread, so she knew I was getting some nourishment each afternoon. I've been a huge fan of Marmite, and ducks, ever since.

Even as young children, Geminis will be perfectly happy doing at least two things at once. There's nothing wrong in this – in fact, it's perfectly normal behaviour for Geminis of all ages – and their parents should allow them to continue in this dual vein. Something that's less easy for their parents to encourage, however, is a bit of sticking power, so the Gemini child learns to start projects and then complete them. This will teach them to follow activities through from beginning to end, rather than abandon them at the first hint of tedium.

Geminis make excellent siblings, even if sometimes it is a case of "she's my sister and I hate her". They love being with children of any age and will happily play for hours with their brothers and sisters. Older Gemini children enjoy looking after their younger siblings and generally taking care of them.

When a Gemini child learns to talk, one of the first words you'll hear is "why". Why do birds have wings? Why do I have to eat my lunch? Why has that man got a bald head? (Naturally, the most embarrassing questions will be asked in the loudest voice.) And so it will go on. Gemini children genuinely want to know the answers to these questions, so their parents should be prepared to respond with honesty and good humour. And they should keep responding, because the Gemini child will keep asking questions.

Most Gemini children start to walk at an early age. It's as though they can't wait to get on their feet and begin exploring the world. They'll dash around all over the place, sometimes getting in their parents' way and sometimes, unless firmly supervised, going for an unaccompanied wander up the road.

At least life will calm down slightly once the little Gemini has learnt to read and write, because they'll spend many happy hours scribbling away or with their nose stuck in a book. This is definitely something to be encouraged, although their parents may be astonished at the way they turn family dramas into copy for the stories they write (which means their entire class will know about the day Daddy dented the car and said a lot of rude words). They should also be given toys that will allow them to fully explore their imaginations. When we were small, my Arien brother and I had endless fun with a chest of dressing-up clothes (in reality, old family cast-offs) and a box of greasepaint.

School will be good fun for a Gemini child, provided that they've got some friends there. It won't be so nice if the Gemini can't find any kindred spirits. Gemini children have excellent brains that are waiting to be filled with knowledge and encouraged to blossom, but they do get bored easily and can drift off into a world of their own if the lessons aren't very interesting. This doesn't mean they're stupid. Far from it, as they are often extremely bright and might be one step ahead of all their classmates, but they don't have very long attention spans. Once they lose track of what the teacher is talking about, they may feel too embarrassed or anxious to ask for help. Although Gemini children may seem very confident, they are often slightly worried by life. Ideally, they need to be taught in small classes so they don't have the chance to get distracted or fidgety. And if at an early age they fall in love with a subject, such as English or history, they will never lose their affection for it. It might eventually have a big bearing on their choice of career.

Health

Geminis have rather a happy-go-lucky approach to their health. In fact, they tend to take it for granted and trust to luck that every bit of their bodies is behaving itself as it should and they don't need to worry about it. If they do have to visit their doctor, they treat the entire exercise as an opportunity to observe their fellow patients and to catch up on any magazines they've missed. They'll be really disappointed if they're the only one in the waiting room and there's little to read. What kind of sloppy service is that, for heaven's sake?

The parts of the body ruled by Gemini are the lungs, arms and hands. This means that Geminis need to pay particular attention to these areas to make sure they're working well. For instance, they can be very shallow breathers, and should really do breathing exercises to increase the oxygen circulating around their bodies. But can they be bothered? Probably not! Many Geminis smoke throughout their lives, even though it doesn't do their sensitive lungs any good at all. Because they're ruled by Mercury they tend to live on their nerves, and cigarettes help to calm them down. Many Geminis end up with broken or badly bruised arms and hands at some point because they tend to wave them about a lot when they're talking, and also because they are easily distracted and often don't look where they're going or think about what they're doing. The result can be lots of trips to the casualty department of their local hospital and a wealth of knowledge about plaster casts.

One of the most noticeable things about Geminis is the fact that they can be very highly strung. This is especially likely if they're worried about something (and they're good at worrying – that bubbly persona conceals all sorts of fears and demons) or they're going through a very hectic phase in their lives. They can get very worked up, making it almost impossible to relax. Their sleep suffers, which makes them even more highly strung than ever. It's a vicious circle.

The result of this is the typical Gemini body shape – tall and skinny. Even the Geminis who like to eat three regular meals a day tend to be slim because they have so much nervous energy. It's a rare sight to see a Gemini who can sit still for long, as most of them are restless and fidgety, and that's another way of burning up calories even if they aren't aware of what they're doing. They might keep changing position, playing with their hair, tapping their feet on the floor or biting their nails. It's as though they're in constant motion.

Speaking of constant motion, regular exercise is very impor-tant for Geminis. They need to keep on the move, and to make it part of their daily routine, as a way of burning off all that excess nervous energy. They might sign up at their local gym in a fit of enthusiasm, especially if there's a great café where they can drink coffee and read the papers, but they won't be very good about actually doing any exercise there unless they have someone to keep them company and set a good example. Sports in which they play with a partner, such as tennis or squash, suit them down to the ground, as proved by the number of famous Gemini tennis players. These include Björn Borg, Steffi Graff and Pat Cash.

Sagittarius is the opposite sign to Gemini, so sometimes Geminis can suffer from Sagittarian-related health problems. These can include problems with their hips, as well as over-sensitive livers that protest if they drink too much alcohol or eat too much fatty food.

Most Geminis are lucky because they age very slowly, so they often look much younger than they really are. This means they can be lulled into a false sense of security about being immortal and never getting ill, so they're outraged when they spot the first wrinkle or grey hair when they look in the mirror. But even then they still manage to look as though they've discovered the secret of eternal youth, even though they don't look after themselves very well. It's so annoying for the more health-conscious signs, such as Virgo!

Money

This is often a sore point for Geminis because they aren't very good at salting away their cash for a rainy day. They are creatures of impulse so they enjoy splashing out whenever they feel like it. This means they can alternate between counting every penny while feeling incredibly virtuous, and blowing a startling amount of money on items that take their fancy. And, because this is the sign of the Twins, Geminis often buy things in pairs, which involves even more expense. If they can't decide which pair of shoes to buy, they will probably buy both of them, even if they don't really need either pair. They may then forget all about them when they get them home and only rediscover them a couple of years later. If they're in luck, the shoes will still be fashionable. If they look ridiculously dated, the Gemini will give them away and start the whole process all over again.

For many Geminis, it's their social life that eats up the most money. Geminis are very convivial, gregarious souls and they love getting together with friends whenever they can. This invariably costs money, whether they're meeting for a quick lunch in a favourite café, going out to dinner or inviting everyone round to their place for a meal. Even when they're on their own, they often can't resist buying a lunchtime sandwich or a takeaway for supper instead of making something from scratch for a fraction of the cost. It's more exciting, somehow.

Another typical Gemini expense is gadgets. They adore them. If you've ever wondered who buys the latest appliances and household gadgets when they've just been launched, and who doesn't wait until they've come down in price because they've been superseded by something newer (a favourite Taurus and Capricorn trick), it's Geminis. Mind you, Ariens usually aren't far behind. The development of computers, the internet, iPods, digital cameras and all those other technological toys has created an entirely new range of products for Geminis to buy. Many of them feel they can't function without the latest mobile phone, to which they'll spend as much time as possible glued.

Geminis love reading, so books, magazines and newspapers can be another significant expense for them. They have a relatively short attention span so enjoy books that won't get bogged down in too much complex detail and send them to sleep. Not that Geminis are idiots, because they're one of the most intelligent signs of the zodiac.

When it comes to keeping track of their money, balancing their chequebooks, making sure they haven't gone overdrawn at the bank and paying bills on time, most Geminis are pretty hopeless. They know they should be doing all these things but somehow they rarely get round to them unless they've a bad scare from their bank manager and put themselves on their best financial behaviour for a couple of months. Even then, they gradually slip back into their old ways. It doesn't help that they usually have several credit cards on the go at the same time, and possibly even a couple of bank accounts. Remember, this is a sign that loves variety and likes to have more than one of most things, so it's not surprising that they can lose track of what needs to be done. When they do get into financial hot water, they tend to rely on their charm to get themselves out of it again, and it's a tactic that's surprisingly successful provided that they don't rely on it too often.

Geminis who want to invest their money need to remember their need for variety. It's a good idea for them to spread their money around so they don't put all their financial eggs in one basket, which is a risky strategy and also rather tedious for them. Instead, they enjoy investing in a wide range of stocks and shares, and also in different building societies. It's a good way for them to play the financial field.

Career
Geminis excel at communicating. They belong to the Air element, which enables them to connect with others on an intellectual basis, and they're ruled by Mercury, the god of communication. This means that Geminis thrive in jobs that enable them to make contact with the rest of the world in some way or other.

Of course, there are lots of ways for them to do this. They might work in a shop, so they're in contact with the general public every day. This could suit them very well, provided that there's enough going on to keep them interested. Geminis are excellent at all forms of buying and selling, so they make formidable sales people and negotiators.

Geminis like to keep on the move, so might enjoy delivering the post. This will have the added bonus of giving them lots of people to chat to so they can keep up with the latest gossip. And they'll get paid for it, which is even better.

You will also find lots of Geminis in the media. They're in advertising (both the Saatchi brothers, who have built up an advertising empire, are Geminis), public relations and marketing, and you'll find stacks of them working as journalists and television presenters. Many Geminis are writers, too. This is a more solitary profession, but they create their own company through the people they write about. They include Jean-Paul Sartre, Lillian Hellman, Catherine Cookson, Dorothy L. Sayers, Alexander Pushkin, Margaret Drabble, Federico Garcia-Lorca, Salman Rushdie, David Hare, Ken Follett, Ian Fleming, Thomas Hardy, Thomas Mann, Sir Arthur Conan Doyle . . . the list of Gemini writers is endless.

The world of acting has its fair share of Geminis, too. Take Morgan Freeman, Michael J. Fox, Tony Curtis, Paulette Goddard, Bob Hope, Jonathan Pryce, John Wayne and Marilyn Monroe for a start. There is also the trio of horror film veterans, Christopher Lee, Vincent Price and Peter Cushing, who are not only all Geminis but whose birthdays fall within 24 hours of each other.

Not all signs can cope with being self-employed but it's no problem for Geminis, who thrive on the variety and who like being their own bosses. They can even stand (to some extent) the financial uncertainty that can come from being self-employed. However, they do need people to work with. Geminis who spend too much time on their own can become very despondent and insular, because it doesn't come naturally to them. They can also waste a lot of time ringing up their friends for a chat, surfing the internet or reading the paper, purely to cheer themselves up. Geminis need to have people to chat to and to bounce ideas off, even if they have to wander over to the coffee machine in order to do so.

Geminis make great colleagues. They're good fun, chatty, entertaining, and usually only too happy to go for a drink after work or to try out that new Italian restaurant at lunchtime. When it comes to knowing the latest gossip, Geminis are way ahead of the game. They watch what's going on, eavesdrop shamelessly on other people's conversations and chat to everyone so they can keep their finger on the pulse and discover who's doing what to whom. They come into their own at office parties, although they can also get into trouble if they flirt too much. However, Geminis can be quite distracting to work with because they're so easily bored that they're always looking for diversions. They'll natter away on the phone when they should be working, or chat about what was on television last night when you're trying to finish writing an urgent report.

As bosses, Geminis can be unpredictable and truly mercurial. You're never quite sure where you stand with them. Robert Maxwell, the larger-than-life newspaper tycoon, was a Gemini who was both loved and loathed by his employees. His behaviour may not be a very good example to other Geminis but his ability to control a media empire certainly is.

Love and Friendships

Geminis are some of the most sociable members of the zodiac. They love being with people and some Geminis prefer this to being by themselves. So relationships are very important to them. However, relationships aren't important to Geminis in the way that they are to Librans, for instance. Geminis need the mental stimulation that comes from talking to other people, and the chance to bounce their ideas off friends and partners.

It's often said that Geminis are fickle, and it's true that this isn't a sign that's exactly renowned for its loyalty. Some Geminis enjoy playing the romantic field even after they've settled down with someone, but most prefer to indulge in some harmless flirting (well, OK, fairly harmless flirting) and to leave it at that. However, if their partner has become boring or hideously predictable, the Gemini will feel less guilty about straying from the primrose path of fidelity, and will look for emotional diversions elsewhere. They'll think it's all rather a laugh, pretending that nothing's going on when they're actually conducting a red-hot affair with someone. It helps to keep them amused and they love the cloak-and-dagger aspects of it all. Until they get caught out, of course!

When looking for a partner, it's vital that a Gemini chooses someone who is a good match for them mentally. Gemini belongs to the Air element, after all, which means they're strongly orientated towards communication and thought. So they'll soon get fed up with anyone who can't string two sentences together or whose eyes glaze over whenever the

Gemini starts discussing their favourite subjects or the latest newsworthy events. Geminis are as appreciative of attractive people as anyone else, but very often it's brains rather than beauty that dictate their final choice of partner. They need someone they can talk to. If all a Gemini wants is a pretty face, what's to stop them looking in the mirror?

Gemini is the sign of the Twins and many members of this sign go through life looking for their soulmate – that person who will make them feel complete. Their twin, in other words. Whenever they meet a new friend or partner, they'll think that at last they've found that kindred spirit they've been searching for. But they'll eventually realize they've been mistaken, and will start the hunt again. What they don't realize is that this perfect person is inside them – it's another aspect of their own personality. Once they've discovered this for themselves, it will have a transformative effect on all their relationships because they won't be so dependent on other people any more.

Geminis are very sociable and enjoy keeping in touch with their many friends. The arrival of the internet has been heaven-sent for them, because it means they can conduct a hectic correspondence with people all over the world without spending a fortune in the process. They like the idea of being able to contact so many people whenever it suits them.

As friends, Geminis are lively and entertaining. It's usually very easy for them to make friends because they're so outgoing and chatty, and they can also be great fun to talk to. No wonder they have so many fans. But Geminis have such a low boredom threshold that they can quickly get fed up with their friends, especially if they become tedious or pompous, and will start looking for new ones to keep them amused. This means that most Gemini address books are full of the names of people they used to know but who have long since fallen by the wayside.

When it comes to showing their emotions, Geminis aren't very good at it. They're easily embarrassed by intense scenes and passionate encounters, and prefer to keep things light and airy. This doesn't mean they don't have feelings because they do, and they can feel things very deeply, but they may draw the line at letting anyone in on the secret.

Family Relationships

Being part of the family isn't as important to Geminis as it is to some signs of the zodiac, such as Taureans and Cancerians. Nevertheless, Geminis do enjoy being part of a gang of people because they're so inherently sociable and friendly. If they happen to be related to this gang then that's great because it means they've got a ready-made group to belong to. Gemini is the sign that rules brothers and sisters, so it's not surprising that many Geminis get on particularly well with their siblings. They share a lifelong bond.

The Gemini's fear of boredom follows them wherever they go and whatever they do, so it's just as likely to surface when they're with their nearest and dearest as when they're with friends. They'll enjoy talking to any member of the family, provided that they can have an entertaining and stimulating conversation. They won't care if this person is the same age as them or if there's a big generation gap between them, because such things don't matter to Geminis. But they'll soon switch off, or make an excuse and leave, if they're stuck with someone who only has one topic of conversation and the Gemini has heard it many times before. It won't matter if this boring person is a parent, sibling or any other blood relative, because the Gemini will still find them hard-going and want to spend as little time with them as possible. So any relatives who can only drone on about their favourite TV soaps or complain about the pensions crisis will soon find they're talking to thin air because the Gemini will have wandered off.

When it comes to being parents, Geminis are lively and good fun. They believe that childhood should be entertaining and adventurous, with plenty of opportunities to see the world, so they'll enjoy taking their children on lots of journeys. However, Geminis secretly think that tiny babies are rather boring, even when they're their own flesh and blood, because they have such limited communication skills at that age.

Geminis become much more interested in their children when they reach the toddler stage and start to talk. Then the Gemini parent can have a field day watching their child exploring the world, and will spend a small fortune on toys and books to stimulate the infant's imagination and communication skills.

Older children of Gemini parents soon learn to fend for themselves. It's not that the Gemini parent doesn't care about their children, simply that they've sometimes got more exciting things to do than to cook their children's supper or help them with their homework. At least this helps the children to become more self-sufficient, although other signs might be horrified at what they think is the rather laissez-faire attitude of the Gemini in question.

Because Geminis manage to stay youthful, both in mind and body, long after many of their contemporaries have started serious ageing, they're good companions to their children. They will want to know all about the latest slang, music and film stars, even to the point of behaving more like a middle-aged teenager than a parent. Yet they will also subtly introduce their children to books at an early age, as well as to a whole world of knowledge and information. Their children will be encouraged to use their imaginations and their intellects as much as possible.

Geminis aren't very strict as parents. They have quite a relaxed attitude to their children's upbringing, and are far more likely to get angry about their child's inability to string a sentence together or voice an opinion about world politics, than about the untidy state of their bedroom or the fact that they've dropped their school tie in a puddle.

Creativity and Potential

Geminis must be allowed to communicate. It's their main reason for being on the planet, and therefore their potential is completely tied up in their ability to make contact with the rest of the world, no matter how they choose to do it.

Writing is one of the most obvious creative outlets for Geminis. We've already discussed the number of famous

Gemini writers, so there are plenty of role models for other Geminis to follow. This means a Gemini might want to write a novel in their spare time or put together a non-fiction book on one of their favourite topics. If that sounds a bit ambitious, they can still get a tremendous amount of satisfaction from writing a private journal in which they record their thoughts and experiences. It doesn't have to be published, and that might be just as well considering that most Geminis love gossip and won't be able to resist recording all the latest exploits of their friends. If they long to see their name in print, the Gemini might write letters to the newspapers in the hope that they're published, or set up their own website.

Many Geminis get involved in local groups and societies, so they might volunteer to be the secretary or to put together a short newsletter every now and then. It will be great fun and also introduce them to lots of people, which is always a plus for a sign as sociable as Gemini.

Geminis are noted for their ability to think quickly and analytically, so they might enjoy teaching themselves to do logic puzzles or cryptic crosswords. Such skills will hone their brains and keep them active, especially as they get older. You'll also find plenty of Geminis on the winning teams at pub quizzes, because they automatically remember all sorts of strange facts that other signs dismiss as being too trivial for words. Alternatively, they could make a serious hobby out of taking part in competitions, so they gradually amass all sorts of booty in prizes.

Geminis also love playing card games (probably because they often win them), so might enjoy becoming part of a club that meets regularly to play bridge or whist. Alternatively, they may dismiss such games as being far too safe and polite, and opt for poker instead. Not that they'll be very good at keeping poker faces (leave that to the Capricorns), but they'll love pitting their wits against everyone else and analysing what their opponents are doing.

Gemini is the sign that rules the hands, so a Gemini looking for a sideline might consider training to be a manicurist or they might like to teach themselves palmistry. They're good at doing fiddly things with their hands, too, such as needlepoint or knitting, although they tend to do these in short bursts of enthusiasm before getting completely fed up with them and moving on to something else. The trick is for them to take up small projects so they complete them before they have time to get bored. Many Geminis enjoy dressmaking, too, especially if they can run up an outfit in a day. But they'll soon get very fed up if they're working on an intricate project that won't be completed for weeks. That simply isn't the way they're made.

In common with their opposite sign of Sagittarius, Geminis never stop learning. A Gemini may have left school in their teens but they will have a lifelong love of information and knowledge, and will soak it up without even noticing that they're doing so. However, some of them leave school early or without going on to university simply because they get bored with academic subjects, which can leave vast gaps in their education. They might therefore benefit from going back to school later in life, whether as a full-time student at a university, a member of an evening class or a participant in a correspondence or internet course. Very often, Geminis spend their lives investigating one topic in detail before moving on to something else, so they end up knowing a little bit about almost everything.

Holidays

Although some signs can't help doubting the wisdom of going on holiday, citing the expense and the problems with long-distance travel, Geminis have none of these qualms. The expense may make them gulp a bit at first, and they may have to scale down their ideas if they're far too ambitious or budget-busting, but once these considerations have been taken care of they will probably pay for the entire holiday with a credit card and hope for the best.

As for the disadvantages of long-distance travel, most Geminis don't really mind this. It's an opportunity to catch up on their reading, for a start. Have you ever seen those people who board an aircraft clutching a massive collection of newspapers and magazines, plus a bulging carrier bag of books bought at the airport bookshop, and wondered who they are? Well, I can tell you. They're probably Geminis. Especially if they only read for half an hour before staring out of the window or around at their fellow passengers.

Geminis even enjoy in-flight meals. They love peeling back the foil on their hot meal to discover what it is, even if they don't recognize it when they see (or taste) it. They are also endlessly entertained by all those cellophane-wrapped items that come with it, such as sweaty chunks of cheese, soft biscuits and strange-tasting muffins. They may not eat them but they'll love unwrapping them. It's all part of the holiday as far as Geminis are concerned.

If they're driving to their holiday destination, the Gemini will want to stop at as many motorway service stations as possible to see if there is any difference between them. They will even put up with inferior food purely for the enjoyment of sitting and observing their fellow travellers. Besides, they can nip into the shop on the way out and indulge in a little retail therapy.

Variety is the spice of life for Geminis, so they won't want to visit the same destination year after year. Instead, they like the thought of trying somewhere completely different each time, because half the fun is reading about the destination before they go and then trying to cram a selection of indispensable travel guides and phrase books into their already bulging luggage. They need to keep on the move, too, so are happiest if the local transport is excellent or they can hire a car to get around. Although Geminis might enjoy spending a couple of days lying on a beach, especially if they're armed with a varied selection of reading matter, they get bored if they do it day after day. Besides, many Geminis find it hard to cope with very hot weather. Therefore, beach holidays are only OK if there are other places to visit besides the sea.

Geminis are thrilled by bustling cities, especially if they can sit in a café and watch the world go by, then shop to their heart's content. Destinations that are steeped in history or culture also appeal to them, although they must offer some light relief, too. Another option is to take an activity holiday in which they'll learn something new, and it could be anything from watercolour painting to belly-dancing.

When Geminis go on holiday, they will always make the effort to send postcards to everyone back home. For some Geminis, writing and sending these postcards becomes a bit of a marathon because they don't want to leave anyone out. They also feel they've got to write different messages on each card, rather than follow the example set by Ariens and Aquarians of using one standard message for everyone. It all takes time. Geminis also enjoy buying souvenirs, whether for themselves or for loved ones they've left behind. They prefer to buy good-quality items, preferably reflecting the culture of the country they're visiting, rather than anything jokey or kitsch.

Home

Geminis need plenty of space. They may not be very large people but they have a tremendous number of possessions. They simply seem to acquire things, and often they're surprised themselves when they realize how many belongings they have. But Geminis are the magpies of the zodiac, so it's hardly surprising.

As a result, they need a home that will swallow up all that paraphernalia, as well as have room to spare for all the stuff they have yet to acquire. Most Geminis have plenty of books, so they need lots of bookshelves or the space to build them. They may also have an extensive library of tapes, CDs, videos and DVDs to find room for, not to mention the magazines they haven't yet got around to reading and the ones they're keeping because they're so interesting. Add box files full of essential pieces of paper (although they'll probably be all jumbled up so looking through them for something specific will take hours) and carrier bags full of old letters (it seems such a shame to throw them away because one day they might inspire the Gemini to write their memoirs or a thinly-disguised autobiographical novel), and you'll realize that a Gemini really needs to live in a mansion. Failing that, their local library would do nicely.

It's a fact of life that Geminis aren't very tidy. They tend to file things on the floor, especially books and other reading matter, and then forget about them. Every so often they'll have a blitz on the pile of clothes they've left on their bedroom chair, or they'll sort through the teetering tower of newspapers waiting to be read, but it may not happen very often unless they live with a very tidy companion. In which case there will be lots of screaming matches.

Geminis need plenty of entertaining space. They're very sociable creatures and they like to entertain their friends and family at home. If they're good cooks they'll enjoy showing off their expertise, but they won't produce anything very rich or creamy because foods like this don't suit them. Instead, they'll make something that's interesting to look at and fun to eat, such as lots of pizzas with different toppings (remember the Gemini need for variety).

Typical Gemini furnishings are light and bright. They may dispense with curtains altogether, or push them right back against the wall in order to let in as much light and sunshine as possible. They like simple, unostentatious fabrics, although they sometimes have a tendency to put so many patterns and colours together that it's difficult to be in the room for long without developing a headache.

Geminis don't like heavy, solid furniture. They think it's ugly and depressing, and can't bear to think that it cost so much money that they'll have to keep it for years. Instead, Geminis prefer small, relatively delicate pieces of furniture, because they can't breathe in overstuffed, crowded rooms. If they can afford antiques they'll go for timeless pieces that will mix with any style of furniture, because a Gemini décor is truly eclectic. You'll find modern chairs arranged round an antique table or Indian shawls draped over a Victorian chaise longue. There will be lots of prints, posters and paintings on the walls, again in an interesting mix. Geminis prefer bright water-colours to sombre oil paintings, and particularly like the work of three Gemini artists: Raoul Dufy, Henri Rousseau and Paul Gaugin.

Although Geminis need the living space provided by a house, most of them are equally happy in a flat, provided that it has a balcony or roof garden so they can get some fresh air every now and then. They enjoy living with other people close by because this gives them a ready-made collection of friends, and they're such chatty souls that they'll soon settle into their new community.

Clothes and Image

No matter how old a Gemini is, they will aways seem young. There's something about the sparkle in their eyes and their often slim figure, as well as their interest in contemporary culture, that takes years off them. And, most importantly of all, they will always dress in a youthful way unless they are strongly influenced by Saturn, which gives them a much more sober appearance. Paul McCartney, Björn Borg, Tom Jones, Brian Wilson, Naomi Campbell, Joan Rivers, Isabella Rossellini, Lionel Richie and Laurie Anderson are all good examples of Geminis whose looks and image belie their years.

So a typical Gemini adult looks younger than they really are, and they want to keep it that way, thank you very much. This doesn't mean that they walk around looking like mutton dressed as lamb, although you will sometimes see older Geminis who really ought to stop buying their clothes from teenager's shops. Mostly, Geminis choose clothes in bright, fresh colours and in styles that are flattering rather than ageing. They avoid frumpy and dreary outfits whenever possible, and if they've got the money they love splashing out on a whole season's worth of new clothes. Don't forget the Gemini tendency to become bored at the drop of a sock, even where their clothes are concerned. Gemini women, in particular, can have two wardrobes (remember that Gemini duality) crammed full of clothes and still lament that they've got nothing to wear. If money is tight, Geminis are skilled at livening up old outfits with fashionable accessories or wearing their clothes in different combinations.

Casual clothes suit Geminis much more than anything smart or formal. Although a Gemini might enjoy the novelty of wearing a smart suit for a short time they'll soon feel uncomfortable because of the way it restricts their movements. Both sexes are far happier in separates, such as jeans and T-shirts, and many Gemini women prefer wearing skirts and tops to dresses. If they've got to look smart, they'll do their best to stand out from everyone else in some way. This is an androgynous sign, so a Gemini woman might look good in a man's suit, complete with waistcoat and tie. It's a look that worked well for Judy Garland when she tried it, and which also suits Nicole Kidman.

Geminis love accessories. In fact, they can't have enough of them. Gemini women have libraries of handbags, belts, necklaces, bangles and bracelets, which they wear according to their ever-changing whims, while Gemini men like having plenty of belts, scarves, rings, hats and anything else that takes their fancy. Sometimes they can take this to extremes, so you'll spot a Gemini who looks as though they're taking part in a competition to see who can wear the greatest number of accessories at one time without keeling over under the weight of them. Johnny Depp and Ronnie Wood are two Geminis with a very distinctive and eclectic way of dressing, and who can wear clothes in all sorts of unlikely combinations with panache.

Of course, it definitely helps that most Geminis are tall, lean and leggy. Some of them never seem to gain any weight at all, thanks to their fast metabolism and habit of skipping meals. Even those that do put on a few pounds manage to carry them lightly or disguise them cleverly. Hugh Laurie and Clint Eastwood are just two examples of rangy, tall Geminis.

Yellow is said to be the classic Gemini colour, although in practice it's a difficult colour for many people to wear. Instead, you'll see Geminis in every colour of the rainbow, and especially in punchy, summery shades such as vivid orange, lime green, scarlet and bright blue. And sometimes they'll wear them all at once, which may or may not be such a good idea.

Famous Geminis

Henri Rousseau (21 May 1844); Naomi Campbell (22 May 1970); Joan Collins (23 May 1933); Bob Dylan (24 May 1941); Padre Pio (25 May 1887); Peggy Lee (26 May 1920); Pat Cash (27 May 1965); Kylie Minogue (28 May 1968); John Fitzgerald Kennedy (29 May 1917); Benny Goodman (30 May 1909); Clint Eastwood (31 May 1930); Ronnie Wood (1 June 1947); Marquis de Sade (2 June 1740); Raoul Dufy (3 June 1877); Rachel Griffiths (4 June 1968); Federico Garcia Lorca (5 June 1898); Björn Borg (6 June 1956); Liam Neeson (7 June 1952); Joan Rivers (8 June 1933); Johnny Depp (9 June 1963); Judy Garland (10 June 1922); Hugh Laurie (11 June 1959); Anne Frank (12 June 1929); W. B. Yeats (13 June 1865); Donald Trump (14 June 1946); Edvard Grieg (15 June 1843); Stan Laurel (16 June 1890); Igor Stravinksy (17 June 1882); Isabella Rossellini (18 June 1952); Aung San Suu Kyi (19 June 1945); Nicole Kidman (20 June 1967); Françoise Sagan (21 June 1935).

The Top Ten Gemini Characteristics

Versatile; Easily bored; Communicative; Intelligent; Highly strung; Inconsistent; Flirtatious; Restless; Superficial; Inquisitive.

Are You A Typical Gemini?

Try this quiz on the Geminis you know to find out whether they're typical members of their sign.

1 Do you always have several projects on the go at one time?
2 Are you a bit of a fidget?
3 Do you suspect that you're rather superficial?
4 Are you an incorrigible gossip?
5 Can you do two things at once?
6 Do you start at the back of magazines and work your way to the front?
7 Do you need plenty of changes of scene?
8 Do you love meeting new people?
9 Do you love making puns and jokes?
10 Do you enjoy being spontaneous?

Score
Score one point for every "no" and zero points for every "yes".
0–3 You couldn't be more Gemini if you tried. You're entertaining, lively

and intelligent, although your dread of boredom can make you abandon projects at the first sign of trouble.

4–6   You have a strong Gemini streak but it's tempered by the influence of other signs. Read the Top Ten Characteristics of the other signs to see which ones ring a bell with you.

7–10   Although you were born under the sign of Gemini you don't have many Gemini characteristics. Look through the Top Ten Characteristics of Taurus and Cancer to see if either of these sounds more like you.

Cancer

22 June–22 July

The Cancerian Adult

Cancer is one of the most sensitive signs of the zodiac. That's all thanks to the Water element to which they belong and the Moon, which is their ruling planet. Put these two factors together and you've got a sign that feels things very deeply. Cancerians are compassionate, affectionate and loving, especially towards their families and close friends, and have an instinctive need to take care of other people. They're warm and welcoming, and are prone to worrying about the people they love. They often have a rather sentimental streak, making them prone to tears. Sometimes, it has to be said, they use tears to get their own way, but at other times they simply can't help having a good cry.

This is the sign symbolized by the Crab, and it's a great clue to the typical Cancerian personality. Crabs are soft, juicy creatures protected by hard, crusty shells, with long pincers that wave about, ready to take nips out of anything that looks dangerous or aggressive. And Cancerians are pretty much the same. They're very defensive, so they arm themselves against possible attacks and pain by appearing to be rather tough and uncompromising. When you first meet a Cancerian you may even be rather intimidated by them because they give the impression of being so difficult and hard-boiled. However, they soon soften up when you begin to know them (and they begin to trust you), revealing the much gentler and more affectionate side of their personality. Before you know where you are, they'll be bringing you home-made cakes and home-grown vegetables, or inviting you round for a blow-out meal (make sure you haven't eaten for hours beforehand so you've got plenty of room for all that food).

Another similarity between crabs and Cancerians is their inability to do anything directly. Crabs inch along the beach sideways and Cancerians do the same through life. They tend to approach problems at an angle rather than head-on, and can find it very difficult to ask outright for what they want. They'd rather skirt around the subject, dropping hints and hoping that the other person catches on to what they're really saying. Sometimes this policy works and sometimes it doesn't.

Being ruled by the Moon makes Cancerians very moody and changeable. You never know if you're in or out of favour with some of them, and the only clue will be whether they're talking to you. They can be incredibly huffy and touchy when they're feeling attacked, so can retreat into a prickly, aggrieved silence at the drop of a hat. This is a tendency that they need to guard against, because it can make life very difficult for everyone around them.

Cancerians can hold on to a grudge for ages because they have such long, retentive memories. They're rather like elephants in this respect, because they never forget. They'll remember if you were kind and polite to them, but they'll also remember the times when you weren't. They won't plot their revenge in the way that a Scorpio might, but they'll file the information about you in a corner of their mind so they're prepared for the next time that you transgress in some way.

This means that the past is very important to Cancerians. For some of them, it's more valid and real than the present, and they love disappearing into nostalgic reveries about what they consider to be the good old days. They might be completely engrossed in their own past or they could be fascinated by events that go back much further than that. Many Cancerians have an instinctive love of history and they can be particularly fascinated by the story of their own family.

This love of the past can make Cancerians very reluctant to relinquish their grip on it. That means they may hold on to a relationship long after it should have ended, or they might continue to live in a house that's got too big or expensive for them purely because they can't bear to leave it. And it's the same story when it comes to getting rid of possessions that they no longer need. Rather than chuck them out, Cancerians tend to hoard their old possessions. This is the sign that has wardrobes crammed full of clothes they can't wear any longer, shelves full of books they'll never read again and drawers full of old Christmas and birthday cards that they can't bear to throw away. In some cases, Cancerians can take this hoarding instinct to extremes, surrounding themselves with clutter until they're in danger of being submerged in a sea of old newspapers, knick-knacks and toys they've kept from their childhood.

These are all examples of Cancerian tenacity. This is a Cardinal sign, which means that Cancerians fix on a goal and then work steadily towards it. And they won't give up. Helen Keller was a Cancerian who embodied this Cardinal quality to an extraordinary degree. She became blind, deaf and mute as a toddler, but despite that she learnt to read, write and talk in several languages, eventually becoming a scholar and teacher.

With their great sensitivity, it's no surprise that they are many successful Cancerian artists and musicians. The artists born under this sign include Edgar Degas, Antoni Gaudi, Frieda Kahlo, Amadeo Modigliani, Jean Cocteau, Jean Jacques Rousseau, Peter Paul Rubens, Marc Chagall, David Hockney, Camille Pissarro, J. M. Whistler, Gustav Klimt and Rembrandt. As for Cancerian musicians, they include Richard Rodgers, Lena Horne, Buddy Rich, Stanley Clarke, Jeff Beck, Deborah Harry, Willie Dixon, Leos Janacek, Huey Lewis, Ringo Starr, Bill Haley, Gustav Mahler, Percy Grainger, Carl

Orff, Arlo and Woody Guthrie, Julian Bream, Linda Ronstadt and Carlos Santana. It's a pretty impressive list by anyone's standards!

The Cancerian Child

The most important things to remember about a Cancerian child are their sensitivity and their capacity for emotion. These are two of their strongest characteristics, but ideally they should be handled carefully from an early age to stop the child getting into any bad habits later in life.

For instance, tears will never be far away with a Cancerian child. They should be allowed to cry when they want to, because it's an important part of their self-expression. So it's no good a parent saying "Don't cry, it doesn't hurt", because that will only confuse their little Cancerian. However, the Cancerian child shouldn't learn to use tears as a weapon and a means of always getting their own way, no matter how tempting that might be.

Cancerian children have enormous emotional needs, and these are best catered for within a happy, loving family. Ideally, they should have two parents, rather than one, otherwise they may start to feel slightly responsible for their lone parent and will feel they have to take care of them, even from an early age. In addition to having a full quota of parents, it will be even better if the Cancerian child has doting grandparents, aunts and uncles as well, because then they'll thrive and will feel loved. It's important for them to receive plenty of hugs and kisses, as well as emotional support. After my Cancerian niece was born, she was happiest whenever she was being cuddled and she would protest whenever she was left on her own. She needed to have her family around her, even when she was fast asleep.

In common with the other Water signs of Scorpio and Pisces, Cancerians have a tendency to bottle up their deepest feelings, so ideally Cancerian children need adults or young friends who are prepared to coax them into talking about what's worrying them. Because something inevitably will worry Cancerian children most of the time, whether it's considered trivial or important by everyone else. Even as children, Cancerians are mentally chewing their fingernails about something or other, and they need to talk about what's bothering them.

One of the most attractive and engaging Cancerian qualities is their concern for others, and even as a child the Cancerian will want to look after their family and friends. If they have any younger brothers or sisters, the Cancerian child will enjoy helping to take care of them, doing anything from changing their nappies to playing with them in the bath and teaching them how to read and write. But their parents should try to make sure that the little Cancerian has some fun as well, and isn't simply an unpaid nanny. If the Cancerian has older siblings, they will want to be included in their games and will feel very left out if this doesn't happen.

If the Cancerian is an only child, they will spend hours playing with their toys. Don't be surprised if the Cancerian converts their bedroom into a hospital for all their soft toys, so they can pretend to nurse them. There will be teddies and dolls swathed in bandages, while the little Cancerian makes sure they are all right.

Another way for a Cancerian child to bring out their innate maternal or paternal instincts is to have a pet. This may be the family dog or cat, or the child might have their own pet which they help to feed and clean. They'll do this very conscientiously, but the parents should be prepared for heartbreak when the pet becomes ill or dies. Even so, the rewards of loving the pet, and being loved in return, will outweigh any sadness for the Cancerian.

Many children love the idea of being sent away to school, but not Cancerians. They feel trepidation at the prospect of being separated from their parents, especially if they have younger siblings who are still at home, and there will probably be some tears and tantrums before the Cancerian settles down happily to life at school. For this reason, it may not be a good idea to send a Cancerian child to boarding school because they will suffer agonies of home-sickness, especially if they're quite young. It won't be so bad if they have a sibling or friends at the same school, but even so they may worry that they've done something wrong and have been sent away as a punishment. They'll need plenty of reassurance and love before they feel happy about it. And a well-stocked tuck box to take with them, to give them some edible comfort.

Health

Cancerians are so intuitive and sensitive that they easily absorb the atmosphere around them. That's great when they're in happy, easy-going surroundings because they'll feel relaxed and really good. But it can be a problem if they're with people who are agitated, angry or depressed because the Cancerian will probably pick up the prevailing mood in no time at all. Cancer is a Water sign, which means Cancerians can behave like human pieces of blotting paper, absorbing what's going on around them faster than they realize. So it's important that they find ways of protecting themselves from other people's disturbing or disruptive emotions. This might involve anything from deliberately limiting the amount of time they spend with people who set them on edge to carrying protective crystals in their pockets to ward off unpleasant vibes. Whatever they opt for, they need to find a solution that works for them.

The sign of Cancer rules the stomach and breasts, so Cancerians need to take particular care of these areas of their anatomy. A Cancerian's stomach can quickly react to difficult situations, either by becoming upset or by feeling as thought it contains a cage full of butterflies. Learning relaxation techniques is one good way to counter this tendency, and the Cancerian may also find it helpful to alter their diet and avoid any foods that make their digestive problems worse.

Before we go any further, let's clear up something I'm frequently asked. Is the sign of Cancer more susceptible to cancer than other signs? No, it isn't. Of course you will find members of this sign who develop the disease, but no more so than any other Sun sign.

One of the greatest problems for Cancerians is worry. They could turn it into an Olympic sport with no trouble at all, and they would all get gold medals without even trying (although they'd still worry that they weren't good enough at it). Cancerians, just like their Capricorn counterparts, will worry about absolutely anything, given half a chance. They don't understand those signs that shrug off worries and believe in living in the moment. It's a concept that's utterly foreign to Cancerians, who spend most of their time living in the past and a small amount of time living in the future – and fretting about what it might involve. They get anxious about the welfare of loved ones, about the cost of the mortgage, about the heating bills, about whether their clothes are going to be munched by moths in the wardrobe . . . you name it, a Cancerian will agonise about it. This, of course, will eventually interfere with their health. They'll start to lose sleep, their sensitive stomachs will play up and they'll feel washed out. It's no good telling a Cancerian not to worry, because you might as well tell a dog not to bark, but at least they can find some strategies to help them relax.

This is a Water sign, don't forget, so an excellent way for a Cancerian to relax is in or near water. Having a fragrant soak in the bath is one answer, or they might regularly go swimming, which will give them many health benefits. Walking beside a river, lake or ocean can also help them to unwind when things threaten get on top of them.

Another potential Cancerian health problem is weight gain. Even if a Cancerian starts life looking slim and lithe, they eventually begin to fill out and may even become quite plump. Their slow metabolisms and love of food don't help, and nor does their tendency to comfort-eat. It's also a fact that Cancerians tend to have rounded rather than angular bodies. They have soft tummies and rounded faces, so they're never going to look like stick-thin supermodels. And nor would they want to.

Another Cancerian characteristic that can have an impact on their health is their delicate skin. Many Cancerians have very pale, sensitive, soft skin, which reacts badly when it's exposed to too much sunlight or wind. Cancerians therefore need to learn to cover up when necessary, whether that means slathering themselves in a high-factor sun cream or wearing protective clothing, rather than run the risk of getting burnt. This is especially important if they live in a hot country or they spend a lot of time outdoors.

Money

Cancerians value money because of what it can buy them – security. Money may not be able to buy you love, as the Beatles pointed out so successfully, but (as they didn't say) at least it means you can be miserable in comfort. Emotional security is the number one priority for Cancerians, but material security isn't far behind in their list of must-haves. As a result, Cancerians have their heads screwed on straight when it comes to finance.

This is a sign that enjoys collecting things (Cancerian Imelda Marcos collects shoes, among other things), so why not collect money? Interestingly enough, some of the richest men in the world have been born under this sign, including the oil magnate Stavros Niarchos, John Jacob Astor I and John Jacob Astor IV, John D. Rockefeller, and Nelson Rockefeller. There are also several contemporary examples of Cancerians who need never worry about paying the gas bill, including George W. Bush, Richard Branson, Georgio Armani, Tom Cruise, and Tom Hanks. Money and this Sun sign definitely go together.

As you will have gathered by now, Cancerians take money very seriously. They have this in common with Capricorns, their opposite sign of the zodiac. Both signs can be somewhat stingy with their cash when the occasion demands it, although Cancerians are more generous when it comes to giving money to loved ones. Even so, they won't throw it around with reckless abandon. They're shrewd when stretching their money and making it work for them, so no one should imagine that they're easy prey or a soft touch because they most definitely aren't. They'll take great pleasure in tracking down bargains when going shopping, and will often buy in bulk in order to save money.

Cancerians acquire their respect for money and what it can buy from an early age, and they never lose it. They may have saved up all their pocket money as children so they could buy what they wanted or put it in the bank, even if their siblings and friends spent their money as soon as they got it. The small Cancerian would have privately gloated over how much money they were acquiring.

Even if they're rich, Cancerians aren't comfortable with the idea of spending money purely for the sake of it or wasting it on items they don't really need. However, if they have the money they can't see the point of making false economies, either, so are much more interested in investing in items that are built to last rather than buying cheap versions that will fall apart in no time at all. Even then, they'll scour the shops and internet sites for the best deals, rather than fork out the full price without quibbling about it.

Probably the biggest expense that most Cancerians will have in their lives is their homes. Cancerians, like Taureans, believe in the security that comes from bricks and mortar. They will invest in a home, even if it's a tiny two-up, two-down house, as soon as they can afford it, and will be delighted to have got a foothold on the property ladder. If they can bear to move house (and many Cancerians can't, because they get so attached to their homes), they can make a good return on their money. They are canny investors, so will always do their best to buy property that's a good bet rather than something that simply takes their fancy. Yes, they've got to live in it but they'll have to sell it at some point, too, and they want to know that someone else will pay good money for it.

Even if a Cancerian already has one home, they'll think long and hard about investing their spare cash in other properties as well. They might buy a second home and rent it out to cover the mortgage payments, make money out of it as a holiday let if it's in a suitable location, or buy up some business premises and lease these out at a sizeable profit.

Other suitable investments for a Cancerian include antique furniture, porcelain, jewellery and silver, provided that they know what they're buying. Many Cancerians enjoy amassing collections of things, as well, as these might eventually turn out to be worth a lot of money even if that isn't the Cancerian's reason for collecting them in the first place.

Career

If a Cancerian wants a career that makes the most of their natural abilities, anything that involves caring is an obvious choice. Cancerians are very skilled at taking care of the rest of us and do it instinctively, so it makes sense for them to make money out of it as well. And they can do this in many different ways. Children are a particular love of many Cancerians, so they might enjoy being a teacher, a nanny or working in a nursery. Princess Diana was a Cancerian who loved children, and who worked in a nursery before she married Prince Charles. Alternatively, the Cancerian could run a shop that sells children's clothes or toys. If they're medically-minded, they might train as a nurse and minister to us in hospital, or become a district nurse who visits people in their homes. Elisabeth Kübler-Ross was a Cancerian doctor who devoted much of her life to taking care of people who were dying, enabling them to have what has come to be known as a "good death".

Food is another area where Cancerians come into their own. Many of them are ace cooks so they are often drawn to the catering business. You'll find Cancerians doing everything from producing modest amounts of home-cooked food to sell in their local farmer's market to being a professional chef or running a restaurant. They also do well as waiters and waitresses, because they will do their best to make sure their customers have a good time. Alternatively, a Cancerian might be drawn to the idea of working in a hotel, where they can welcome people and make them feel at home. Another option is for them to take in lodgers (who will inevitably be cooked for and treated as one of the family) or turn their home into a small hotel or family-run bed and breakfast place. They'll probably get lots of repeat bookings, and many of their customers will become friends.

Antiques have a big appeal for many Cancerians, so they might enjoy working in an antiques shop or for an auctioneer's. They'll be really fascinated by the provenance of the antiques that pass through their hands, especially if they're silver or good furniture. Cancerians often have a great interest in history, so they might enjoy studying the subject, writing about it or teaching it.

Bricks and mortar are so important for Cancerians that it makes sense for them to earn money from something connected with property. They do well as estate agents (when they'll be surprisingly hard-boiled about negotiating good prices for the properties on their books), interior decorators, furniture designers, makers of soft furnishings and house-sitters for people going on holiday.

Professions connected with water can also appeal to Cancerians, and you'll find them working in the fishing industry, as swimming instructors, chartering boats, on cruise ships and as marine biologists. Conservation of marine life is particularly dear to their hearts.

Whichever way a Cancerian earns their daily bread, they'll want to do it in congenial surroundings. They'll also enjoy making a big fuss of their colleagues, perhaps bringing in home-made biscuits or cakes for special occasions (such as every Friday!) or instigating regular evenings when they all go out for a meal so they can get to know one another better. The Cancerian will probably end up giving sympathy and sensible advice to lovelorn colleagues or hearing about their family problems, and will be genuinely concerned about them.

This is a Cardinal sign, meaning that Cancerians always want to get ahead and make progress, and you'll see this reflected very clearly in their careers. These are people who want to get on in life and who don't mind doing lots of hard work in the process. They certainly don't expect things to land in their lap without any effort on their part. They're far too realistic for that.

Love and Friendships
This is one area of life in which Cancerians specialize. Being a Water sign means they're full of emotion, and they can't help showing it. This is not a sign that's able to hide its feelings for long, although they'll do their best. Just like crabs hiding inside their tough, protective shells, Cancerians can come across as rather tough and, well, somewhat crabby at first. What they're actually doing is protecting themselves from possible dangers and are waiting to see what sort of person you'll turn out to be before they get too involved with you. But behind that often rather difficult and uncompromising exterior beats a heart of gold, and once you've won it it's yours for ever. Whether you want it or not.

A Cancerian can't imagine not having other people in their life. Who would they take care of, for a start? Cancerians love to look after people and they instinctively respond to them with sympathy and compassion once those initial difficult moments are over. One of their favourite ways of showing that they care is to feed people. It gives them great pleasure to cook someone a meal or bake them a cake, for no other reason than that they want to make that person feel special.

In fact, Cancerians have a very strong paternal or maternal streak in them, whether or not they ever become parents. They can't help taking care of others and worrying about them. "Are you all right?" is a classic Cancerian phrase, normally uttered in a rather anxious tone of voice. And it may have been sparked off by something as innocent as you refusing a third slice of home-made cake to avoid your waistband getting so tight that it cuts off your circulation. Sometimes this is reassuring and comforting but at other times it can be rather claustrophobic and oppressive.

This is where we reach the potential emotional problems that a Cancerian can experience. Because they have such a strong need for emotional security, Cancerians are often reluctant to let partners out of their sight for long. Perhaps they're worried that they won't come back, or they genuinely feel they can't survive without them. Even if the Cancerian simply enjoys the other person's company, occasionally their concern can tip over into smother-love. So it's important for Cancerians to give their nearest and dearest plenty of room to breathe. They should be especially careful not to place heavy emotional demands on their loved ones, or to use emotional blackmail (such as staging a sulk or going into a major huff) in order to get their own way. It's often difficult for Cancerians to be direct when asking for things that they need, which can lead to misunderstandings and bad feeling all round. When dealing with problems in a relationship, they find it hard to talk about what's wrong. They hope that their partner will somehow read their mind and prevent them having to put their feelings into words. Not surprisingly, this approach often doesn't work.

A Cancerian is the sort of person who wants a relationship to last forever, which means they can be very resistant to the idea of endings. This applies to friendships as well as love affairs. Cancerians like to stay in touch with their school friends throughout their lives, even if they have nothing in common any longer. They're loyal friends, although they can be quite possessive and demanding when they feel insecure.

A Cancerian's tenacious instincts may tell them to cling on to a relationship long after it should have finished, but this can lead to unhappiness and stop both people moving forward. Even if the relationship does come to an end, the Cancerian may struggle to acknowledge this emotionally. The song "Never Can Say Goodbye" could have been written for them. They can't throw out belongings they no longer need and neither can they let fading relationships come to a natural end.

Family Relationships
Family is everything to a Cancerian. They need to belong to a group of people that they love. In an ideal world, these people are their flesh and blood. But sometimes that isn't possible for some reason, in which case the Cancerian will

create their own family from friends, neighbours, colleagues, customers or pets.

Many astrology books tell you that Cancerians always get on wonderfully well with their families but that isn't true. I've met many Cancerians who have no time for their relatives because they don't get on, but who have created a tight network of close friends who are their family to all intents and purposes. These people will always come first as far as the Cancerian is concerned, and they'll lavish plenty of love and attention on them.

Some Cancerians are so wrapped up in their families, whether these are created or ready-made, that they don't really bother with anyone else. It's as though no one else really matters, or they're relegated to a much lower rung in the pecking order. You will even come across Cancerians who spend so much time with their families that they don't feel the need for anyone else in their lives. In fact, they may even be slightly offended when members of their family have outside interests because they will think they shouldn't need them when they've got each other. Taureans and fellow Cancerians will understand, but more freedom-loving signs such as Sagittarius and Aquarius will feel suffocated and trapped by such a strong need for enforced togetherness.

Cancerian parents should be very careful not to let their natural protectiveness turn their home into a prison for their children. They won't mean to do this and would be mortified to think that was how it felt, but they can definitely create a smothering atmosphere in which their children are tied to their apron strings. Unlike many families where it's the other way round, it will be the Cancerian parents who experience acute separation anxiety when their children start going to school. The mother who stands in tears at the school gates, watching her child starting his first day at nursery school, is either born with the Sun in Cancer or with several other planets in this sign. And it will be the same story throughout the child's life, especially when he leaves home. That will trigger a major crisis in the life of the Cancerian parent, who will have sleepless nights fretting about how their child is coping in the great big world without them.

However, if they can manage to avoid this pitfall, Cancerians make wonderfully caring and tender parents. They will absolutely dote on their children, recording every significant event from their birth onwards. And the moment they hold their first child in their arms, they will feel as though they've finally achieved something that they've been searching for their whole lives. It's as though everything makes sense at last, and they will vow to look after their child throughout their life.

If the Cancerian doesn't have children of their own for some reason, they will take an avid interest in the children of their friends and family. For instance, they'll be adoring aunts and uncles who spoil their nephews and nieces absolutely rotten, buying them special presents and taking them out on treats. Above all, the Cancerian will let the children know how deeply loved they are, and that will be their greatest gift of all.

Creativity and Potential

This is the sign of the homemaker, so it's an area where most Cancerians are very gifted and have a lot to offer. Many of them have got this down to a fine art, creating homes that are comfortable, welcoming and relaxing. It's a wonderful way for them to express their creativity, whether they're making their own curtains and loose covers for the furniture, dreaming up subtle decorative schemes or creating a safe, happy environment in which their children can grow up. Some of them are so good at transforming their homes into truly desirable residences that they can easily do this to make money.

Cancerians are fascinated by the past and therefore love antiques. However, these are often expensive to buy when they're in good condition, so the Cancerian could learn to restore tatty antiques to their former glory. They can either teach themselves or, preferably, take some proper courses in restoration so they don't do the wrong thing and end up wasting both their time and money. Equally, they might be interested in buying up an old house that's seen better days and painstakingly putting it back together again.

While we're on the subject of the home, a Cancerian might enjoy growing lots of their own fruit and vegetables, or even running a smallholding if they get really ambitious. It will give them a huge glow of satisfaction to produce their own food. Many of them also love baking bread, partly because there is such a wealth of tradition wrapped up in it.

Cancerians are Water signs, so almost anything connected with water could appeal to them and help to bring out their potential. They could take swimming lessons so they become accomplished swimmers, or learn how to use a surfboard if they live near a suitable stretch of sea. Deep-sea diving, snorkelling and fishing might also suit them. If such activities are unsuitable for some reason, a Cancerian could create a pond in their back garden so they can sit quietly and observe what's going on in it. Another option would be to decorate objects, such as mirrors and small boxes, with shells. They could give them away as presents or, if they become very skilled, sell them to interior design shops.

With their love of family and the past, it makes sense for a Cancerian to research their family tree. They'll be fascinated by what they discover and it will give them a very strong sense of connecting with their roots. Mind you, they could also discover a few skeletons which might not be such fun but would at least be interesting. Alternatively, they could organize all the family photographs into chronological order, complete with little labels to identify everyone for the benefit of future generations. If the Cancerian wants to take this one step further, they could sign up for a history course or teach themselves about a particular period of history.

Many Cancerians enjoy photography because it's a way of recording the moment for posterity. They can become very skilled photographers, whether they're taking snapshots of their family or they want to turn their photography skills into an art form. George Eastman, who was a nineteenth-century American pioneer of photography, was born under the sign of Cancer.

Another way of recording what has happened to a Cancerian is for them to write their memoirs, even if they never want to get them published. Once they get started, they'll love writing down the story of their life and they may even want to augment it with photographs, letters and other keepsakes (of which the Cancerian will inevitably have many), and leave it for future generations of their family. Marcel Proust, who spent years shut up in a cork-lined room for health reasons, was the Cancerian who wrote *Remembrance of Things Past*, a Cancerian book title if ever there was one.

A rather less gentle pursuit that Cancerians could take up is boxing. A surprising number of world-class boxers have been born under this sign, including Mike Tyson, Jake La Motta, Leon Spinks and Jack Dempsey. Even Sylvester Stallone, who had such a success in the Rocky films, is a Cancerian.

Cooking is another wonderful way for a Cancerian to express themselves, and if they're any good at it they can expect plenty of encouragement from their family and friends!

Holidays
These can be rather a sore point for many Cancerians because, quite simply, they don't like leaving home. In fact, they would often much rather stay at home than wrench themselves away from all that's dear and familiar, and have to cope with strange beds, a disrupted routine and all the other difficulties that holidays can bring. Besides, they may have treasured family pets that will have to go into a cattery or kennels if the Cancerian goes away on holiday, and they can't bear the thought of that.

Familiarity breeds content for Cancerians, so if they do manage to tear themselves away from their home comforts they'll still feel uneasy when visiting somewhere for the first time. What if they don't like it? Actually, they're the sort of person who is welcomed with open arms by hoteliers because if they like the place they'll return year after year, and they'll take their nearest and dearest with them. What started off as a strange hotel will become a home from home, and the Cancerian will probably exchange Christmas cards with the owners each year. They'll love knowing that they can spend their holiday in familiar surroundings and, being a thrifty soul, may even have managed to negotiate a decent discount for being such a loyal customer. However, this arrangement may not go down very well with the rest of the Cancerian's family, especially if they belong to some of the more adventurous signs of the zodiac. Catch an Aquarian or Sagittarian going back to the same place year after year? Never!

It's a rare Cancerian who doesn't enjoy eating, so they'll want to choose a destination in which the food is to their liking, and they'll hope that there's lots of it. Cancerians can't cope with anything too exotic or strange, and they need to take care of their sensitive tummies, which rules out some of the more far-flung corners of the world. They also can't tolerate extreme heat or humidity, because they quickly start to wilt. With their propensity to worry over the slightest problem, it's not a good idea for them to stray too near to war zones or other places of potential unrest. Countries in which animals and children are treated badly won't appeal either, because the Cancerian will be so upset about what they see going on around them.

Cancerians love being near water and would enjoy a relaxing beach holiday or staying at a hotel on a large lake. Alternatively, they could hire a boat or go on a cruise, which gives them the chance to make lots of friends while living in comfort. Another option is a self-catering holiday in which the Cancerian can create a home from home. However, this isn't such a good idea if the Cancerian is going with the rest of the family because they'll probably end up being chained to the sink and cooker, while everyone else goes off and has a good time. Many Cancerians own caravans or mobile homes, which neatly solves the holiday dilemma of being in unfamiliar surroundings but still means they may spend the entire time taking care of their loved ones.

Thanks to the Cancerian tendency to acquire objects, most members of this sign will return home with many more possessions than they had when they left. They won't be able to resist buying lots of souvenirs, not only for themselves but for the loved ones they left behind. They'll choose foods that are easily transportable, such as salamis or tins of expensive delicacies, as well as items that can have rather sentimental overtones. While on holiday, they'll make sure that they send postcards to all their favourite people, and will secretly feel hurt if they don't see them on display next time they visit them.

Home
It's putting it mildly to say that home is where a Cancerian's heart is. It's the most important place in the world for them, because it's where they feel safest and most comfortable. And if it isn't, then something is very wrong in the Cancerian's life and they will be acutely aware of it.

Cancerians put a lot of time, money, effort and love into their homes. They would rather buy property than rent it, because they consider that to be a much better investment and also because it then means they won't run the risk of being turfed out by their landlord. Even if a Cancerian's home is not much bigger than a shoebox because that's all they can afford, they will still want it to be as cosy and comfortable as possible. If they've got the money to pay for something bigger, the Cancerian will always watch what property prices are doing, even if they have no intention of moving, purely so they can keep an eye on their investment. However, it will be a huge wrench for them to move when the time comes. And as for packing up their many belongings . . . it doesn't bear thinking about!

One of the most notable features of any Cancerian's home is the amount of possessions it's able to hold. To look at some Cancerian homes you'd imagine they needed a shoehorn to fit everything in. It's a rare Cancerian who goes for minimalist living, with clear surfaces and everything tucked neatly out of sight. Instead, a typical Cancerian home is positively bulging at the seams. You will probably have to be careful where you stand or sit for fear of knocking over a prized possession or squashing the cat which has got lost amid a towering pile of plump cushions. Every table top, every mantelpiece and every wall will be covered with the Cancerian's belongings, some of which are meant to be there and others of which have been put there temporarily and then forgotten. There will be endless photographs of loved ones past and present, paintings of ancestors, copies of old family trees, pictures of the Cancerian's previous houses and snapshots of their beloved pets. If they have children, the Cancerian may even have framed their tiny shoes or a lock of their hair and put these on the wall as well.

It's a Virgo's idea of a dusting nightmare. Not that the Cancerian will care (unless they happen to live with a Virgo), because they will simply feel that their house has character and personality. Many Cancerians are avid collectors, whether by accident or design, so there will probably be a few of their collections dotted about too.

Be careful if a Cancerian ever asks you to get something out of one of their cupboards because you should be prepared for an avalanche of possessions to come tumbling out all over the floor. It's the same story in the Cancerian's kitchen, which they consider to be the hub of the house. The kitchen cupboards will be groaning with china and food, and the drawers crammed full of kitchen equipment as well as other things that might one day come in handy, such as short lengths of string (which the Cancerian will tell you are too good to throw out, even though they can't think of a single way of using them). Once opened, it's hard to close the drawers again without getting something trapped. And it could be your fingers.

Ideally, a Cancerian's kitchen is big, with plenty of space for all their family and friends to sit around the table. Their idea of heaven is to have a big farmhouse kitchen with an Aga (and a cat sleeping on top of it), a scrubbed kitchen table, a few armchairs for flopping about in, and trays of freshly baked bread and cakes that have just come out of the oven and are waiting to be eaten by the hungry hordes.

When choosing furniture, Cancerians like to go for things that will last. They aren't interested in fashionable pieces that will look out of date in a couple of years or flimsy items that look in danger of falling apart. Instead, they go for well-made, classic furniture. If it's old or antique, so much the better. It may also have been in the family for a long time, as Cancerians love the idea of owning family heirlooms. Their sentimental value will far outweigh any monetary considerations.

Clothes and Image

As in every other area of their lives, Cancerians like their clothes to be comfortable. Although very fashion-conscious Cancerians will wear whatever has just come off the catwalk, they'll still hope that they can sit down and stand up in their designer threads without wincing or having to wipe away tears of pain. Most Cancerians, however, want to be able to move around easily and aren't keen on waistbands that dig in or collars that threaten to choke them. They also aren't quite so bothered about keeping up with the latest fashions.

But that doesn't mean they want to look frumpy, dowdy or as if they don't care. Many dress designers have been born under this sign, including Georgio Armani, Bill Blass, Pierre Cardin, Oscar de la Renta, Bruce Oldfield and Elizabeth Emmanuel (who, with her then husband, David, designed the wedding dress for Lady Diana Spencer, a fellow Cancerian). Perhaps it's something to do with the idea of clothes providing some form of protection, just as a crab's shell protects the soft flesh concealed within it.

Having said that, some Cancerians have turned out to be great trendsetters. Diana Rigg's sexy, leather-clad persona as Emma Peel in *The Avengers* during the 1960s launched a plethora of slinky women on the high street, and Lady Diana was transformed into a worldwide fashion icon after she became the Princess of Wales. Another Cancerian woman noted for her dress sense was Barbara Cartland, who always wore frothy pink dresses.

Cancerians like to wear soft, natural fabrics. They aren't happy in anything that's too starchy or rough, and they much prefer cottons, silks and linens to nylons and other synthetics.

Many Cancerians love wearing woolly cardigans and jumpers, especially if they've knitted them themselves, because they're so warm and comforting, and when they're at home they're quite happy to slop around in old clothes. Naturally, they'll have plenty of these because they won't be able to throw them away.

Classic Cancerian style tends to be timeless. These aren't people who throw away their clothes at the end of every season and then completely replenish their wardrobes with the latest offerings. That seems wasteful in the extreme and, besides, Cancerians can rarely bring themselves to throw anything away. As a result, they tend to wear a lot of old favourites, some of which stand the test of time admirably while others can look sadly dated. If they've got the space to hold on to their clothes for long enough, they can come round in fashion again. Even if the Cancerian can no longer fit into them (and many of them do tend to put on a lot of weight as they get older, much to their chagrin), they can either pass them on to their children or sell them to shops specializing in vintage clothes.

Cancerian men can look very good in smart suits and ties, while Cancerian women like floaty, romantic clothes. Both sexes usually have pale skins, so can easily look washed out in very strong, dominant colours. As a result, they look good in subtle shades, especially if they are reminiscent of the sea. This is, after all, a Water sign. It's ruled by the Moon, and so iridescent colours and silvery greys also suit Cancerians.

Cancer is the sign of the Crab. These are creatures that carry their homes around with them and Cancerians like to do the same by cramming as much stuff as possible in their pockets or bags. A Cancerian woman may not go to the gym each week but she certainly does unofficial weight-training each time she lifts up her handbag because it's bound to weigh a ton. She'll have everything in there, including the essentials such as her wallet, purse and chequebook, but also lots of other things that she believes she needs. For instance, as well as her own set of keys she'll probably have those of her parents, best friend or closest neighbour, so she can let herself into their houses in an emergency. She'll have her diary, which will be chock full of dates and scribbled notes, and a selection of photos of her nearest and dearest. She may also have some seashells that she collected during her last beach holiday, indigestion remedies and goodness knows what else. A Cancerian man will have all these things too, but they'll be stuffed into his pockets (which will completely spoil the line of his trousers and jackets), rolling around in his briefcase or littering the floor of his car.

Famous Cancerians

Billy Wilder (22 June 1906); Joséphine de Beauharnais (23 June 1763); Jeff Beck (24 June 1944); George Orwell (25 June 1903); Claudio Abbado (26 June 1933); Helen Keller (27 June 1880); Kathy Bates (28 June 1948); Antoine de Saint-Exupéry (29 June 1900); Mike Tyson (30 June 1966); Amy Johnson (1 July 1903); Hermann Hesse (2 July 1877); Tom Cruise (3 July 1962); Dr Thomas Barnado (4 July 1845); Jean Cocteau (5 July 1889); HH The Dalai Lama (6 July 1935); Gustav Mahler (7 July 1860); Elisabeth Kübler-Ross (8 July 1926); Tom Hanks (9 July 1956); Marcel Proust (10 July 1871); Gough Whitlam (11 July 1916); Julius Caesar (12 July 100 BC); Harrison Ford (13 July 1942); Emmeline Pankhurst (14 July 1858); Iris Murdoch (15 July 1919); Margaret Court (16 July 1942); Donald Sutherland (17 July 1935); Nelson Mandela (18 July 1918); Edgar Degas (19 July 1834); Sir Edmund Hillary (20 July 1919); Ernest Hemingway (21 July 1899); Rose Kennedy (22 July 1890).

The Top Ten Cancerian Characteristics

Sensitive; Imaginative; Sentimental; Protective; Defensive; Family-minded; Loving; Money-minded; Tenacious; Moody.

Are You A Typical Cancerian?

Try this quiz on the Cancerians you know to find out whether they're typical members of their sign.

1　Can you put the past behind you without a qualm?
2　Is it difficult for someone to hurt your feelings?
3　Are you happiest in your own company?
4　Where food is concerned, can you take it or leave it?
5　Do you find it easy to end relationships?
6　Do you tan easily?
7　Are you very tidy?

8 Generally speaking, do you like being away from home?
9 Is it difficult for you to shed tears?
10 Do you believe in travelling light through life?

Score
Score one point for every "no" and zero points for every "yes".

0–3   You couldn't be more Cancerian if you tried. Your emotions run deep, making you sensitive and easily hurt. You can be moody and you like to protect yourself by being in familiar places as much as possible.

4–6   You have a strong Cancerian streak but it's tempered by the influence of other signs. Read the Top Ten Characteristics of the other signs to see which ones ring a bell with you.

7–10   Although you were born under the sign of Cancer you don't have many Cancerian characteristics. Look through the Top Ten Characteristics of Gemini and Leo to see if either of these sounds more like you.

Leo

23 July–23 August

The Leo Adult

Leo is the zodiac sign connected with royalty, and there's always something regal about a Leo. It may be their dignified manner, their air of calm authority or perhaps it's the tiara perched on their head! It's an entirely fitting association, though, because Leo is the sign of the lion, and what is the lion but the king of the jungle? Many words connected with lions also apply to Leos. They have a lot of pride, for instance, and it's often completely justified. They may also have a mane of hair, just like their feline counterpart. Very often a Leo is easily identifiable by their hair, and in suitably royal style it's often referred to as their crowning glory.

You only have to look at a list of famous Leos through the ages to realize that this is definitely the sign of royalty. Even if a Leo doesn't have blue blood flowing through their veins they seem to belong to an indefinable A-list that excludes lesser mortals. Here's a sample of just a few well-known Leos who fit into this glittering category: Omar Khayyám, Carl Jung, George Bernard Shaw, Aldous Huxley, Dag Hammerskjöld, Henry Ford, Henry Moore, Claudius I, Queen Elizabeth the

Queen Mother, Neil Armstrong, Alexander Fleming and Malcolm Forbes.

A typical Leo likes being in the limelight every now and then. They may not want to be the centre of attention twenty-four hours a day (although some Leos do), but they certainly like people to take notice of them. They aren't comfortable with the idea of playing second fiddle to someone, and even if they are initially happy to be in someone's shadow they soon want to emerge into the spotlight themselves. After all, it's where they belong, and a Leo who continually lurks in the shadows is denying an essential part of their character.

Leos like things to be done properly, and they're certainly fantastic at organizing people and making systems run smoothly. Sometimes, they may have a tendency to switch from being a good organizer to someone who's a bit bossy and who thinks they know best. Not surprisingly, this isn't very popular with other people. However, the Leo's irrepressible sense of humour usually asserts itself sooner or later, enabling them to laugh at themselves and tone down their act a bit.

Leo is a fixed sign, which means they can have very fixed opinions. In fact, not to beat about the bush, Leos can be incredibly stubborn, opinionated and inflexible at times. They know they're right and are determined not to concede to anyone. They will hold their ground come what may, even if it makes them unpopular. Henry Ford was a Leo car manufacturer who famously said his Model T Ford was available in every colour as long as it was black. You will also encounter Leos who can be rather pompous and full of themselves, almost as though they really are royalty and everyone else is a lesser mortal. They look down their noses at everyone and can't help boasting about themselves, their connections and their fantastic taste. They may also be incredibly vain about their own good looks. Happily, these puffed-up Leos are few and far between, because the vast majority of the members of this sign are dignified without being starchy, proud without being self-obsessed, and they have high standards without being snooty.

Leos have some wonderful characteristics, which is why they're such a popular sign of the zodiac. They're kind, big-hearted, funny, entertaining, generous, magnanimous, trusting, idealistic, romantic and creative. They care about their friends and family, are staunchly loyal and reliable, and never forget other people's acts of kindness to them. When you have a Leo on your side you feel you can take on the world and win, partly because you know they'll go into battle on your behalf if necessary and partly because they boost your confidence to such an extent that you start to think you really must be rather special after all. After all, a Leo loves you, and that's really saying something!

Bees need honey and Leos need praise. You must show them your appreciation on a regular basis, and you've got to mean it, too, because they'll soon see through you if you're faking it. But this isn't usually a problem because there's always some reason to praise the Leo in your life, whether it's their cooking, their sense of style, their organizational skills or their sheer good-heartedness. They're generous with their praise, too, and will encourage you to do all sorts of things you'd never have dared to contemplate without them cheering you on.

This is the sign ruled by the Sun and it belongs to the Fire element, too, so there is plenty of heat associated with Leos. They love sunshine, they're warm and affectionate, and they're full of enthusiasm and optimism. Even when life gives a Leo some terrible knock-out punches, they'll eventually get back on their feet and carry on, although it may take a few years to do so. They won't be defeated because they have such a love of life and a determination to do their best. You can't help loving them for it, and being thankful for having them in your life. Where would you be without them?

The Leo Child
Leo children are compact balls of energy and enthusiasm. They are also very entertaining, because they love making people laugh and keeping them amused. My small nephew is a Leo and he loves clowning around, pulling faces and doing silly

things to make everyone laugh. He's always endearing and he loves having an appreciative audience, in true Leo style.

There are two things that Leo children need more than anything else – love and praise. This is the sign of love, after all, so it makes sense that Leo children need plenty of affection, hugs and kisses. They must know that they're cherished and treasured in order to feel safe, otherwise the world will seem a very hostile place. For this reason, it can be very confusing if their parents blow hot and cold, being loving one minute and angry the next, because the Leo child won't know where they stand. They are very honest, too, and therefore expect everyone else to be the same. If their parents or other relatives lie to them over something important, the little Leo's faith in them will be shaken and in future they will always wonder whether they can trust them.

It's important for parents and siblings to praise the Leo child whenever they deserve it. They need to know that they've done well because this encourages them to do even better in the future. Some people believe that praising children gives them swollen heads, but it's really important for little Leos to receive lots of pats on the back. Of course, it's no good if the Leo is praised to the skies indiscriminately, but parents must be very careful when ticking off their Leo child because any criticism will really sting. They certainly shouldn't be deliberately hurtful or scathing about what the Leo is trying to do, because that will make them reluctant to try again. Despite that bouncy, effervescent and enthusiastic façade, Leos can be very sensitive and are easily hurt.

From an early age, Leo children should be encouraged to express themselves artistically and creatively. That might mean painting lots of pictures or writing stories, dressing up, learning how to sew or anything else that takes their fancy. They'll play by themselves if necessary, but it's much better for them to play with siblings, friends or their parents. Leos love to join in and be a part of a group, even from an early age, so they aren't very happy if they're left by themselves for too long. Ideally, older brothers and sisters should spend plenty of time with their little

Leo sibling. That way, the little Leo won't feel left out. Siblings are very good at knocking the corners off each other, so they will probably be the ones to teach the Leo to take their turn rather than to expect, in true royal style, to always come first. They will also stop the little Leo being incredibly bossy, or showing off and expecting to be the centre of attention all the time.

As this is such an affectionate and demonstrative sign, a Leo child must have plenty of people to love. A Leo child needs regular hugs and kisses from their family, which they'll usually return with gusto unless they're busy with something more important, such as eating a chocolate biscuit or playing with a new toy. But, even then, they normally relent at the last minute. Leos love being around animals, too, whether it's the family pet, they're visiting sheep in the countryside or looking at the animals in a zoo.

Leos are very image-conscious, even as young children. A Leo child will have firm ideas about what they will and won't wear, and if you disagree with them you'll get a good example of that strong Leo will and stubbornness. You'll go blue in the face before you can persuade the Leo to do what you say.

Most young Leos enjoy rushing around and keeping busy, which helps to burn off any excess energy and keep them fit, and they should be encouraged to do so. It will help them to sleep well at night and might even become a good habit that they can keep throughout their lives. Other activities that suit small Leos include gymnastics, dance, swimming and athletics (even if it's a rough and ready egg-and-spoon race with their siblings in the garden).

If you're choosing toys for your favourite small Leo, they love cuddly toys such as teddy bears and will lavish masses of affection on them. Little Leo girls normally like to play with dolls, and Leo boys enjoy train sets, toy forts and bows and arrows. Both sexes will like being given clothes, even at an early age, especially if they can have their picture taken in their new finery.

Health

If health is wealth, most Leos are pretty well-off. Because this is a Fire sign, Leos tend to be fit and in good health. They have robust constitutions and their natural enthusiasm for life helps to stay them well because there's always something interesting for them to look forward to. Their innate optimism and their sunny tempers (well, most of the time, anyway) have very beneficial effects on their health.

The Leo's element of Fire and their ruling planet, the Sun, give them plenty of energy but it can burn out quite quickly sometimes. This is when a Leo can run out of steam, especially if they feel their efforts aren't being appreciated. After all, Leos always need praise and they will go into a decline if they don't get it. Their energy levels can also be depleted when their relationships aren't going according to plan, because love is such an important part of their lives. If a Leo has been let down in love, they need to restore their faith in human nature by spending time with other people they care about. They will also benefit from being with a cherished pet, whose unconditional love will help to make them feel better.

Leo rules two areas of the body – the heart and the spine. Since all Leos have big hearts, it makes sense that this sign rules this particular muscle. However, it does mean that Leos need to take care of their hearts. They might be interested in eating a diet that is good for their heart and in taking plenty of regular cardiovascular exercise. This is another area where a pet can be beneficial to a Leo, because scientific tests have proved that stroking an animal can reduce high blood pressure.

It's very important for Leos to learn to take care of their backs, too, since this is the other area that's vulnerable for them. Ideally, they should learn how to lift heavy objects without placing a lot of strain on their spine, and choose chairs that support their back rather than allow it to go into a slump. They should also make sure they're sleeping on a good mattress, rather than something that has seen better days (or nights) and which has collapsed in the middle like a soggy cake.

Exercise is good for all of us but it's good for Leos because it allows them express themselves – something that is essential to any Leo's mental and emotional well-being. If the Leo doesn't fancy working up a sweat in the gym, they could consider taking up dancing, skating or any other sport that combines balletic grace and self-expression with muscle-power. Yoga and Pilates are also good for Leos because they help them to strengthen their back muscles and improve their posture.

With their love of the good life, Leos need to keep a watchful eye on their weight. It can creep up on them without their really noticing it, so it seems that one week they can fit into their clothes without any trouble at all and two weeks later they can't do up their waistband without taking really deep breaths. It can take a lot longer than this for them to put on weight, of course, but the effects will be the same and the Leo will be horrified to find that their clothes don't fit properly any more. So Leos should make sure they get plenty of regular exercise, even if it's nothing more than a brisk walk around the block every day, and they should also try to monitor their intake of rich foods. Some Leos adore cream, butter and cheese, and will happily munch away at them even when they shouldn't. They also can't resist biscuits, cakes and puddings, none of which will do their waistlines any favours. Fine wines can be another downfall, unless the Leo is very strict with themselves.

Money

This is often a sore point for Leos! Their innate generosity and their appreciation of all the good things in life mean they're frequently out of pocket. Even if they earn good money, it can all vanish in a series of delicious spending sprees, weekend breaks and trips to their favourite restaurants. Leos like the idea of picking up the tab for things because it means they're taking care of people and making them feel good. But it can lead to hideous credit card bills or bright red bank accounts. What's more, Leos like to do things properly so will want to give someone the very best that they can afford. And sometimes, they'll still spend the money even when they can't afford it.

Leo

If a Leo is honest (which most of them are), they'll admit that they like the idea of having money. They enjoy the cachet it brings and the things it can buy. For instance, given the choice between staying in a luxurious hotel and roughing it in a bed and breakfast, guess which option a Leo is going to choose! They have the same luxury-is-best approach to everything in life, and they believe that quality rather than quantity wins every time. Why buy something shoddy when they can save up their money and buy the real thing? No wonder gold is the Leo colour!

For some Leos, it's very important to maintain their high standards and give everyone the impression that they're doing very nicely, thank you. They also find that it cheers them up. I've known Leos who don't have two pennies to rub together but who still like to put on a good show by serving decent wine and looking prosperous. They would also far rather splash out on an expensive but delicious cup of coffee in elegant surroundings than have two cups of indifferent coffee and a sandwich in their local cheap cafe where the smell of burning fat clings to their clothes for the rest of the day.

Having said that, some Leos attract money in the way jam attracts wasps. If you look at a list of famous Leos you'll notice that a lot of these people will never need to worry about keeping up with the Joneses because they are the Joneses.

If a Leo has got some spare cash and is looking for interesting ways to invest it, they might be attracted to antique jewellery. Made from gold, of course! However, they should take expert advice before investing heavily, just as they should with any other sort of investment. Another classic Leo investment is property. Leos are no fools and they know that bricks and mortar can represent one of the best returns on their money. This means they'll want to own the roof over their heads as soon as possible, and they'll continue to move up the property ladder until they can afford to buy the home of their dreams. If they've got the money, they'll consider buying another property as well and renting it out, possibly as a holiday home so they can let their friends use it sometimes.

With their organizational skills, Leos are very good at keeping track of how much money they've got. They take pride in knowing how they're doing financially, even if the facts themselves are depressing enough to keep them awake at night. They certainly don't believe that out of sight is out of mind, and like to take a practical, down-to-earth approach to their finances. Leos are also concerned about passing on their money and belongings to the next generation, so are keen to keep their wills up to date. It gives them pleasure to think that their children, relatives and friends will have something to remember them by.

Career

Leos need to shine in everything they do, and that's especially true when it comes to their careers. Even if a Leo has quite a humble and mundane job, they will want to feel that they're contributing something of value and that they're appreciated by the rest of the team. This isn't someone who is happy working away by themselves, rarely having any contact with others, or whose efforts are taken for granted and exploited. Instead, a Leo must receive regular doses of sincere praise and encouragement, otherwise they tend to wither up like plants that don't get enough water.

One of the marvellous things about Leos is that they can turn their hands to almost anything, given half a chance. They have tremendous ability and talent, and they also have a streak of dogged determination that makes them work away at something until they've triumphed at it. You will find Leos in all walks of life, but especially in those careers that put them in the public eye. That doesn't necessarily mean they have to be famous (although we'll come on to that in a moment), but simply that they have to be noticed by someone.

Showbusiness is a calling for many Leos. A list of famous Leo actors and actresses reads like a Who's Who of the theatre and cinema. Here are just a few Leo names to conjure with: Kevin Spacey, Jennifer Lopez, Arnold Schwarzenegger (who's now running a political career too), Wesley Snipes, Peter

O'Toole, Lucille Ball, Robert Mitchum, Dustin Hoffman, Melanie Griffith, Antonio Banderas, Sean Penn, Robert De Niro, Rosanna Arquette, Halle Berry, Ethel Barrymore, Coral Browne, Martin Sheen and Robert Redford. Leos are renowned for their organizational skills, so there are lots of Leo film producers and directors, too, including Peter Bogdanovich, Peter Weir, Alfred Hitchcock, Roman Polanski, Sam Goldwyn and John Houston.

Politics is another sphere that attracts Leos, thanks to the power it enables them to wield and also the chance to make the world a better place. Sometimes, the power can go to a Leo's head, as it did in the case of Louis XVI, who lost his head as a result. Napoleon Bonaparte is another Leo whose ambitions ended up working against him. Other suitable Leo careers include anything that involves them giving a performance. Mick Jagger is a Leo who's got this down to a fine art.

Leos make good bosses, provided that they don't become too bossy and dictatorial. Perhaps they should be wary of believing their own publicity, as it can make them behave in rather pompous and overbearing ways. Once the Leo ego is over-inflated it will take a lot to make it return to its normal size. Nevertheless, Leos have fantastic leadership abilities which they can demonstrate in many different jobs. They are loyal and trustworthy employees, provided that they believe they're being appreciated, and they're also warm and encouraging employers.

It's always good to have at least one Leo in an office or working environment because their warmth, enthusiasm and sheer personality can always be guaranteed to cheer up everyone else. They are also very generous souls, so will happily stand everyone a round of drinks in the pub after work or bring in a home-made cake (which will be beautifully iced) on Friday afternoons. They excel at arranging parties, too, because they have such a good idea of how to make special events go with a swing. However, they should be given a strict budget in case they get carried away and splash out on caviar and champagne all round.

Leos make fantastic teachers, too. It's probably because teaching gives them the chance to get up in front of their students and perform. What's more, the Leo will take a great interest in the welfare of their pupils, and will want to help them out when necessary. They may even be aware of a little hero-worship going on, which will secretly thrill them to bits even if they make light of it and pretend it's all a big joke.

Love and Friendships
Leos know all about love. It's a very important part of their lives, whether it's heady romance, enduring friendship, parental care, sibling affection or any other category you care to think of. In fact, a Leo without love is like a plant without water, because they'll start to wither up. Not that this is likely to happen because most Leos have a tremendous capacity to give and receive love. Love is a Leo speciality and members of this sign spend a lifetime working on getting it right.

Leos are tremendously loyal, which is one of the reasons why they excel at relationships. People know they can rely on Leos, and the fierce Leo pride makes sure they won't let anyone down. Of course, there are bound to be occasions when a Leo can't fulfil everyone's expectations, in which case they'll feel wretched and worried about it. They'll feel they haven't done their best, even when they have.

Leos are born romantics, which is a trait they share with Librans and Pisceans. Whenever they fall in love, they become completely starry-eyed and put their beloved on a lofty pedestal. Leos adore the notion that love will triumph in the end, especially when it comes to their own lives, and are always crushed if it doesn't work out like that. There is definitely a side of them that likes to get their own way, so they'll not only be heartbroken but angry too when their dearest wishes don't come true. It's not supposed to be like this! The Leo is supposed to waltz off into the sunset with their own true love by their side, preferably surrounded by several adorable children.

Leos are wonderfully affectionate, kind, demonstrative and loving. They have big hearts and see nothing wrong in proving that fact at every opportunity with endearments, hugs and confidence-boosting comments. When you have a Leo on your side, rooting for you, you feel as though you could conquer the world because they've got so much faith in you. It's the same story whatever your relationship with a Leo – you'll still feel as though you're something special, and they'll keep reminding you of that fact in case you forget. This is the sign ruled by the Sun, after all, and the warmth of a Leo's love can make you feel as though you're basking in the sunshine.

Having said that, you'll have to do something to justify your Leo's faith in you. Leos aren't fools, so they'll want to see evidence that you've got what it takes. That's because Leos need to feel proud of their loved ones. Perhaps they're worried that a lack of application or motivation in you will somehow reflect badly on them. Whatever the reason, they'll want to cheer you on from the sidelines and pop open the champagne to celebrate your triumphs.

So love with a Leo can be a wonderful, heady and romantic experience. But sometimes it can also be an exercise in power. Leos are named after lions, which are the kings of the jungle, and Leos definitely like to be top cat. They want to be the one who calls the shots and who's in charge, and they'll make sure you don't forget it. This means they can sometimes be rather imperious and bossy, as they find subtle and not-so-subtle ways of putting you in your place. This is the sign of royalty, after all!

Being so loyal themselves, Leos expect loyalty from their loved ones and friends in return. You must support them as they support you. They place a strong emphasis on fidelity and will be bitterly hurt if they discover their partner has been unfaithful.

Leos make wonderful friends. They're good fun to be around and are very entertaining. They're also keen on having lots of treats, so rarely need any persuading about going out for a meal or doing anything else that you'll both enjoy. Even if you're both broke they'll still dream up inexpensive ways of enjoying yourselves. And if you're both feeling flush, the world will be your oyster.

Family Relationships

Lions are family-minded animals. They like to be surrounded by their cubs and Leos are exactly the same. A happy family is very important to them, and they like having children around. It's great if they're the Leo's own children, but they're equally warm and friendly with other people's offspring. A Leo also enjoys having a partner they can depend on. They place a strong emphasis on fidelity and will be bitterly hurt if they discover their partner has been unfaithful.

Leos are very sociable creatures so they aren't very happy when they have to live on their own. They're much better at being part of a contented family group, particularly if they can take care of everyone. They like to feel that they're providing for their loved ones, whether as the breadwinner or the cook, and will place a lot of emphasis on family togetherness. They don't like the idea of every member of the family eating what they want at different times. Instead, they like everyone to gather round the table for a shared mealtime in which they can all talk and catch up on one another's news. Besides, it's an opportunity for the Leo parent to keep an eye on their children's table manners and to make sure they're eating properly. But most of all, the Leo's big heart swells with pride and happiness whenever they're surrounded by their family, and they're always relieved to know that everyone is at home, safe and sound.

When a Leo becomes a parent for the first time, you'd imagine that no one has ever had a baby in the history of the world before. They'll be incredibly proud of their child, taking masses of photos and praising the infant's talent, good looks, intelligence and all-round-wonderfulness to anyone who'll listen. And the Leo will never lose this delightful adoration of their child, no matter how old they both become.

Mind you, this doesn't mean that Leo parents are pushovers or soft touches, because they aren't. A Leo parent can be very strict when necessary, laying down the law and telling their child how to behave. They don't want the child to let down themselves or their family, so they'll do their best to keep them on the straight and narrow.

Sometimes this means that a Leo has very high, and rather unrealistic, expectations of their children. They don't want them to be little saints, exactly, but they will expect them to do well at school and to aim high in life. A Leo parent can also be quite strict about the company that their child keeps, and can be rather snobby about some of the friends their child brings home with them. They must make sure that they don't impose their own values and beliefs too strongly on their children, even if they do believe that they're doing it for the children's own good.

When it comes to education, a Leo parent will want their child to have the very best that's available. That may mean moving house to be near a good school or, if there's enough money to pay for it, sending their child to a good fee-paying school. The Leo will be quite happy to make some economic sacrifices if it means that their child has an excellent education and mixes with the right people.

But don't get the idea that a Leo parent is nothing but an old-fashioned taskmaster, because they aren't. They believe strongly in having fun with their children, and will happily crawl around the carpet with them, play games with them, take them on exciting expeditions, teach them magic tricks and generally make them feel completely special and cherished. They'll also encourage their children to explore their potential in whichever way takes their fancy, and will always give them their whole-hearted support. What child could ask for anything more?

Creativity and Potential

Leo creativity and potential? How long have you got? Leos are so full of creativity that it's difficult to know where to start describing their talents. They also have plenty of potential because there is bound to be something that they haven't turned their hands to but which would work out very well if they did. They also have a deep-seated need to express themselves in whichever way most appeals to them.

This is one of the most creative signs of the zodiac, so Leos have a head start on almost everyone else. In fact, it goes against the grain for them to not to express their creativity somehow or other. Many Leos are born artists, as they soon discover when they pick up a pencil or paintbrush. If a Leo doesn't fancy doing that (or has already got it down to a fine art, if you'll forgive the pun), they could try something slightly different, such as painting silk scarves, making stained-glass windows or creating their own jewellery. They need to experiment until they find something that suits them and which they can fit into their undoubtedly busy life.

Many Leos have a secret yearning to be centre-stage, so they might enjoy joining an amateur dramatics group. They may not end up taking the part of the leading man or lady but they'll have a jolly good try. Alternatively, the Leo might want to express their organizational skills by becoming an essential member of the backstage crew, such as being in charge of the wardrobe, lighting or make-up. They'll do their best to ensure that the entire production runs like clockwork.

Several giants of the poetry world were born under the sign of Leo, including Percy Bysshe Shelley, John Dryden and Rupert Brooke (who also had typically Leonine film-star good looks). Maybe a modern-day Leo would like to follow in their eminent footsteps. Alternatively, they could write fiction, encouraging themselves with the knowledge that P. D. James, Enid Blyton, James Baldwin, Danielle Steel, John Galsworthy, Emily Brontë, E. F. Benson, Georgette Heyer and Hermann Melville are all Leos. As will you will see from this list, Leo writers fall into many different categories, so a budding Leo author has plenty of scope to choose from.

Leo is the sign of the Lion and many Leos have a special affinity with cats. They make excellent cat-breeders because they have the interest in these animals as well as the organizational skills needed to breed them successfully.

Alternatively, a Leo could run a cattery that's frequented by cats when their owners go on holiday. Even if all that is too ambitious or doesn't appeal, a Leo will get a tremendous amount of pleasure and entertainment from taking care of their own cats. They might want to paint them or write poems about them, too.

Another classic Leo skill is interior design. Some Leos have an instinctive flair for it, which is perfectly obvious the moment you walk into their own homes. They love decorating rooms and finding the perfect objects for them.

Leos are also dab hands in the kitchen. They aren't so keen on producing everyday, simple food because that can get rather mundane, but they love creating spectacular centre-pieces, such as massive cakes or splendid roasts. They need to remember their flair for the dramatic, and to pull out all the stops. It will give them tremendous satisfaction to spend hours in the kitchen and then be deluged with compliments about all their efforts. Leo food not only tastes good but it looks good, too, as the Leo will spend ages choosing the right plates and presenting it as attractively as possible. It's yet another example of their instinctive showmanship.

Holidays
The one thing a Leo craves above all else is sunshine, so it's very high up on their list of holiday priorities. This is, after all, the sign ruled by the Sun, so it's no wonder that Leos need plenty of its warmth and light in their lives. They feel better when the Sun shines, it's as simple as that.

Leos really come into their own when they're in a hot climate, although even they will wilt if the temperature rises too high. They find it particularly difficult to cope with high levels of humidity, especially if they were born on the Cancer/Leo cusp.

If a Leo could have their heart's desire, they would stay in a luxurious and exclusive resort on a tropical island, where they could do lots of celebrity-spotting while sipping cocktails on a palm-fringed beach. Think of the potential for holiday photos that would turn all their friends green with envy! Alternatively, they could have a wonderful time in one of the most glamorous and sophisticated cities in the world, shopping in the best boutiques, seeing the sights, eating in the swankiest restaurants and staying in a hotel with more stars than the night sky. Too expensive? Then a Leo would love going on safari and seeing their namesake lions prowling around, provided that they didn't have to hammer in their own tent pegs every night. Leos do have their standards!

Something else that would appeal to a Leo is driving through a warm and friendly country in a chic or classic car, staying at delightful hotels along the way and buying lots of lovely clothes to wear when they get home. However, they would want to go at their own pace and not have it dictated to them by a hectic holiday itinerary.

If all of these options are out of the question because the Leo is flat broke, they still need to go on holiday. They lead such busy lives that they need to have a complete break every now and then, partly for their own health and sanity and partly so everyone who's left behind can realize how much they depend on the Leo's organizational skills. Maybe the Leo could hire a cottage by a beach or in the countryside, so they can surround themselves with some of their favourite people. They can combine self-catering with occasional excursions to local restaurants as their budget permits.

Leos are brainy creatures so they won't want to go on a beach holiday in which they mindlessly lie on the broiling hot sand for two weeks without any intellectual stimulus. If nothing else they'll want to take some fat books with them so they can catch up on their reading. They will also develop writer's cramp from scrawling masses of postcards while they're sitting in cafes and restaurants.

At least they won't have to worry about keeping fit, though, because most Leos worthy of the name will take about three times as much luggage with them as they really need. They'll pack clothes for every eventuality, many of which are unlikely to crop up (such as being invited to dinner on Steven

Spielberg's yacht), so will build up a set of bulging muscles merely from hauling their luggage off the baggage carousel at the airport and into a taxi. And they'll do even more weight-training when they come home again because they'll be bringing so many souvenirs with them. Some of them will be for themselves but the vast majority will be to give to their friends and family.

Now we get on to a tricky subject here. Some Leos have exquisite taste, only choosing the most beautiful and delicate objects to take home, while others go for rather more flamboyant and showy souvenirs. Gold is one of the colours associated with this sign and some Leos can't get enough of it. So be warned next time a Leo you know goes on holiday!

Home

A Leo's home is their castle. Literally, in some cases. After all, this is the sign of royalty and some Leos won't settle for anything less than a stately home. Even if they have to create it themselves.

A Leo will lavish love and affection on their home, even if it's tiny. Despite its size, they will be as proud of it as though it were an expensive mansion. They will expect their guests to be equally appreciative of it, so visitors should be prepared to "ooh" and "aah" at every little detail. The Leo will be genuinely thrilled that all their hard work is being noticed, even if it isn't always to everyone's taste. Some Leos like rather gaudy furniture and objects, the sort that you can even see in the dark because they're so bright. Other Leos prefer more restrained and subdued items.

Either way, the Leo will go for the best that money can buy. This isn't a sign to skimp on the essentials or be cheese-paring about their comfort, so you can expect to sink into the sort of sofa and armchairs that envelop you and won't let you stand up again without a struggle. The rooms in which the Leo entertains will contain many of their favourite objects and possessions, purely to give them the pleasure of displaying them to their guests. This doesn't mean they'll want to show off, merely that they'll want other people to get as much enjoy-ment out of their belongings as they do themselves.

This is a Fixed sign so Leos like furniture that's built to last. They don't care for anything flimsy unless it's a valuable Georgian antique, in which case it will be kept discreetly out of harm's way while still being on show. Instead, they like furni-ture they can use without having to worry about breaking it. It's got to be comfortable and practical, especially if there are lots of children and pets in the Leo's life.

If they can afford it, the Leo will enjoy treating themselves to the best that money can buy, from cushions to cookers. You can expect to see some big brand names in most Leos' houses, because they can't see any point in buying inferior makes that no one has ever heard of and which will probably go wrong in no time at all. With their love of the dramatic arts, the tele-vision set will probably have pride of place, as will a CD player and some big speakers.

Leos are very generous so they will want enough space to do some entertaining and, preferably, to have people to stay. Some Leos I know have so many friends who drop in unannounced that they almost need a revolving door instead of an ordinary front door. They need a big kitchen or dining table around which everyone can eat, and they'll bring out the best silver and finest napkins when they're entertaining. They may also have some very expensive china and glassware tucked away for special occasions, such as holidays or birthdays.

When decorating their home a Leo will choose plenty of oranges and yellows, because these colours remind them of sunshine. If they draw the line at having yellow sofas or orange curtains, they'll choose paintings with these colours, small arrangements of brightly decorated china or vases full of the most splendid and flamboyant flowers, such as massive sunflowers, lilies or dahlias. Many of these flowers will come out of the Leo's garden, because this is a sign that loves gardening. Leos especially enjoy growing their own fruit and vegetables so they've always got freshly picked produce. If they have a glut of anything they'll send their guests home with bags full of scarlet tomatoes or green beans.

Leos are good at creating at atmosphere, so may have a weakness for pot pourri, scented candles and aromatherapy oils. But only if they smell nice!

Clothes and Image

Leos always want to be seen at their best. They take pride in their appearance and don't want to look messy or sloppy. Even when they're lounging around at home, with only the cat to see what they look like, they'll still aim to be decorative and attractive. If they unexpectedly catch sight of themselves in a mirror, they don't want to get a nasty shock. Besides, what if someone were to visit on the spur of the moment and the Leo opened the door looking like a member of the Addams family? It would ruin their image.

When choosing clothes, many Leos go for something dramatic and eye-catching. They want to make a statement and they want to stand out from the crowd. They certainly don't want to blend into the background or look as though they're wearing someone else's cast-offs. And if they do happen to be wearing second-hand clothes, you can bet they'll be so expensive and well-made that they look as though they're brand new. The Leo won't want to give the game away by wearing anything tatty or shoddy.

Mae West was a suitably theatrical Leo who dressed to impress. Madonna and Mick Jagger are also Leos who believe that clothes create a powerful image and who are both style icons. Jacqueline Kennedy Onassis was another Leo style icon, especially when she was America's First Lady. (How Leo can you get?) Sometimes the Leo look can be extremely flamboyant and showy, but classic Leo style is typified by the supremely elegant and sophisticated designs of Yves St Laurent and Coco Chanel. Naturally, they are both Leos.

If you want to know how to recognize a Leo at fifty paces, it's easy. Look at their hair. Most Leos have masses of hair and it's a very important part of their image. Classic Leo hair is thick and curly, just like a lion's mane. Robert Plant, Whitney Houston, Martha Stewart and Melanie Griffith all have typically luxuriant Leo hair. Even when Leos have their hair short, you still can't help noticing it. Think of Robert Redford, Sean Penn and Bill Clinton, who all have thick Leo locks.

Another noticeable Leo characteristic is their ability to stand up straight. They understand the importance of good posture, not only for health reasons (especially as many of them have bad backs) but because they know it makes them look sleeker, more youthful and better dressed. You will never catch a Leo slumping or slouching, unless they really have no choice.

In the days when it was considered acceptable to wear fur coats, Leos loved them. (And probably wore them with sunglasses, to create a truly movie-star image.) I have a Leo friend who went through a phase of buying old fur coats at jumble sales and wearing them with jeans. She was simply expressing her Leo nature. Nowadays, Leos are more likely to buy good-quality fake furs rather than wear the real thing.

Jewellery is a very important part of the Leo image, for both sexes. If the Leo can afford it, they'll wear precious stones and a discreet amount of gold (but not too much because they don't want to look vulgar or as though they've just won the lottery). Having said that, you will sometimes find a Leo who can't resist looking showy and flashy, with an if-you've-got-it-flaunt-it attitude. They'll be loaded down with so many earrings, necklaces, bracelets and rings that you'll be dazzled by the glare whenever the sun comes out.

Mind you, most Leos prefer to create a more subtle image, even if they do have ways of letting you know that their clothes cost more than you'll earn in a year. For instance, a loaded Leo will casually take off their jacket and fold it so the designer label is just visible, drop lots of designer's first names into the conversation or carry the latest handbag that you know has a year-long waiting list of potential buyers who are desperate to get their hands on it.

Famous Leos

Haile Selassie (23 July 1892); Amelia Earhart (24 July 1898); Iman (25 July 1956); Kevin Spacey (26 July 1959); Hilaire Belloc (27 July 1870); Beatrix Potter (28 July 1866); Benito Mussolini (29 July 1883); Arnold Schwarzenegger (30 July 1947); Evonne Cawley (31 July 1951); Yves St Laurent (1 August 1936); Peter O'Toole (2 August 1932); Martha Stewart (3 August 1941); Louis Armstrong (4 August 1901); Neil Armstrong (5 August 1930); Andy Warhol (6 August 1928); Mata Hari (7 August 1876); Dustin Hoffman (8 August 1937); Melanie Griffith (9 August 1957); Antonio Banderas (10 August 1960); Enid Blyton (11 August 1897); Cecil B. DeMille (12 August 1881); Fidel Castro (13 August 1927); Halle Berry (14 August 1968); Oscar Peterson (15 August 1925); Madonna (16 August 1958); Mae West (17 August 1892); Robert Redford (18 August 1937); Bill Clinton (19 August 1946); Robert Plant (20 August 1948); Peter Weir (21 August 1944); Henri Cartier-Bresson (22 August 1908); Gene Kelly (23 August 1912).

The Top Ten Leo Characteristics

Proud; Creative; Organizational skills; Affectionate; Flamboyant; Dignified; Stubborn; Loyal; Needs to be appreciated; Enthusiastic.

Are You A Typical Leo?

Try this quiz on the Leos you know to find out whether they're typical members of their sign.

1 Do you have a burning need to express yourself creatively?
2 Does love make your world go round?
3 Are you idealistic?
4 Do you like your clothes to make a statement?
5 Do you prefer quality to quantity?
6 Do you think that only the best is good enough?
7 Do you pride yourself on your loyalty?
8 Have you ever been accused of being a snob?
9 Is your enthusiasm easily aroused?
10 Have you ever been accused of being bossy?

Score

Score one point for every "no" and zero points for every "yes".

0–3   You couldn't be more of a Leo if you tried. You're loving, positive and enthusiastic. You're good at organizing other people as well as yourself, and you're a staunch supporter of loved ones.

4–6   You have a strong Leo streak but it's tempered by the influence of other signs. Read the Top Ten Characteristics of the other signs to see which ones ring a bell with you.

7–10   Although you were born under the sign of Leo you don't have many Leo characteristics. Look through the Top Ten Characteristics of Cancer and Virgo to see if either of these sounds more like you.

Virgo

24 Augus–22 September

The Virgo Adult

If there were a prize for being methodical, efficient, practical and modest (despite this list of virtues), a Virgo would win it hands down. No one else would even come close. Virgos are extremely reliable and you can always count on them, especially in a crisis, which is when they really come into their own.

This reliability is one of their greatest strengths, but also one of their biggest curses. It's a strength because it makes Virgos so dependable and trustworthy. The world may be falling down around your ears but your Virgo friends will always stand by you. And it's a curse because this reliability is often exploited by others or taken for granted. What's more, the Virgo's innate need to be of service to other people means that they often do things that are above and beyond the call of duty. They feel that they'll be letting themselves and others down if they do any less. Mother Teresa, who spent her life looking after the poor in Calcutta, was a Virgo who was world-famous for her service to humanity. We've all heard of fair-weather friends but Virgos are foul-weather friends instead, because they'll rally round when times are hard. They'll sit and listen as you tell them all your troubles, or they'll take on all the catering if it's a family emergency and will make sure everyone has clean clothes to wear, too.

At the risk of embarrassing the Virgos who are reading this, they are the unsung hero and heroines of the zodiac. The world would come to a grinding halt without Virgos making sure that everything is ticking over nicely, yet somehow they rarely receive the applause they deserve. Their innate modesty, their habit of underestimating themselves and their tendency to retreat from the limelight, all prevent them elbowing other people aside and grabbing the glory they deserve. Such behaviour doesn't seem right to them somehow, so often the Virgo will be overlooked in favour of someone who's done less work but made more of a song and dance about it. Sometimes, a Virgo is like Cinderella, working away behind the scenes while others take all the glory. And if you do manage to pay them a compliment, they won't want to hear it and will shrug it off. Praise makes Virgos very uncomfortable, whereas it makes Leos purr like cats. You can't help loving Virgos for their modesty, because they go very bashful and quiet.

Virgo is definitely the sign of the perfectionist. Members of this sign have a tremendous love of detail, so they're very careful to dot all the Is and cross all the Ts. It's a way of controlling their own world. They want everything to be in as much order as possible, although whether they're able to achieve that is another matter. I've known some Virgos who live in a permanent state of complete muddle even though they wish they didn't, while others have remarkably organized and ordered lives in which nothing is out of place. Sometimes, the Virgo will take this love of order to extremes, losing their sense of perspective, obsessing about the tiniest detail and not being able to see the wood for the trees. It doesn't help that they live on their nerves, thanks to their ruler, Mercury, so they can get very het up about the smallest problems.

Virgo is an Earth sign, which is where their practicality comes from. But their Earthy element also makes them rather conservative and unadventurous. Virgos don't like to stick their necks out too far or take huge risks because that isn't the way they're made. As a result, they have a tendency to play very safe, especially where money is concerned. Their innate caution often serves them well because it stops them rushing into situations without thinking them through first, but it can also prevent them living life to the full because they're so concerned about the potential snags of what they're proposing. "Yes, but what if . . ." the Virgo will say when you make a suggestion that they don't like. Ideally, they need to be with people who aren't as hidebound as they are, and who can encourage the Virgo to let their hair down once in a while.

However, although Virgo is an Earth sign it's also a Mutable sign. This means Virgos are much more adaptable to change than their fellow Earth signs of Taurus and Capricorn. Their Mutable quality, combined with their planetary ruler, Mercury, gives them quicksilver brains that are able to take in information, process it and spit it out again faster than other signs can say "Sorry, could you repeat that?" They're fantastic at analysing situations and information, and at working out exactly what is going on. Virgos share this Mercury-Mutable combination with Geminis, although they aren't quite as mentally agile. Nevertheless, Virgos are highly intelligent, even if they don't advertise it by showing off.

A typical Virgo is very astute and very sharp. No one can pull the wool over their eyes because they've already smelt a rat and are watching to see what will happen next. They also have a highly developed critical sense. It enables them to spot the difference between deceit and truth, gold and dross. This powerful sense of discrimination also makes the Virgo extremely tough on themselves because they always think they could do so much better if they only tried harder. Yet the Virgo's idea of being second-rate is often everyone else's example of exemplary behaviour. Maybe they should let themselves off the hook every now and then?

The Virgo Child

Small Virgos tend to take life rather seriously. In common with Capricorns, they often have old heads on young shoulders, with an overdeveloped sense of responsibility. As a result, Virgo children need to be encouraged to enjoy their childhoods, rather than to spend their early years being very conscientious and painstaking. For instance, a Virgo child will always do their homework before having fun, rather than spending the evening in front of the television and then frantically doing their homework over breakfast. They must be encouraged to enjoy themselves and to relax, otherwise they will be storing up a lifetime's habit of worrying, being stressed and experiencing general anxiety.

Most Virgos have a very neat and tidy appearance, even as children. Their brothers and sisters may get covered in mud (or worse), and get grass stains on their clothes, but Virgo children often manage to avoid such dramas. This is just as well as it upsets them when they get in a mess. As a result, the classic image of a Virgo child is of Alice in Wonderland, with immaculate hair, clean shoes and a freshly pressed apron.

Virgo is ruled by Mercury and is a Mutable sign, which makes members of this sign very versatile. As a result, Virgo children, like their Gemini cousins, are often able to do two things at once. They should be encouraged to develop this skill because it's an important part of their nature and it comes instinctively to them. However, they must also be encouraged to concentrate on what they're doing rather than to switch from one project to the next as the fancy takes them and when they get bored.

That typical Virgo modesty kicks in early, so Virgo children need to be given plenty of encouragement and praise. Their parents should give them lots of pats on the back to avoid the child feeling that they'll never live up to expectations. If the Virgo child doesn't do well in their exams or any other sort of test, their parents should let them discuss their feelings so they can talk them through, rather than bottle them up and secretly feel guilty at letting everyone down. If the child does keep their feelings to themselves, they will almost inevitably start to feel ill, probably with tummy problems. It's at this stage that their parents, or an older sibling, should persuade them to talk about what's really wrong.

Virgos are born teachers, so you're quite likely to find that a Virgo child has arranged all their soft toys and dolls in rows and is giving them lessons. The Virgo interest in medical matters can also kick in early, so a Virgo child might turn their bedroom into a hospital ward, complete with dolls wearing bandages round their heads and teddies with their paws in slings.

Other signs may have to be coerced into helping with the household chores as children but young Virgos are usually quite willing to roll up their sleeves and lend a hand. If anything, they can be too eager to do this, so they miss out on playing with their friends because they're too busy helping Mummy in the kitchen or watching Daddy mend the car. This can make them seem rather like goody two-shoes, especially if they have brothers and sisters who are much naughtier. As a result, they need to find ways to relax and have fun.

Virgo children enjoy reading from an early age, and they also have a thirst for knowledge. They love books on wildlife and will happily roam the garden looking for butterflies or birds, although they may be put off by less attractive creatures such as flies and worms. Virgo children are highly intelligent, and will beat everyone else in the family when playing logic games or anything that requires good hand and eye co-ordination. They like toys with a practical slant, such as kits for pressing flowers. With their love of outdoors, they might also appreciate being given a child-size spade and fork, so they can cultivate their own little patch of garden. They'll get a huge thrill out of growing flowers or easy vegetables.

Something else that can appeal to a Virgo child is a microscope. Virgo is the sign of detail, so a microscope is the perfect way for a child to examine the world in miniature. My Virgo father had a microscope as a small boy and took it everywhere with him. He once disgraced himself by taking it along when he and his parents went out to tea. They were given blue cheese which he immediately put under his microscope. The hostess wasn't amused when he excitedly exclaimed that he could see lots of mites crawling through the cheese, but that's classic Virgo for you.

Health

Before we go any further we need to get one thing straight. We're on home ground here! Health is a very important subject for most Virgos, and they take it seriously. This sign has a very powerful affinity with all aspects of health, from worrying about it to treating people when they're ill. Even if a Virgo doesn't work with health in some way, they are probably very, very interested in the subject. They may subscribe to a health magazine or read lots of books on health, especially if they're on the subject of complementary health.

One of the first things to learn about Virgos is that they're often confirmed hypochondriacs. No sooner have they read about an ailment than they start to imagine that they've got it, even if they belong to the wrong sex. For instance, when a Virgo man's pregnant partner is about to deliver their baby, he's quite likely to experience labour pains as well, having come out in sympathy with her. Let's hope he hasn't spent months experiencing morning sickness as well!

Virgos are very tuned into their bodies, but they have a tendency to interpret every twinge and ache in the worst possible light, thinking they've got all sorts of terrible diseases. What might be a simple cold to most people can be interpreted as something much more sinister by a Virgo, who imagines it's the beginning of flu, tuberculosis, cancer or some strange tropical disease contracted during their last holiday and which has been lying dormant ever since. Some Virgos take their hypochondria to such an extreme that they almost have their very own chair in their doctor's waiting room. They will certainly have read all the magazines in there and are probably on first-name terms with all the staff.

Very often, the worst thing a Virgo can suffer from is worry and anxiety, which can play havoc with their body and make them feel pretty wretched. Virgos are so prone to worry that it's second nature to them, and some of them always have some sort of worry that they're mulling over. When they get rid of one, they replace it with another. None of this does their health any favours, and it can interfere with their sleep patterns. It has also been shown scientifically that worry, anxiety and a negative outlook can deplete the body's immune system, creating an increased susceptibility to disease. So perhaps worrying really can make you ill.

Virgo rules the digestive processes in the body, and many Virgos suffer from stomach and digestive problems. Once again, typical Virgo worrying may make the situation worse. Such embarrassing ailments as irritable bowel syndrome are especially prevalent among Virgos, and their natural modesty makes such problems quite difficult to cope with. Virgos can also have problems with constipation, so it's important for them to eat plenty of fibre and to drink lots of fresh water.

Actually, eating a healthy diet often comes very easily to Virgos. Many of them place tremendous importance on eating properly, even if that means they're the only one in the family who eats their greens (although they'll do their best to nag everyone else into submission). Having said that, many Virgos have such sensitive bodies (a characteristic that they share with their opposite sign, Pisces) that they have food allergies that call for special diets. I have one Virgo friend who is dramatically allergic to fish and another who is wheat-intolerant.

When looking for treatments for their health problems, Virgos are often instinctively drawn towards complementary therapies such as reflexology, acupuncture, healing and homeopathy. Such therapies suit their delicate nervous systems, although most Virgos will avoid anything that they consider to be too off-the-wall or New Age. Ideally, there should have been some research into their chosen therapy so they can read about how effective it is before handing over their hard-earned cash.

Money

This is an area where Virgos really come into their own. They have a natural empathy with money and are very keen on what it can buy, so they usually manage their own finances very well. Besides, they're such organized creatures that it would be very unusual for them not to know what's happening to them financially. If they do lose track of what's going on in their bank account, it's probably because they're going through some sort of crisis. But it's a rare Virgo who makes the same mistakes twice.

They have two factors to thank for this sensible attitude towards money: their planetary ruler, Mercury, and their element of Earth. Mercury gives Virgos plenty of brainpower and also an enviable ability to analyse situations in detail so they can see precisely what's going on. It also enables them to talk to people who might be able to help them, so they get a better idea of what their options are. Their Earth element gives Virgos a practical streak, so they have a sensible attitude to money. It also makes them rather conservative about spending money and averse to taking financial risks.

Many Virgos are drawn to banking and accountancy, but even if a Virgo's career doesn't involve handling money they may still find themselves acting as an unofficial financial adviser to their friends. Something tells people that a Virgo will know the best credit card deals or which bank is most suitable for small businesses. If the Virgo doesn't know, they'll do their best to find out because the information could come in handy for them as well. Virgos also have a refreshingly no-nonsense attitude towards money, with the accent on practicality and common sense. They certainly aren't sentimental about it, and believe in sorting out problems as they arise. For instance, if you've got to sell your car because you can't afford to run it and must buy something cheaper, the Virgo will fail to understand why you don't simply get on and do it. What's the problem?

When it comes to spending money, Virgos aren't always over-generous. There are usually perfectly good reasons for this (such as being unable to afford to throw their money around in all directions), but sometimes it's because of a careful attitude towards money that verges on the penny-pinching. Virgos get great satisfaction from trawling supermarket aisles looking for special offers, and they're also eagle-eyed for bargains when their favourite shops hold sales, even if they could easily afford to pay the full price. They like to set aside some cash for a rainy day, so they don't believe in spending their money as soon as they get it. Instead, they salt their spare money away in savings accounts or stocks and shares (but only the very safe ones), and watch it grow steadily over the years. Virgos aren't interested in get-rich-quick schemes because their common sense tells them there has to be a catch, such as the threat of losing their entire investment. Instead, they will research their options very carefully and methodically before weighing up all the pros and cons and reaching a considered decision.

Another reason why Virgos aren't keen on spending lots of money is their natural modesty. They hate the thought of appearing showy and flamboyant, and shudder at the financial excesses and extravagance of some signs. It's so distasteful! Instead, the Virgo likes to preserve a sense of modesty and discretion about the state of their finances, and if they do buy anything very expensive it will also be extremely discreet. If they buy a designer outfit they're quite likely to remove any labels that might be visible, because they hate the thought of being swanky and showing off.

Virgos are especially reluctant to spend money on themselves, even if they lavish it on their children or partner. Perhaps they think they don't deserve it?

Career

It may be a truism, but when it comes to work Virgos definitely believe in service with a smile. They have such a strong urge to be of service to others that it can even interfere with the rest of their lives, because they'll put in more hours than everyone else and be much more conscientious than their colleagues. Some

Virgos see nothing wrong in regularly working overtime or bringing their work home with them. And if a colleague is ill or the office is short-staffed, a Virgo will gladly do even more work until everything gets back to normal. This means they're in grave danger of being exploited by unscrupulous bosses and also by workmates who want an easy life.

Virgos are reliable, dependable, meticulous, full of common sense and highly practical. They believe in the values of hard work, preparation and organization, so a tremendous amount of effort goes on behind the scenes in whatever they choose to do. They also have a perfectionist streak, so will never allow themselves to get away with doing the bare minimum at work. Instead, they want to do their very best, purely for their own sense of satisfaction. They're used to burning the midnight oil, even if it doesn't do much for their health. It's as though they can't let themselves relax or take things easy – they have to drive themselves on otherwise they feel they're letting themselves (and everyone else) down. Sometimes they can get so bogged down in details that they lose track of the main picture, which is the point at which they need to take a well-deserved break and get things back into their proper perspective.

Among the careers that suit Virgos are anything to do with accountancy, banking, statistics, systems analysis, agency work, secretarial work, the medical profession, veterinary work and religion. They're a whizz at running an office and making sure everyone is doing what they're meant to. Virgos enjoy setting up systems to make everything run more efficiently, and will try to take advantage of the latest technology to keep track of phone calls, emails and other forms of communication. However, they will blanch at paying massive amounts of money for brand-new technology because they think it's an unnecessary extravagance most of the time, so everything in their office will probably be slightly out of date for financial reasons.

Put a Virgo in charge of the petty cash if you want to make sure that each penny is accounted for, but don't be surprised if they're really strict and harsh with employees who lose their receipts or borrow money from petty cash without asking. I once worked for a publishing company where the stationery cupboard was run with a rod of iron by a rather scary Virgo. Not only did she insist on drinking her tea out of her own tea cup (probably worried about germs), she was a terror at interrogating us all about why we needed more Tippex. She once told me, in true Virgo style, "You aren't paid to make mistakes."

However, this doesn't mean that all Virgos are Tartars in the office. The vast majority of them are actually very kind and considerate, and their sensitivity means they want to work in a happy and harmonious atmosphere. Virgos like turning their colleagues into their friends, although they may find it difficult to become very chummy with someone who isn't particularly bright. Somehow, they'll never manage to forget that this person's IQ is smaller than their waist measurement.

Virgos are ultra-dependable, so their bosses and colleagues always know they can count on them in a crisis. They'll work round the clock if necessary, but should try not to get into a situation where they're the only one who does this while everyone else enjoys their eight hours of sleep each night. They are also immensely modest. Some signs aren't good at taking criticism, but Virgos aren't good at accepting compliments. If you tell a Virgo what a good job they're doing, they'll change the subject quickly or laugh off what you've said. They definitely don't want to hear how wonderful you think they are. Virgos always believe that they could do better if they tried.

Love and Friendships
This is often a difficult area for Virgos. And to prove it, there are more single and/or celibate Virgos in the world than any other sign. The Virgo's high standards tell them that if they can't be with someone very special, they'd rather not be with anyone at all, thanks very much. Virgos don't want to settle for second best. However, this perfectly acceptable attitude is complicated by the natural Virgo modesty. Virgos often can't

help seeing themselves in a rather unfavourable light, because they concentrate on what they see as all their faults and tend to ignore all their good qualities. They can't imagine what other people can see in them, so they may not even bother to pursue someone they fancy because they're so convinced that they'll be rejected.

Relationships can also be difficult for Virgos because it's sometimes hard for them to express their feelings. They tend to clam up in times of high emotion and may even think there's something rather embarrassing about open demonstrations of affection. As a result, they can give the impression of being very buttoned up and distant. Even if they know you very well indeed, they may only give you a peck on the cheek, and if you hug them you can feel them wondering how to respond. It's as though they'd like to hug you back but something stops them doing so.

It can take a lot of love and patience from other people to make a Virgo become more demonstrative. This is especially likely if they grew up in a family where affection was only shown on special occasions. Sex, however, is another matter! Many Virgos have a very red-blooded approach to sex, which is definitely encouraged by the Earth element to which they belong. They can be very raunchy and uninhibited when the fancy takes them, although not every Virgo is like this. Some are very modest, even between the sheets.

Virgo's ruling planet, Mercury, gives members of this sign a tremendous respect for intelligence. Even if they meet someone who's so attractive that they belong on the cover of a magazine, the Virgo won't be interested in a long-term relationship if the other person is as stupid as a fence post. The Virgo has better things to do with their time!

Virgos are very critical of themselves, always finding fault and telling themselves that they could do better, and very often this spills over into criticism of their loved ones. The Virgo may think they're doing their loved ones a favour by pointing out their flaws, but that isn't how it comes across. To the Virgo's nearest and dearest, it can feel like one long nagging session in which they can't do anything right. So the Virgo must try to temper their criticisms and nags with some praise every now and then, otherwise they'll find that they're either very unpopular or are left talking to themselves.

Virgos are lively and sociable friends, and they can be real chatterboxes when the mood takes them. They're great at organizing social events, and are often the friend who makes the running. So you can expect your Virgo friends to ring you up to suggest getting together, or to tell you that they've booked a table at a local restaurant and you mustn't be late. Just as with their lovers, Virgos don't want to bother with dim-witted friends, so you can take it as a compliment if you have several Virgo friends in your life. You can expect to have wide-ranging conversations, especially about current news stories and other important issues of the day. But you should also be prepared to do lots of gossiping. All my Virgo friends are inveterate gossips, and with their love of detail you can usually rely on them to get their facts straight, too. Most satisfying!

Family Relationships

It does Virgos good to be part of a family unit. When they're by themselves they can become very cut off from the rest of the world and rather insular. But it's not quite so easy for the Virgo to be emotionally isolated when they're surrounded by the rough and tumble of family life. Of course, if the Virgo is a workaholic who's never at home they will be somewhat disconnected from everyone. But that won't stop them worrying about their loved ones. Virgos simply can't help it. They fret about everyone, whether they're flourishing or having a bad time. It's as though they can't switch off the worry section in their brains. Virgos are usually extremely discriminating except when it comes to worrying, because they will worry about anything and everything.

When the Virgo becomes a parent, they'll want to do everything as efficiently and properly as possible. They'll read all the books they can find about looking after babies and bringing up children, and will follow the rules slavishly for their first child.

However, they'll be much more relaxed when they have their second child and won't feel so duty-bound to do all their child-rearing by the book.

Virgo parents place particular emphasis on ensuring that their child has a decent education, and will start teaching their infant many skills long before school age. For instance, the Virgo will take their baby to special swimming, dance or music classes, to encourage the child's co-ordination and sense of rhythm. They will also give the child plenty of educational toys, such as building blocks and alphabet jigsaws, so they can learn through play. The Virgo parent will also place a tremendous importance on improving the child's literacy skills, and will introduce books when the child is still in the cradle. However, the Virgo needs to do all these things with a light touch, to avoid their child feeling as though every game they play has an educational purpose and that life is one long, dreary lesson. So the books should be fun and entertaining, to ensure that the child reads them for enjoyment more than anything else. The Virgo might even want to invent their own bedtime stories to keep their children amused.

The Virgo parent will enjoy taking their children out on day trips to the zoo, museums and other places that combine education with enjoyment. They'll enjoy dreaming up lots of interesting games, too, such as a special treasure hunt for the whole family. This is where the Virgo love of puzzles and crosswords really comes into its own, and some of the clues will be fiendishly clever. I remember my Virgo father once organizing an Easter egg hunt for my brother and I when we were small. He went to enormous trouble hiding eggs in the house and garden, and we had great fun searching them out.

If the Virgo parent is keen on educating their child from almost the moment he or she emerges from the womb, you can imagine the importance they place on that child's education once school starts. Virgos are canny with their cash so they won't automatically consider sending their child to a fee-paying school. However, if they can afford it and there are no other options, they won't think twice about paying for their child's education. And, with that Virgo persistence, they will research the best options ceaselessly until they're happy with their choice.

Something else that the Virgo parent will be concerned about is their child's diet. They will want to make sure that their child is eating properly, and may be particularly concerned about them following the approved family diet when they aren't at home. For instance, if the family is vegetarian the Virgo won't want their child eating meat at school. If the Virgo is a fussy eater, with a long list of things they don't like, they should be very careful not to transfer their own likes and dislikes to their child.

Finally, the Virgo must keep their perfectionist streak under control. They've got to learn to encourage their child to do well without making them feel wretched when they don't. And that means curbing their natural tendency to criticize and find fault, giving the impression that nothing the child does is ever good enough. If the Virgo behaves like this it won't make for a happy home life at all. And that will really give them something to worry about.

Creativity and Potential

Virgos have a tremendous amount of potential. The trouble is that they don't always know it. That's because Virgos are modest to a fault, and can have very low opinions of themselves. "Oh, no," they say, when you suggest something they could do and which they'd be successful at, "I couldn't possibly do that." The fact is that Virgos don't know until they try, at which point they could be pleasantly surprised.

Assuming that a Virgo is able to get over this potential hurdle, they will be astonished at how many things they can turn their very dextrous hands to. They also benefit from having a very sharp eye for detail. Virgo is ruled by Mercury, which has a strong connection with hands, and Virgos are marvellous at doing fiddly things with their hands. For instance, they might enjoy making lace, which is a remarkably painstaking and complex operation, perfectly suited to

Virgoan patience and manual dexterity. Alternatively, they might prefer needlepoint or knitting, especially if they're working on something intricate. Beadwork could be another hobby that they enjoy, and they would get particular satisfaction from looking at their array of different coloured beads which they've organized into neat rows. The Virgo might become so good at one of these skills that they're able to sell their work, should they want to. Other fiddly tasks that please Virgos are making mosaics (they'll love fitting the shapes together and then carefully glueing them in place) and découpage.

Another classically Virgoan pastime is jigsaws, and it's a great way for them to relax. However, the Virgo will want to have a special place in their home where they do jigsaws, especially if it doesn't interfere with everyday living. Geminis, who also like jigsaws thanks to their Mercury ruler, are quite happy to eat on their laps for a few weeks if the dining room table is covered with a mammoth jigsaw project, but Virgos can't cope with such disruption.

Virgos have tremendous brainpower and enormous reserves of patience, so they might get a kick out of writing in their spare time. They could write fiction, biography or some other form of non-fiction equally well. Frederick Forsyth is a Virgo author whose novels are renowned for their detail and research. Jessica Mitford is another Virgo writer who carried out a tremendous amount of research for her book on the American funeral industry. (And, in typical Virgo fashion, she wrote with great relish and detail about what happens to decomposing bodies.)

If the Virgo doesn't want to write a book, they could use their intellect to complete crossword or logic puzzles instead, which are hobbies they share with Geminis. Virgos also do well at competitions, such as dreaming up clever tiebreakers or answering detailed questions.

With their interest in health matters and their need to serve others, some Virgos might consider taking up medicine professionally even if it involves a change of career. If the Virgo feels it's too late to train as a doctor or nurse, they could learn chiropody or one of the complementary therapies. They might have a particular interest in homeopathy, with its very detailed symptoms that they'd find endlessly fascinating. Another option would be flower remedies, as Virgos are very keen on natural products.

Speaking of which, another pastime that Virgos might enjoy is making their own beauty products, such as soap. They will enjoy using natural ingredients whenever possible, and might become so successful at the entire process that they start a small cottage industry.

If the Virgo doesn't fancy any of these options, they might like to do something with figures instead. For instance, they could consider taking a course in higher mathematics or accountancy. Both of which could come in very useful!

Holidays

Here's a tricky subject. Virgos work so hard, and are so conscientious and such worriers, that they need plenty of holidays. But they're often reluctant to take them, and for the very same reasons that tell us they need them. Virgos worry about what will happen to their job, their home, their pets, their car, their fridge, their bills and their money if they go on holiday. "What if . . . ?" they'll say in justification, listing a series of potential disasters. They can spend so much time and energy on getting ready to go away that they're exhausted by the time they reach their destination. Before they leave they'll have lists in every room in the house, itemizing the things in there that should be moved, cleaned, packed or thrown out. I have even known some Virgos who have lists of lists, so they have a superlist that covers everything they need to think about and then subsidiary lists that go into more detail. Then the Virgo will take another list away with them so they know what to bring home. After all, they don't want to discover, when they're on the plane and it's too late, that they left their alarm clock on their hotel bedside table. That's right, Virgos take their alarm clocks on holiday with them. How else are they going to know what time to get up in the mornings?

Virgo

When you're finally able to persuade your Virgo that they need a holiday, it can be difficult to choose a suitable destination. Although a Virgo may sound enthusiastic when their friends tell them about their trips to exotic locations, or describe meals containing the sort of wriggly items that the Virgo would squash to death if they found them in their garden, in reality they avoid such places like the plague. Actually, the Virgo would probably rather have the plague than visit anywhere with dodgy hygiene, unsafe drinking water, poisonous creepy-crawlies, stomach-churning food or primitive plumbing. They simply can't cope with such challenges and would prefer to stay at home than have to face them. Virgos are not the most adventurous travellers in the world, and they don't care!

The choice of holiday destination is definitely determined by the sort of food the Virgo can expect to find there. They aren't good with foods they don't recognize or meals where they can't see the individual ingredients. It doesn't help that they have a special infrared vision that switches on when they go to unfamiliar restaurants and enables them to see (or imagine that they can see) bacteria incubating around the rims of drinking classes, cholera germs suspended in ice cubes, fingerprints on the lettuce, botulism in the olives and weevils in the bread. They're much happier when they're able to cook their own food in a self-catering apartment, although only after they've disinfected the fridge, scoured the cooker and washed the floor. You can't be too careful, you know. I have one Virgo friend who insisted on leaving the hotel she and her husband had just checked into because she didn't like the look of the carpets.

Ideal holiday destinations for Virgos include ski resorts where they can combine exercise, hot chocolate and fresh air, or luxurious health farms that serve more than just a single lettuce leaf once a day. They would also adore a specialist holiday which caters for one of their interests and keeps their very clever brains fully occupied.

While they're away, Virgos will be very conscientious about

buying and sending postcards to everyone back home. They won't lick the stamps, of course (are you mad? – who knows what bugs are lurking on them), but will moisten them on a damp sponge instead. They will buy presents for their loved ones who have been left behind, and also for neighbours who are looking after their home while the Virgo is away. But they won't bring back any food, in case it goes off on the way home.

Home

A place for everything and everything in its place. That's the Virgo motto when it comes to their homes. Most Virgos are extremely tidy and well-ordered creatures, and their homes reflect this very strongly. Mind you, they might think that they're living in a pigsty, although (unless you're a Virgo too) you may struggle to see how this could be possible. Everything is so neat and tidy! Paintings are arranged symmetrically on walls, cushions are plumped up to perfection and books are arranged on shelves either in alphabetical order or by colour. They even wash their dirty plates before putting them in the dishwasher. Sometimes these Virgos long to muddle things up and be more disorganized, but it's virtually impossible for them to live like this and the sight of an untidy desk or dressing table will probably give them indigestion. They have to get everything back in order before they can relax.

This idea that cleanliness is next to godliness can drive other signs mad with irritation. I used to know a Virgo who put a limescale remover in her toilet one night, which meant it couldn't be used until the following morning. Naturally, her Aries boyfriend woke up in the night desperate to use the loo. In the end, after a furious row in which he begged to be allowed to use the bathroom, he had to find a discreet corner in the garden.

But not all Virgos are paragons of cleanliness and tidiness. Virgos go to extremes, so they're either obsessively well-organized and neat, or they're complete slobs who never pick up a duster from one year to the next. I've known some pretty messy Virgos, but what they lack in housecleaning skills they more than make up for in personality.

Being an Earth sign means that Virgos believe in owning property because it's such a good investment. So a Virgo will do their best to buy their home as soon as they can afford it, even if they have to put in hours of overtime each week to pay the mortgage. However, when you talk to them about their homes, Virgos often turn out to be rather dissatisfied with them. They aren't what the Virgos really want, perhaps because they'd like a different kitchen or a new bathroom suite but it seems such a waste to rip out the offending fittings and install new ones. As a result, they put up with what they've got, sometimes for decades. You will also meet Virgos who don't even like their houses very much, but think it's too much expense or trouble to move and therefore they'll soldier on and put up with what they've got.

Gardens are important to Virgos because they appreciate the chance to sit outside. They also enjoy gardening as a pastime and many of them get enormous satisfaction from growing their own food. I had a Virgo uncle who grew so many vegetables and fruits that he was completely self-sufficient in them. His kitchen garden was, predictably, very neat and well-organized, and it's certainly a rare Virgo who has a messy garden. If a Virgo doesn't have a garden, they will have plenty of house plants instead, and probably some herbs growing on their windowsills. All the plants will be flourishing, with shiny leaves. (Yes, of course they polish them!) You'll also see plenty of books in most Virgo households, because they love reading and believe in the importance of acquiring knowledge. And you can bet there won't be any dust on the bookshelves, either.

Virgos are conventional souls so they choose traditional furniture and furnishings for their homes. They don't want anything too contemporary in case it dates, but nor do they want anything too old in case it's very delicate and gets damaged. Very often, Virgos keep most of the furniture throughout their lives because they can't see the point of getting rid of it while it's still useful. As a result, you can find wealthy Virgos living with furniture that's rather shabby or old-fashioned, and which suggests they're a lot poorer than they really are.

When it comes to choosing fabrics, Virgos love patterns. They're especially fond of small floral patterns, and need to limit the number of them they use in a room at one time to avoid inducing migraines in their visitors.

Clothes and Image

As you will have gathered by now, Virgos don't like looking messy. It simply isn't in their natures. Even if they aim to look casual and relaxed, they will still give the impression that everything they're wearing has just been ironed. That's simply the way they're made, and they can't do much about it.

So the classic Virgo look is clean, cool, calm and collected. Ingrid Bergman, Greta Garbo and Lauren Bacall are three Virgo women who epitomize their sign. They all give the impression of being confident and self-assured in order to hide an inner vulnerability. Typical Virgo men include Richard Gere, Jeremy Irons and Hugh Grant, all of whom are slightly hesitant and shy, and try to disguise their innate sensitivity. But don't get the impression that every Virgo looks as though butter wouldn't melt in their mouth. Some of them might have this image, but Virgos like Chrissie Hynde, Freddie Mercury and Bill Murray give a very different impression. They embody the naughty, sexy side of Virgo.

Because they're ruled by Mercury, the typical Virgo is tall, lithe and looks as though they need feeding up. With their instinctive interest in health and diet, it's a rare Virgo who becomes severely overweight, and most of them do their best to keep in trim throughout their lives. Twiggy, the 1960s model, is a Virgo who got her nickname because of her very slender figure.

Virgos are so cautious about spending money, thanks to their Earth element, that they are reluctant to splash out on the latest fashions. They're far more likely to buy end-of-season stock in the sales, which immediately means they'll never be in the vanguard of fashion. Not that most of them care, because they're rather dismissive of people they consider to be fashion victims. Virgos are more interested in getting value for money when they buy clothes than in being at the cutting edge of fashion. Sometimes they will wear particular outfits for years after they stopped being fashionable, simply because they haven't yet worn out and it seems a shame to throw them away. Equally, if they put on weight they'll keep the clothes they've grown out of in the hope that one day they'll manage to wear them again. The fact that the clothes might be out of date by then doesn't cross their minds. However, Virgos aren't sentimental about their clothes, so don't have any qualms about throwing away special items such as their wedding outfits when they no longer need them. For goodness sake, what's the point of keeping them, they'll ask. They'll only attract moths!

Very often, Virgos don't have to worry about keeping up with changing fashions because they like to choose classic clothes that don't date very much. Hemlines may go up or down, trouser legs may widen or narrow, and collars may wax or wane, but a Virgo's clothes will somehow manage to ride these fashion waves. Typical Virgo colours are safe and go with almost everything – navy blue, grey and brown, often in neat checks and floral prints. I used to know a Virgo man who wore nothing but white and grey, and whose home was completely furnished in grey as well. However, these safe colours can become rather dreary, so it's good for Virgos to go mad every now and then and wear splashes of much brighter colours.

In common with their Gemini cousins, Virgos enjoy jazzing up their outfits with accessories. They love bags, whether they're briefcases, handbags or luggage, especially if they combine practicality with style. You'll never catch a Virgo woman with a tiny handbag, even when she goes out to dinner, because she likes to carry around so much stuff that it would never fit into something so small. Instead, she'll carry a bag filled with so many belongings that lifting it is like doing weight-training.

Virgo

Famous Virgos

Stephen Fry (24 August 1957); Sean Connery (25 August 1930); Macaulay Culkin (26 August 1980); Mother Teresa (27 August 1910); Johann Wolfgang von Goethe (28 August 1749); Ingrid Bergman (29 August 1915); Mary Wollstonecraft Shelley (30 August 1797); Maria Montessori (31 August 1870); Lily Tomlin (1 September 1939); Keanu Reeves (2 September 1964); Charlie Sheen (3 September 1965); Anton Bruckner (4 September 1824); Freddy Mercury (5 September 1946); Joseph P. Kennedy (6 September 1888); Queen Elizabeth I (7 September 1533); Peter Sellers (8 September 1925); Hugh Grant (9 September 1960); Fay Wray (10 September 1929); D. H. Lawrence (11 September 1885); Barry White (12 September 1944); Roald Dahl (13 September 1916); Sam Neill (14 September 1947); Agatha Christie (15 September 1890); Lauren Bacall (16 September 1924); Anne Bancroft (17 September 1931); Greta Garbo (18 September 1905); Jeremy Irons (19 September 1948); Sophia Loren (20 September 1934); Stephen King (21 September 1947); Fay Weldon (22 September 1931).

The Top Ten Virgo Characteristics

Modest; Practical; Critical; Thrifty; Health-conscious; Cautious; Perfectionist; Quick-witted; Industrious; Happy to be of service

Are You A Typical Virgo?

Try this quiz on the Virgos you know to find out whether they're typical members of their sign.

1 Do you do your best to be neat and tidy?
2 Do you like to do things properly?
3 Is worrying second-nature to you?
4 Do you put other people's needs before your own?
5 Have you ever been told that you underestimate your abilities?
6 Do a lot of people rely on you?
7 Are you methodical?
8 Are you a bit of a nagger?
9 Have you got lots of nervous energy?
10 Do you get caught up in too much detail sometimes?

Score

Score one point for every "no" and zero points for every "yes".

0–3 You couldn't be more Virgo if you tried. You try to do things to the best of your abilities, even though you never really think you've done well enough. Yet other people admire and respect you.

Virgo

4–6   You have a strong Virgo streak but it's tempered by the influence of other signs. Read the Top Ten Characteristics of the other signs to see which ones ring a bell with you.

7–10   Although you were born under the sign of Virgo you don't have many Virgo characteristics. Look through the Top Ten Characteristics of Leo and Libra to see if either of these sounds more like you.

Libra

23 September–22 October

The Libran Adult

Here is the natural diplomat of the zodiac. Librans have such a strong desire for harmony and peace that they're always weighing up the atmosphere and trying to keep things sweet. Librans have their ruling planet, Venus, to thank for this. She gives them charm, tact and an ability to put other people's needs before their own. Librans have an instinctive dislike of scenes, tantrums and arguments, and will bend over backwards to stop these going any further. However, this can sometimes work against them because they may adopt the policy of anything for a quiet life, and will therefore give into other people rather than endure the fuss they're causing. All Librans have a tendency to give their power to their partners, with the result that they're under their thumbs or so dependent on their love and approval that they are always keen to pacify them.

Having said that, Librans don't always want peace and harmony. Sometimes, they like to liven things up by creating trouble. It's as though they even have to balance out harmony with disruption. This can be difficult for other people to cope with, because it seems as though the Libran has completely changed character and has become hard to deal with. Luckily, these episodes never last long but they can cause ructions in the meantime.

It's often said that Libra is the sign of indecisiveness. A Libran prefers to sit on the fence or have other people reach decisions for them, rather than to make up their own mind. There are many reasons for this but one of them is the Libran dislike of being unpopular. If a Libran can get someone else to make their decisions for them, this person is more likely to be happy with what's decided. Whereas if the Libran makes the decisions, the other person may start to complain if they aren't happy. It's all because Librans like to be seen in a good light as often as possible.

Actually, they have such a strong need to be liked and admired that they're highly susceptible to flattery. They love to be loved. They also need to know that they aren't being taken for granted, so if they do you a favour you must always thank them fulsomely. If you don't, they'll start to feel resentful about what they consider to be your ingratitude and rudeness. And that's definitely not good news.

You only have to pay a Libran a few compliments to have them eating out of your hand, and they'll tell everyone how wonderful and what a good judge of character you are. Not that it's hard to compliment a Libran because they have so much going for them, including a very attractive image. Some members of this sign are absolute stunners, and even the ones who aren't so good-looking have delightful and lively personalities that more than compensate.

Librans also have an ingrained ability to see at least two sides to every argument, so it's very difficult for them to favour only one point of view. This is because Libra is the sign of balance and is represented by the scales. When you see images of a pair of scales, both sides are level, but in real life one side is usually higher than the other. Librans continually try to balance their own psychological scales, which is quite a feat!

A Libran's relationships are the single most important part of their life. Everything else comes second. If a Libran doesn't get on with other people, or has few friends, they feel as though something is very wrong indeed. This is partly thanks to their Air element, because it encourages them to make intellectual connections with other people. As a result, Librans choose to spend time with people who are intelligent and good company. Just like themselves, in fact. They have no interest in dolts and idiots, even if they do have pretty faces. Their ruling planet, Venus, gives Librans an overwhelming desire to love and be loved in return, which is another reason why relationships are so important to them.

Although Librans give the impression of being sweet pussy cats who would never hurt a fly, in fact they're much tougher than this. In fact, they can be very tough when the need arises, although they'll do their best to disguise this by being so utterly charming and polite. Libra is the iron hand in the velvet glove, and Librans often get what they want through flattery and a few well-chosen words. Not that there's anything wrong with this. It's simply how they operate. You have only to think of such powerful Librans as Margaret Thatcher, Bob Geldof and Benjamin Netanyahu to realize that members of this sign don't always get their own way through sweetness and light. Sometimes they have to borrow some of the aggression and determination of their opposite sign, Aries. Their Cardinal nature also helps, because it makes them go after what they want. Actually, some Librans have been downright scoundrels, with Bonnie Parker, Richard III, Pancho Villa, Heinrich Himmler and Aleister Crowley being just a few examples. So you mess with Librans at your peril!

In common with Taureans, who are their fellow Venusians, Librans love the good life. They can't think of anything nicer than eating lots of delicious food, lazing around with a drink and taking life easy. Let someone else run around in ever-decreasing circles, chasing their tail and meeting deadlines. The Libran has better things to do with their life, thank you! Of course, they will get on with things when they have to, but they certainly know how to relax when the work is over. And, ideally, they should have someone attractive by their side to help them to unwind and forget all about their cares and woes.

The Libran Child

That Libran charm kicks in at an early age. Even as a baby in a pram, a Libran will instinctively know how to make the best of themselves, and how to wow everyone who comes to say hello. A few dimples, a sweet smile, a wave of a chubby hand, and the little Libran's new family will be besotted.

Libran babies are usually easy to look after. They eat, they sleep and they gurgle at you. They're particularly keen on eating, which is why many of them are quite curvaceous. As they start to grow, they enjoy being held and fussed over by doting relatives, and are the sort of babies who don't like being put down. They much prefer to be cuddled than left on their own, so their parents may have some difficult times trying to persuade their Libran baby to go to sleep by themselves.

This is an Air sign, don't forget, so Libran children aren't stupid by any means. They will enjoy learning to read and write because these skills will help them to communicate with the rest of the world. If they're given children's stationery sets they'll take a lot of trouble writing letters to their loved ones, or sending notes to their favourite soft toys.

Speaking of toys, these are very important to Libran children. They are especially important if the Libran is an only child, because the toys will be treasured companions. The parents of the child may also have to get used to hearing lots of stories about the little Libran's imaginary friends, because even as toddlers Librans have a strong need for relationships. This means that, in an ideal world, Libran children should always have siblings. They'll keep each other company, and the Libran child will be very protective towards their brothers and sisters if they're younger, or very admiring of them if they're older.

Libra is often called 'lazy Libra', and Libran children should be encouraged to be active from an early age. Their parents and siblings need to do this in tactful and subtle ways, so the

Libran doesn't realize what's going on. For instance, they could all go for brisk walks along their local beach and stage competitions to see who can collect the most shells or who can run the furthest. The Libran will soon want to win the races and beat everyone else in the competitions. But they won't be so keen if they're told to go outside and play by themselves. They'll probably find the nearest patch of sunny grass and flop down on it, and that will be the end of that. The child's parents should be especially careful to restrict the amount of time their little Libran spends in front of the television set or computer, otherwise they'll only move when it's time to eat.

Speaking of eating, Libran children can be quite fussy about their food. Their parents need to coax them out of this habit as well, otherwise the Libran child will only eat the foods that they like, which might be chocolate ice cream and doughnuts, and will refuse to even touch anything else.

It will help if the parents, or an older sibling or other relative, can teach the little Libran how to cook. This will give them a valuable skill, but it will also make the Libran more inquisitive about different foods and more willing to try them, especially if they've helped to cook them.

Libran girls are usually very feminine, and will enjoy playing with their dolls. They will also take a big interest in their own appearance from an early age. Libran boys are normally very masculine, although they are also very sensitive emotionally. They're particularly keen on playing with guns and staging fights with their friends, which are two ways for them to explore their opposite sign of Aries. But both sexes will be delightfully demonstrative and friendly, making them very popular both at home and at school. It's all thanks to that Libran charm!

Health
The typically Libran balanced attitude to life means that members of this sign can give the impression of being very peaceful and easy-going, people who take things in their stride. The reality isn't quite like this! Librans can feel tense and

wound up a lot of the time, simply because they're trying to create harmony out of crisis and it's rarely possible. They may also go through phases when they wish they could be more vocal about what they want, rather than always putting other people's needs first or not knowing what they want and therefore being unable to ask for it.

It can take a lot to make a Libran lose their temper, and this isn't always very good for their health. While other signs can get involved in a huge row that clears the air and lets them work off their tension, a Libran will rarely allow themselves to do this, which makes them feel even more fraught than before. Finally, they'll reach the point where a row is inevitable, and it's usually much more unpleasant than it would have been if it had been allowed to take place earlier. The more the Libran bottles things up, the more potent these emotions will be when finally allowed to escape.

Above all, Librans need plenty of exercise. Unfortunately, this is anathema for many of them, because they simply can't work up the energy and enthusiasm to get all hot and sweaty in the gym or on the racetrack. Frankly, they'd rather lie back on a nice, soft, comfortable sofa with their feet up and sip some champagne or nibble a few chocolate truffles. Isn't that enough exercise for one day? Sadly, it isn't, especially as they often have very low metabolisms, with the result that many Librans spend their lives battling with their weight. When it comes down to it, they would rather be overweight and happy than slim and unhappy. Of course, this can have very bad effects on their health, not only leading to weight gain but also to the medical problems that can go with it, such as diabetes and heart problems.

Ideally (and this is a very Libran word, by the way), the Libran should take exercise with a partner. And I'm not necessarily talking about sex, although that is often an important part of a Libran's life. If the Libran can take someone with them to keep them company, chivvy them along and then relax with afterwards, they won't be nearly so chary about being energetic. For instance, they could go for a brisk walk together, share a cycle ride around some country lanes in search of a nice lunch or accompany each other on visits to the gym. The fact is that a Libran won't want to do any of this by themselves, because they'll start to feel lonely and then they won't bother to do it any more. Another option is for the Libran to join an exercise class full of potential kindred spirits, so they have a good reason to go every week. Mind you, they may undo all the good they've done in the class by going out for a drink or a meal afterwards.

Libra is the sign that rules the kidneys, which means that Librans need to take care of this area of their bodies. They must make sure that they drink plenty of water each day in order to flush out their kidneys, especially if they enjoy drinking alcohol. If the Libran is susceptible to kidney stones they should take expert advice about altering their diet to reduce the likelihood of getting any more stones. Librans can also suffer from gout, which is caused by too rich a diet. You see, it all comes back to food with Librans!

Money

We're on dodgy ground here! Let's put it simply – Librans and money can be a tricky combination. It's nothing to do with the Libran intelligence. How could it be, when they belong to one of the cleverest signs of the zodiac? It's more to do with the Libran reluctance to face up to unpleasant facts coupled with their enjoyment of the good things in life. This means that if a Libran wants something, they'll buy it. Only later will they think about whether they can afford it or not. I've had several Libran friends who have lurched from one financial crisis to the next, always living in fear of receiving nasty letters from their banks and never opening these missives when they do arrive for fear of what they might contain. It's an unsettling and uncomfortable way to live, and it rarely does them any good. Librans tend to spend first and think later, which means they can rack up monstrously high balances on their credit cards and they rarely have any money in their bank accounts by the end of the month.

Librans certainly appreciate quality, and that usually comes at a price. They aren't interested in being swanky or showing off because that's the sort of behaviour they loathe. It's simply that they have excellent taste and they like to indulge it as often as possible. Some signs will deliberately buy a designer outfit because they want to tell everyone who made it and how much it cost. A Libran will buy a designer outfit simply because it fits them beautifully, is very flattering (probably cleverly hiding a few bulges) and is made from a fabulous fabric. They'll tell you that it's a false economy to buy cheap clothes because they don't last, and that they'll get years of wear out of their expensive clothes. It's the same story when you go out for a meal with them. You might suggest going somewhere inexpensive, out of consideration for the Libran's parlous financial state (or for your own, of course), but the Libran will probably insist that you go somewhere much more costly. They won't stint themselves when they get there, either, and will airily order whatever they want rather than keep one eye on the prices.

As you will have gathered by now, it's important for Librans to learn some horse sense when handling their finances. For a start, they should steel themselves to put away a little money each month so they can build up some savings. They may dip into these savings whenever they need bailing out, but at least they've got them as a financial standby. It will be even better if the Libran puts their money into the sort of account that can't be touched for a year or two, so there's less danger of them raiding it in order to splash out on a new pair of shoes or a weekend away.

However, many Librans are so indecisive that they find it difficult to make decisions about what to do with their money. Which savings account should they choose? Which bank would be best for them? If they've got some money to invest, should they choose stocks and shares? It will help if they have a trusted adviser to give them a guiding hand, but they must make sure this is someone who really is trustworthy and honest. Some Librans are trusting to the point of being completely gullible, so they run the risk of giving their money to someone who will swindle them out of it or who hasn't got a clue about what they're doing.

Most Librans will have at least one credit card, and they'll use it on a regular basis. That's fine, but sometimes they can forget to pay the minimum monthly payment, and that can land them in hot water. So they really need to get themselves organized financially. It could save them a lot of money.

Career
Librans have a tremendous amount to offer the world, especially in their working lives. They should play to their strengths, which means emphasizing all their good points and finding jobs that will bring out the best in them.

One of the greatest Libran qualities is their tremendous tact. These people are rarely stuck for the right phrase or the most polite way to say something awful. They have a way with words that means they're the most diplomatic sign in the zodiac, and they should capitalize on it whenever possible. This means they're perfect in a job like customer relations, in which they have to deal with complaints from the public. A Libran will always do their best to smooth a customer's ruffled feathers. In fact, if a Libran can't do it, no one can! Librans are also good at personnel work or human resources, for the same reasons. Another option for a Libran is to go into the diplomatic service, especially if they want a career that offers lots of travel opportunities.

Librans also excel in the beauty and fashion industries. After all, Librans are one of the most attractive signs in the zodiac, so it makes sense that they're interested in appearances and in looking good. A Libran would enjoy being a beautician, make-up artist or dress designer. If none of those careers is suitable, the Libran might enjoy selling expensive make-up or clothes in a department store. Note the word "expensive", because they won't want to peddle anything cheap and nasty. With their Venusian love of scents, a Libran could be interested in becoming an aromatherapist or working for a perfume company. Alternatively, they might enjoy the music business.

Another classic Libran option is to become an interior designer. Most Librans have very good taste, so they would enjoy making a living out of it. They would also excel at calming down frazzled clients and coping with their giant egos.

In fact, a Libran will do well in any job that makes the most of their charm, good taste, equable personality, powers of attraction and their intelligence. Librans understand the importance of solid relationships, so they might be interested in working for a dating agency in which they find suitable partners for their clients.

Being a Cardinal sign means that Librans are full of drive and ambition. They want to get ahead in life, and sometimes they will do that by setting up their own business. However, they will fare much better and be much more successful if they can work in partnership with someone rather than on their own. This is one way of countering the Libran's inability to make up their mind about anything because, if necessary, the business partner can make all the decisions. The partner will certainly have to be strong-willed so they can stop the Libran only working a two-day week or spending all the profits on long lunches while they're still struggling to make a name for themselves. The Libran may also hire staff on the basis of how attractive they are rather than their level of skills. When questioned about this, the Libran will say quite logically that if they're going to spend so much time with their employee, they've got to like them and they must be easy on the eye.

Bosses and colleagues find Librans a great asset to have around, because they're decorative, courteous and interesting to talk to. They're also very popular. And no wonder, because they'll do their best to turn workmates into friends. Sometimes, it has to be said, they'll also turn them into lovers. A lot of Librans seem to get involved in office romances!

It's important for a Libran to work in pleasant surroundings and preferably with pleasant people. They don't like being in dirty, noisy or scruffy places for longer than they have to. They may even leave a job because they can't tolerate the unpleasant conditions any longer. So if you work with a Libran and you want them to stay, you must make life pleasant for them.

Love and Friendships

Relationships mean everything to Librans. They can't exist happily without them because they are completely attuned to having other people in their lives. Some signs, such as Capricorns, can be loners, but that's impossible for Librans. They simply don't function like that. They need people around them for most of the time, and when they are alone they must know that they've got someone important in their life to whom they can return. There is nothing sadder than a Libran on their own, because they will be incredibly lonely and desolate. Even if they put on a brave face to the rest of the world, inside they will feel lost and aware that a very important part of their life is missing.

There are two reasons for the Libran dependence on relationships. The first is their planetary ruler, Venus, which makes them so affectionate and eager to get on well with others. And the other factor is their Air element, which gives them a desire to communicate with the rest of the world. This means a Libran would probably wither up and die if they had to live without other people around them. Even if this didn't happen physically they would feel as though it had happened emotionally. The people in a Libran's life reaffirms their identity and makes them feel valued. It's as though a Libran gains a strong sense of themselves by being with other people. When they're alone, they aren't sure who they are.

For Librans, the focus is on other people. This is in direct contrast to members of their opposite sign, Aries, who focus on themselves. For a Libran, the important questions are whether their is partner happy and what they're doing with their life. And if the Libran can't focus on others because they aren't there, that raises all sorts of questions about the purpose of the Libran's life. Even so, it's a rare Libran who doesn't have their own fan club, because they're so good at getting on with other people and they're such good company. As a result, they usually have plenty of firm friends, who are always willing to hear about the Libran's latest heartache or the new love of their life.

When choosing their friends, Librans are attracted to people who are bright, witty and great company. It's very easy for them to make friends because they're naturally so charming and outgoing. However, Librans do sometimes desert their friends in favour of a new love, and only get in touch again when things start to go wrong. They really should learn to spend more time with their friends even when they are in the midst of a love affair, in case they discover (usually when the affair is over and they're on their own again) that their friends have got fed up and deserted them.

Another major plus point in favour of Librans is their huge romantic streak, which runs through them like letters in a stick of rock. It's very easy for them to fall in love. Sometimes they can fall in love with love, which leads to broken hearts all round when they realize that they're in the grip of infatuation rather than love. They are also very idealistic and tend to have very high expectations of their beloved. In the Libran's eyes, this person will be more divine than human. But when they discover that their beloved has feet of clay just like the rest of us, they can feel let down and disappointed. How dare this person turn out to be human after all!

Many Librans spend virtually all their adult lives in emotional relationships. For instance, a Libran may get married at an early age and spend the rest of their life with this one person. It would be unthinkable for them to do anything else because they would hate to be on their own. Or they might be serial monogamists, only ever moving from one committed relationship when they have another one to go to, so they're never without a partner. It can be extremely difficult for a Libran to end a relationship, partly because they hate the inevitable emotional dramas and partly because they can't bear the thought of being on their own again. So they may stick it out with one partner until they've met that person's replacement. Even then, it can be a struggle for the Libran to sever their ties with the first person, often because they don't want to hurt them. If they're unhappy with their partner and they don't meet anyone else, they may still stay in this difficult relationship simply because they haven't had a better offer. Deep down, Librans believe that any partner is better than none.

Family Relationships

Harmonious relationships are essential to a Libran's well-being, no matter who they're with. It's important to a Libran that they get on equally well with their family as with their friends, and they'll feel quite churned up when they have a disagreement with someone. As a result, Librans will often bite their lips and swallow their anger rather than risk showing it and potentially causing mayhem. I've known Librans who bottled up their anger for years before finally letting rip. Even then, they did it in a moderate and considerate way, which didn't really help matters. Sometimes, their partners didn't even know the Librans were angry with them.

However, there is a strange dichotomy here because, although Librans like a peaceful life, they don't like it to be peaceful all the time. This is another example of the Libran need for balance. If life gets too sweet and easy-going, the Libran will unconsciously start stirring up trouble to make things interesting again. They'll rock the boat in some way, perhaps by starting a blazing row or doing something that will annoy everyone around them, and then deal with the fall-out. They need to balance the harmony with some disruption. Very often, they don't even realize they're doing it, so they can be very surprised when the rest of the family accuses them of being difficult or rude. I used to know a Libran who often made nasty or hurtful remarks, presumably in the hope that I would rise to the bait. Many astrologers have noted that Librans are simply Ariens on their best behaviour, and it's absolutely true. But most of the time, Librans are easy to be around and very considerate.

Librans don't enjoy spending a lot of time on their own, so they like it if their family can provide plenty of company.

They'll go on outings together, and if the Libran has anything to do with it the family will spend a lot more time together than many contemporary families. Librans believe in togetherness.

When a Libran becomes a parent, they'll be thrilled. They'll dote on their children, admiring their beauty, soft skin, sweet smiles and perfectly formed hands. They'll also pay a lot of attention to what their children wear, so even as babies they'll be very well-dressed. Nothing will be too good for the children, and the Libran may even knit or crochet a special blanket for them that will be passed on to each baby in turn. The Libran will show their sentimental side by carefully saving locks of hair from each of their children as babies, as well as treasuring other mementoes from their childhood such as tiny pairs of shoes or teething rings.

The Libran will do their best to instil courtesy and good manners in their children from an early age, and will place enormous emphasis on this. They will also make sure that their children have decent table manners, and understand the importance of such words as 'please' and 'thank you'. However, they aren't good at meting out punishments, partly because they hate to be seen in an unfavourable light, so they may rely on their partner to be the one who ticks off the children. The Libran will also place a tremendous emphasis on their children's education, introducing books at an early age and doing their best to ensure that family mealtimes are opportunities for proper conversations with the children. The children will be expected to keep up with world news and form their own opinions. When the children become old enough to leave home, the Libran will be very sad to see them go. They'll be torn between being pleased that their children are now independent and able to lead their own lives, and being sorry that they're leaving the nest. They'll also have to wrestle with feelings of possessiveness when their children fall in love and bring boyfriends and girlfriends home. Many Libran fathers in particular will be secretly convinced that their daughters' boyfriends aren't good enough for them, even if they would never dare to say so.

Creativity and Potential

Librans have a tremendous amount to offer the world. They're loaded with potential, and all they've got to do is to prove it. Their planetary ruler, Venus, gives them enormous artistic skills which they enjoy using to the best of their ability, and their Air element gives them intellect and the ability to communicate with others. As a result, they have a lot working in their favour.

Many Librans are musical, whether they play an instrument, compose music or simply enjoy listening to other people's musical outpourings. The list of Libran musicians is long and illustrious, and includes every musical taste from jazz to classical. A Libran who plays an instrument may never hope to emulate such celebrated and diverse Libran musicians as Ray Charles, Jerry Lee Lewis, Tom Petty, Art Tatum, George Gershwin, John Lennon, Yo Yo Ma, David Oistrakh or Luciano Pavarotti, but they can have a jolly good try.

Many Librans also enjoy treading the boards as actors. After all, they often have film-star good looks, so they're already halfway there. A Libran could join their local amateur dramatic society, which is how many famous actors and actresses started out. They'll enjoy the camaraderie and the social aspects of belonging to an acting group, and will adore the excitement of getting ready for opening nights. They will also prove that they're surprisingly ambitious when it comes to landing decent parts, and they certainly won't want to take a back seat when they could be in a starring role.

Venus, the ruling planet of Libra, also gives members of this sign a strong ability to reflect the world around them through photography and painting. Linda Eastman and Annie Leibowitz are two successful Libran photographers, while Libran painters include Pierre Bonnard, Odilon Redon, Mark Rothko, Caravaggio and Tintoretto.

Venus also gives Librans their love of silky, tactile fabrics and their interest in clothes. As a result, a Libran might enjoy making their own clothes or even designing them (after all, it worked for Donna Karan and Ralph Lauren). The Libran will love using expensive, luxurious fabrics such as silk and velvet, and will also enjoy receiving lots of compliments when they're able to wear the finished articles.

With their instinctive empathy for other people, a Libran might enjoy doing some voluntary work, such as helping to run the shop in their local hospital or organizing outings for disadvantaged children. They also do very well if they volunteer to work on a telephone helpline, because they're good at listening and their natural charm will help them to cope in difficult conversations. I have a Libran friend who started helping homeless drug addicts in his spare time and eventually did it as a full-time job. His Libran diplomacy made him a natural at it, and he showed genuine concern for everyone who came through the doors of the shelter where he worked. You might think that Librans, who have such a romantic and idealistic view of the world, would shy away from anything unpleasant and potentially upsetting, but they have a streak of steel running through them that enables them to cope remarkably well.

Which brings me on to my next suggestion for ways of exploring Libran potential. Politics. There are some pretty powerful Librans who have run countries or changed society, including Margaret Thatcher, Lech Walesa, Vaclav Havel, Jimmy Carter and Mahatma Gandhi. Despite their need for harmony and balance, Librans enjoy rocking the boat so they make good politicians who want to shake people up and make things happen. The Libran could get involved in politics on a very modest, local level, so they can combine it with their day job. Then they can extricate themselves again if it doesn't work out in the way they want.

Holidays

Librans can take any amount of luxury, relaxation and lotus-eating, especially when they're on holiday. They believe that holidays are opportunities for complete indulgence, so they will do their utmost to take life as easy as possible so they can relax, unwind and recharge their batteries. If you go on holiday with a Libran, don't expect them to be up with the lark every morning, with the day's itinerary already planned and the freshly-made coffee on the breakfast table. You need an Aries or Virgo if you want such a lively holiday companion. Instead, the Libran will still be a snoozing lump under the covers, and they'll be reluctant to stir until they absolutely have to. When they do get up, you'll be the one who has to organize everything while the Libran looks around blearily for their sunglasses or sarong.

Librans are too intelligent to be content with spending a fortnight lying on a beach while they kipper themselves in the sun. It might be relaxing at first but they soon get very, very bored. Besides, they have too much respect for their skin to want to turn it into leather. However, the Libran might fancy visiting somewhere that offers the twin attractions of sparkling blue seas and plenty of culture. Then they can alternate between sunbathing and sightseeing as the fancy takes them. This is also a good way of ensuring that the Libran's holiday companion is happy. And if the Libran's companion is happy, the Libran is happy. (Usually, at any rate.)

However, if a Libran does go on holiday with someone (and they're unlikely to go on their own because they have such a strong need for companionship), the Libran will make as few decisions as possible. That's because they find it almost impossible to make up their mind sometimes, so the holiday companion will have to be the one to suggest what they're going to do for the day. Left to their own devices, the Libran will still be sitting around at lunchtime, wondering where to go and what to do.

Decent food is also high on the Libran's list of holiday essentials, because there's nothing they like better than working their way through a menu full of delicious temptations. They may even choose their holiday destination or hotel purely on the strength of its cuisine or wine, and they'll do their best to sample as much of it as possible while they're there. They certainly won't want to stay in second-rate places if they don't have to, and even if they're having a budget holiday they will still want to enjoy good food and drink. One way for them to do this is to choose a self-catering holiday, although you won't find them spending too much time at the sink and cooker. Either someone else will have to do all those chores or everyone will eat very simply but deliciously, so there's minimum cooking and washing up.

A typical Libran's has very sophisticated tastes and would enjoy visiting the great cities of the world, especially if they can combine sight-seeing with an enjoyable tour of the best shops they can find. However, this could all work out very expensive, so ideally the Libran needs to travel with someone who can restrain them from spending a fortune if they don't have it. They will also need someone to help them carry all the carrier bags!

Librans are good at sending postcards home, but they'll only send them to the people they love and the people who ought to receive one, such as their boss or the neighbour who's keeping an eye on their home. They certainly won't want to send them to all and sundry, because they simply won't be able to work up the enthusiasm. As it is, they will ruthlessly strike off names on their list of potential recipients when lassitude or boredom overtakes them, even if they reinstate them later on when guilt gets the better of them. So if you get a postcard from a Libran you know, thank them profusely because a lot of effort will have gone into it.

Home

Pleasant surroundings are very important to Librans, and they will never be truly happy in anywhere that's mucky or ugly. That doesn't mean they have to live in a palace but they will always make sure that their home looks as good as possible. And they will still lavish love and attention on their home whether they own it or rent it. After all, they've got to live there! As a result, Librans can be ideal tenants because they will paint and decorate their rented homes, tend the gardens and generally take care of everything. And if they can't do it themselves, they'll pay someone to do it for them.

Librans like to furnish their homes with quiet good taste. Even if a Libran is rolling in money they don't want to look as though they're stinking rich. How vulgar can you get! So there will be no ostentatious displays of wealth, no opulent, museum-quality furniture or sideboards covered with highly polished family silver. If there is any silver it will be safely tucked away in a cupboard (which saves having to clean it and reduces the likelihood of it being stolen) and only brought out on special occasions. Keeping quiet about such riches has another advantage, because it means that if the Libran has to sell their treasures in order to raise some cash no one will be any the wiser.

Antiques appeal to Librans, if they can afford them, because they like their traditional shapes and quality. They also enjoy the sense of history that comes with antiques, the notion that lots of people have owned them and they have a story to tell. Many Librans are interested in military artefacts, which is a characteristic they get from Aries, their opposite sign of the zodiac. As a result, you will find lots of Libran homes that contain paintings of battles, figurines of soldiers or collections dedicated to famous military leaders, such as Napoleon Bonaparte.

If a Libran can't afford expensive antiques they may content themselves with going to their local junk shop and buying pieces of furniture that they can restore at home. They will enjoy transforming something that was fit only for the rubbish heap into a thing of beauty, and will give it pride of place.

Librans place a great deal of importance on how things smell, so their homes will always smell fresh and clean. They may also enjoy lighting scented candles or placing bowls of pot pourri on tables, especially if they are quietly expensive rather than something cheap that they picked up in the supermarket.

This is such a sociable sign, with such a strong need for other people, that a Libran won't enjoy living alone if that means they're isolated from their fellow human beings. It's essential for a Libran to have lots of friendly neighbours living nearby, so they can call on them when the fancy takes them. The Libran charm will soon work its magic, turning neighbours into friends and thawing out even the most hostile people. As a result, the Libran will enjoy doing lots of entertaining, and they'll do it really well. Every now and then they'll love pulling out all the stops and hosting a fabulous dinner party or a lavish lunch, where people from all walks of life can mingle and everyone has a wonderful time.

The typical Libran colours are pastels, especially pale pink and pale blue. They like floral patterns, too, such as lovely chintzes. And, of course, it goes without saying that they adore fabrics that cost a fortune, especially if they're hand-blocked or carry patterns from the eighteenth or nineteenth centuries. They're far less keen on inexpensive fabrics bearing ordinary patterns that you'll find everywhere, even if that's all they can afford. Rather than have to put up with something they don't like, the Libran will make sure they're first through the door of their favourite furniture shops the moment their sales start, so they can snap up some bargains. It's one occasion when the Libran can't afford to be indecisive because they'll lose out if they hesitate for too long.

Clothes and Image

Librans love the romantic look. Libran men are at their best when they look as though they've just stepped out of the pages of a nineteenth-century romantic novel, complete with floppy hair, a slim waist and ravishing good looks. They're deliciously masculine without being aggressively so, in the style of Libran actors Roger Moore, Michael Douglas, Christopher Reeve, Tim Robbins, Guy Pearce and Marcello Mastroianni. As for Libran women, they can't resist frills and flounces, and often look great in filmy fabrics such as voiles and chiffons. They love softening up their outfits with long, floaty scarves, and adore the chance to get dressed up, complete with a large-brimmed hat. They are ultra-feminine, as you can gather from this list of Libran ladies: Kate Winslet, Catherine Zeta-Jones, Brigitte Bardot, Catherine Deneuve and Sigourney Weaver. Some Libran women come across as being very demure and rather prim, even if that isn't how they really are. Julie Andrews and

Olivia Newton-John are two examples of this squeaky-clean Libran image.

Because Libra is ruled by the planet Venus, members of this sign can have problems with their weight. Venus gives them a love of delicious food and drink, and also an inability to resist such things. "I can resist everything except temptation," Oscar Wilde famously announced. And what else could he be but a Libran? Thanks to Venus, Librans may start life looking slim and lithe, but they put on the pounds over the years and eventually become rather well-rounded. Even if they aren't fat, they look curvaceous, cuddly and voluptuous. Which is probably no accident, because it makes them look very inviting and seductive. Libran women, in particular, can be very soft and pillowy, with classically feminine bodies. They often have hourglass figures, which they like to accentuate.

As you will have gathered by now if you've read the rest of this chapter, Librans can't resist looking good. These are the sort of people who will get dressed even to take out the rubbish, because they have a horror of being seen at their worst. They will spend a lot of money on maintaining their appearance, although they won't want this to show. It has to look effortless, even if it takes them longer than they'd like to admit. So Libran women believe in buying expensive face creams and good-quality make-up, rather than the cheapest brand they can track down. And they will spend a lot of time applying all these unguents and powders in order to present a polished, beautiful image to the world. They also like to invest in good underwear, especially if they've reached the stage in life where it's got to help to defy gravity and make the best of what nature gave them. Libran women also like to wear pretty or sexy nightdresses, which add to their seductive image. These aren't women who will go to bed in an oversized T-shirt. They want to look attractive, even when they're asleep. After all, what would happen if there were a fire and they had to be rescued by the fire brigade? They don't want to look a fright while they're being given a fireman's lift.

Many Libran women are also incapable of leaving home

without having sprayed themselves with a generous squirt of their favourite scent. Once they've found one that they like (which can take years, given their chronic indecision), they won't want to change it in a hurry and it will become their signature perfume. Very chic. They go for light, floral scents, and will avoid anything that's too cloying or sickly-sweet in case it gives them a headache. Libran men also like to smell nice, and worry that their deodorants will let them down in a crisis. They pay great attention to their clothes, and enjoy spending a lot of money on them if they've got it to spare. And sometimes they'll splash out even when they don't have the money. After all, they do have an image to maintain, especially if they're still single and on the hunt for a partner. They've got to look smooth and sexy. And they usually succeed admirably.

Famous Librans

Ray Charles (23 September 1930); F. Scott Fitzgerald (24 September 1896); Catherine Zeta-Jones (25 September 1969); Bryan Ferry (26 September 1945); Meat Loaf (27 September 1947); Brigitte Bardot (28 September 1934); Lech Walesa (29 September 1943); Angie Dickinson (30 September 1931); Walter Matthau (1 October 1920); Mahatma Gandhi (2 October 1869); Gore Vidal (3 October 1925); Susan Sarandon (4 October 1946); Guy Pearce (5 October 1967); Britt Ekland (6 October 1942); Desmond Tutu (7 October 1931); Paul Hogan (8 October 1939); John Lennon (9 October 1940); Harold Pinter (10 October 1930); Eleanor Roosevelt (11 October 1884); Luciano Pavarotti (12 October 1935); Margaret Thatcher (13 October 1925); Roger Moore (14 October 1927); P G Wodehouse (15 October 1881); Tim Robbins (16 October 1958); Rita Hayworth (17 October 1918); Martina Navratilova (18 October 1956); John Le Carré (19 October 1931); Tom Petty (20 October 1950); Carrie Fisher (21 October 1956); Catherine Deneuve (22 October 1943).

The Top Ten Libran Characteristics

Indecisive; Sees two sides to every argument; Charming; Diplomatic; Romantic; Sentimental; Easily flattered; Idealistic; Resentful; Needs harmony.

Are You A Typical Libran?

Try this quiz on the Librans you know to find out whether they're typical members of their sign.

Libra

1 Is it easy for you to make up your mind?
2 Are you good at saving money?
3 Are you happiest when you're by yourself?
4 Can you eat anything you want without putting on weight?
5 Can you leave the house without checking to see what you look like?
6 Do you enjoy having rows?
7 Are you immune to a pretty or handsome face?
8 Are you indifferent to what people think of you?
9 Do you enjoy being on the go from morning to night?
10 Do you frequently lose your temper?

Score
Score one point for every "yes" and zero points for every "no".

0–3 You couldn't be more Libran if you tried. You're a people person, unable to function without having important relationships. You have a strong need to be liked but you can be very idealistic, which leaves you susceptible to being hurt.

4–6 You have a strong Libran streak but it's tempered by the influence of other signs. Read the Top Ten Characteristics of the other signs to see which ones ring a bell with you.

7–10 Although you were born under the sign of Libra you don't have many Libran characteristics. Look through the Top Ten Characteristics of Virgo and Scorpio to see if either of these sounds more like you.

Scorpio

23 October–21 November

The Scorpio Adult

Intense and passionate about life, Scorpios never like to do things by halves. They believe that if something is worth doing, it's worth doing properly. They launch themselves into it with an all-or-nothing attitude, although of course they aren't in the slightest bit interested in coming away with nothing. They want to get the "all" part of the deal! Scorpios apply this logic to every aspect of their lives, from shopping to sex. Everything must have meaning for them. It's this intensity that makes Scorpios so mysterious to the rest of us. There's a lot more going on inside them than they're prepared to admit, because they're very private and they like to keep their feelings to themselves.

Scorpio's modern planetary ruler is Pluto, which governs secrets and things that are going on under the surface. It also governs buried treasure, and there's certainly plenty of that with Scorpios. They're very complex creatures, and what you see is most definitely not what you get. No wonder that Scorpios don't want to give the game away about themselves, and prefer to retain an inscrutable and mysterious image. It's

165

as though they want to keep everyone guessing, especially if they're secretly worried that no one will like them if they discover the real person hiding beneath all those masks and disguises. Yet they have little to be anxious about because Scorpios are such dramatic, entertaining and life-affirming company.

Before Pluto was discovered, Scorpio was ruled by Mars, the planet of war, determination and aggression. This is what gives Scorpios their drive and ability to get where they want to go, come what may. Mars also gives them their temper, even though it is dampened by their Water element so they tend to smoulder and stew for a long, long time before finally blowing their tops. But it can be very scary when they do let rip, rather like a volcano erupting after weeks of rumblings.

Scorpio's Water element also means that members of this sign are extremely sensitive to situations and people, although they won't want to let anyone in on that particular secret. In fact, they're much more sensitive than most of us give them credit for, even though the textbook Scorpio is portrayed as someone who would stab you in the back as soon as look at you. Yes, Scorpios have a strong desire for revenge when they're betrayed, but they often don't act on it. Instead, they will brood on what went wrong, feeling wretched and angry about it. They may envisage all sorts of horrible ways to get their vengeance but they won't necessarily act on any of them.

One of the interesting things about Scorpio is that it can reach the highest heights and sink to the deepest lows. So you will find some Scorpios who are able to rise above their worst human instincts and transcend them, and others who give into all their urges, regardless of the consequences. But no matter whether a Scorpio is a saint or a sinner, they're never surprised by what human nature can make people do. Scorpios have usually seen it all, either in their private lives or through their jobs. They have Pluto to thank for this, so their lives are often highly dramatic, almost like the plot from an opera. Some Scorpios have had terrible experiences but have managed to survive them.

Pluto is also the planet of transformation, and it shows. The lives of many Scorpios are divided up into distinct chapters. When things go wrong, they have the knack of making a clean break and moving on to something new with barely a backward glance. It could be a new relationship, a new job or even a new country, but they'll cut themselves off from what went before and sometimes it will be as though their old life never existed. This can be very hurtful for the people they left behind but it's simply the Scorpio way of coping with what life throws at them.

It's essential for Scorpios to have power and control over their lives. They loathe the very idea of being at someone else's mercy or whims, and need to know that they're in the driving seat. Sometimes, this can make them seem rather formidable to everyone around them, because they will take charge of situations and people without realizing it. In other words, it's OK for them to boss others around but they don't want to be on the receiving end of the same treatment! That's when their hackles will rise.

Because Scorpio is a Fixed sign, members of this sign know how to stick to their guns. When faced with opposition to something that they think is important, they will dig their heels in and refuse to budge. This can make them very committed to a cause but it can also make them highly obstinate and stubborn, so they'll go blue in the face before conceding defeat. It's as though hell has got to freeze over before the Scorpio will cave in. Sometimes, the Scorpio's ability to concentrate on one thing to the exclusion of all else can make their behaviour rather compulsive and obsessive, which is a warning sign to them to lighten up and not have such a one-track mind.

Never underestimate the power of a Scorpio's emotions. They feel things really deeply, and as a result are often caught in the grip of intense emotional experiences. When they fall in love, for instance, it's a head-over-heels experience and they'll put all their energy into the relationship. Their friendships are equally important and highly charged. But if it's true that you get out of life what you put into it, Scorpios are way ahead of many of the rest of us because they put so much effort and emotion into their lives.

The Scorpio Child

Even when they're babies, Scorpios are controlled by their emotions. They smile more broadly and scowl more fiercely than other children of their age, and are already showing the Scorpio intensity that will be with them throughout life.

It's very important for Scorpio children to feel loved and wanted. Emotional security means a lot to them, and if they have parents who are undemonstrative, always distracted by other things or never around, the Scorpio child will interpret this as being their own fault and will brood on all the reasons why this might be so. They will also learn to shut down their feelings and responses as a form of self-defence, and it might then take them years to open up again. So Scorpio babies and children need plenty of love and affection, and they must also be encouraged to develop their wonderful sense of humour so they can laugh at the world and also (most importantly) at themselves. This is one of their greatest saving graces, because it acts like a safety valve when things get too hot and heavy, so it's essential for them to develop it from an early age.

Something else that's vitally important for Scorpio children is physical security. They need to know that they're living in a safe, protected environment. If their parents are worried about something, ideally they should keep it to themselves and avoid discussing it in front of their Scorpio child in case it alarms them too much. They like to be settled, too, so will struggle to cope if their parents enjoy frequent house moves. All the upheavals will be very traumatic to the little Scorpio who is, after all, a Fixed sign. They don't like too much change because it unnerves them.

If the Scorpio child is the first-born, they may not react very happily when a younger sibling arrives. They'll see this child as a threat and a rival for their parents' affection, so on no account should they be made to feel second-best or as though no one cares about them any more because all the attention has switched to the new arrival. Sometimes, this sibling rivalry can last a lifetime if nothing is done to check it, so it's important for the Scorpio child to become friends with their younger brothers and sisters.

Scorpios have very active imaginations, so parents should pay careful attention to what their Scorpio child is reading and watching. If the child starts having horrible nightmares it may be because of what someone has told them or what they've read. This means that stories or films about ghouls, ghosts and things that go bump in the night may fascinate the little Scorpio when the lights are still on but will terrify them when they're left alone in the dark. Their parents shouldn't minimize these night terrors or ridicule the child about their fears, but instead should discuss them with the child and try to put their mind at rest.

Scorpio children need plenty of discipline when they're growing up. This doesn't mean they need to be bullied or brought up in a restrictive environment, but they do benefit from knowing the rules and being aware of what they can and can't do. They will accept their parents' rules quite happily, provided that they know why they've been imposed. What they won't like are arbitrary rules, or rules that keep changing. Something else that won't impress the Scorpio child is if there seems to be one law for them and a less harsh one for their siblings. Such preferential treatment won't go down at all well!

As the Scorpio child gets older, they will need some privacy, especially if they live in a small house full of people. Ideally, they should have their own bedroom, which will probably display a sign saying "Keep out". They'll also be reluctant to share their possessions with their friends and siblings, and may have to be persuaded to do so. It's therefore very important that the Scorpio's belongings are returned to them in their original state whenever they do lend them out, so they'll be encouraged to do it again.

The teenage Scorpio will also be very cagey about their love life, and will take umbrage if it's treated as a joke. But their parents should try to persuade them to bring their beloved home to meet the family, partly to be friendly and partly so they can make sure that this is someone they want their Scorpio child to spend time with. And they'll also have to stand by with the hankies when everything ends in tears.

Health

The intensity with which a Scorpio approaches life doesn't always do their health a lot of favours. Scorpios often have an all-or-nothing approach to the world, with a tremendous intensity that can give them enormous highs or despairing lows. What's more, most Scorpios tend to bottle up their feelings, so they find it very hard to unburden themselves to a sympathetic listener because they've somehow trained themselves not to do so. This is partly because they're so private but also partly because they have such a strong need to keep control over situations and they fear they may lose this if they're seen as weak or in need of help.

So much pent-up emotion can play havoc with a Scorpio's sleep, and also with their digestion and blood pressure. It's bound to prey on their mind, with the result that they can become quite obsessive about it. This is one of the many reasons why it's good for Scorpios to take plenty of exercise, because it helps them to let off steam and work out their aggression. They may also be able to forget their troubles when they're thumping hell out of their opponent in the boxing ring, tearing around a race track, catching someone in a flying rugby tackle or rushing up and down the cricket pitch. As you will have gathered from this list of typically Scorpio sports, members of this sign enjoy setting themselves tough challenges and getting involved in aggressive activities.

Scorpios also excel at water sports, which is exactly as it should be considering that they belong to a Water sign. But once again they enjoy tough, slightly dangerous water sports, such as water-skiing, kayaking, scuba diving, white-water rafting, jet-skiing and canoeing. If they go swimming, they'll want to be the best in the pool and will thrash up and down the water in an impressively controlled burst of speed and energy.

There's nothing namby-pamby about Scorpios! (After all, this is the sign of James Bond!) When a Scorpio needs some quiet time to themselves, they might gain a lot of emotional satisfaction from strolling by an ocean or lake.

The areas of the body ruled by Scorpio are the bowels and sexual organs. It's highly typical that this sign should rule the two areas of the body that are most likely to cause embarrassment, because Scorpio is the sign that rules hidden, unspoken and secret things. Where the bowels are concerned, Scorpios often suffer from constipation so they need a diet that has plenty of fibre but also lots of liquid to flush everything through their digestive system. With the legendary (and often apocryphal) Scorpio sex drive, it's no surprise that the sexual organs can cause problems sometimes. Another area of the body that can affect Scorpios is their throats, which is a link with their opposite sign of Taurus.

Scorpios have a lot of stamina and endurance, but even so they should take care of themselves. They aren't invincible, even if they like to think so. They should try not to work themselves into the ground too often because it won't do them any good in the long run. They may be able to work round the clock when they're under a lot of pressure but they shouldn't do this regularly because it will eventually wear them out. However, it may be difficult for them to switch off from work when they're busy because they'll become so engrossed in it. It will be almost all they're able to think about.

Another problem with being completely wrapped up in work is that it leaves little or no time for the Scorpio to take any exercise. As a result, they can get quite stocky in later life, especially if they indulge too often in rich foods and plenty of their favourite red wine.

Money
This is a subject that Scorpios understand and respect! They like money because it enables them to stay in control of situations, rather than knowing that situations are controlling them. Scorpios don't like the thought of being dependent on others,

or the State, to pay the bills. It makes them nervous because they don't have the upper hand. It also offends their strong sense of pride and self-worth. They are the ones who should be in charge!

If a Scorpio shares a joint bank or savings account with someone, they will usually try to control the purse strings. For instance, it will be their signature that goes on the cheques or they'll arrange for all the paperwork to be sent to them. The Scorpio may tell themselves that their financial partner is too busy to do it or isn't financially-minded, even though those probably aren't the real reasons for them wanting to be in charge. It's far more likely that, suspicious as ever, they're worried that the other person may not keep them fully abreast of what's going on and might even try to trick them in some way. And no self-respecting Scorpio is going to put up with that sort of behaviour. However, it may be difficult for the Scorpio themselves to share information with their partner, even if they don't share a bank account, so it will seem as though the Scorpio is trying to keep their financial situation a secret for some nefarious reason. They need to be careful about this, because sometimes this cloak-and-dagger approach to finance can drive a wedge between the Scorpio and their partner.

Scorpios are canny and eagle-eyed when checking their own bank statements and other financial paperwork. They will go through statements line by line to make sure there aren't any errors and won't hesitate to query something if they aren't happy about it. If they have stocks and shares, they'll quiz their stockbroker to make sure they know what they're talking about, and if they make their own investments they'll read all the financial pages of the newspapers before reaching any decisions about what to buy or sell.

When a Scorpio has money to spare, they don't like frittering it away. They aren't the sort of person to spend money just for the sake of it, and even if they're very well off they may be reluctant to part with their cash. Sometimes this can make them rather penny-pinching, so they begrudge spending money on little things. Some Scorpios enjoy buying status symbols, such as expensive cars or big houses, because these make a major statement to the world that they're doing OK for themselves. They won't be able to resist showing you what they've bought and casually telling you how much it cost. Owning such things gives them a sense of power. Occasionally, however, having a home or garage full of status symbols can turn out to be a burden because the Scorpio has to work really hard to maintain their lavish lifestyle. Not that they'll want to give up their way of life even then, because that would involve a massive loss of face.

The Scorpio's careful approach to finance means they're equally clever when it comes to finding ways of investing their money. They are often skilled researchers, thanks to their ability to dig deep below the surface of life, so they will enjoy tracking down the best rate of interest available at any one time and doing lots of detective work to see which credit card offers the most attractive deal. And there's no way anyone can fob them off with unfounded sales talk. The Scorpio will spot that coming a mile off!

Career

Whatever a Scorpio does for a living, it has to give them pleasure and satisfaction. If their job is mindless or they always count the hours until it's time to go home, they'll soon start to feel frustrated and as though they're wasting their life. And that's when the rot will set in because they'll feel dissatisfied and resentful.

Ideally, a Scorpio needs a career that offers them plenty of emotional depth, an intellectual challenge and gives them something to get their teeth into. Many Scorpios are fascinated by psychology, psychotherapy and psychiatry, because they enjoy unravelling people's complex personalities. They're intrigued by what lies beneath the surface, so will enjoy digging down into someone's unconscious to find out what's lurking there. Hypnotism is another very Scorpio technique, and the Scorpio will be captivated by their ability to put people into a trance and help them to overcome difficult problems such as smoking or a fear of flying.

Another suitable profession for Scorpios is anything to do with finance. These are very money-minded souls, so they'll are enjoy being in control of money in some way. They might work in a bank, whether as a cashier or the manager (which, of course, they would much prefer), or on the stock market where they're handling massive amounts of money. They'll enjoy the adrenalin and risks that go with working on the stock market, although they'll need plenty of ways to relax so they don't burn out too quickly.

With their forensic minds, Scorpios make excellent detectives. They enjoy picking over the facts and working out exactly what's been going on. Alternatively, they could be interested in working as a pathologist. This isn't for everyone but the job appeals to the Scorpio desire to dig down to the truth. Any other sort of medicine can also suit them, but working as a surgeon is especially appealing to them. Coping with life and death problems will give them a thrill and let them know that they're doing something valuable and important. Another option is for the Scorpio to work in a funeral home. They'll enjoy the intensity of it and the fact that they're able to help people who are in crisis. They may also be rather amused to be working with one of the last taboos – death. Very often, it holds no terrors for Scorpios.

On a lighter note, you'll find Scorpios working in geology and vulcanology, and also in archaeology. As a complete departure from all this, they could also be attracted to the wine trade, because Scorpios often gave a tremendous appreciation for wine (and especially if it's red).

If a Scorpio is working in an office with other people, they won't want to be the minion. Even if they have to start at the very bottom of the office pecking order, they won't want to stay on that lowly rung of the ladder for long. They know they're destined for better things. Besides, they want to experience job satisfaction and they may not get it if they're simply running around at someone else's beck and call. Sometimes this desire to get ahead can make a Scorpio seem very ambitious, and their boss may even wonder if the Scorpio has got their eye on the top job. (And they probably have!)

Scorpios enjoy getting involved in all the office intrigue that's going on around them, and are probably one of the first to know the latest gossip. I used to work with a Scorpio whose radar for gossip and intrigue meant he knew what was happening the moment it started, and sometimes even before that. The Scorpio's tremendous sensitivity, coupled with their ability to keep a secret, can mean they're a shoulder to cry on when colleagues are having a bad time. However, they will be less forthcoming when their own life hits the skids, and they may not breathe a word to anyone even if their world is collapsing around their ears. They'll put on a brave but inscrutable front. When times are good, the Scorpio will happily take part in work expeditions to the local pub or wine bar. No wonder they're a very popular member of the team!

Love and Friendships

As with every other area of life, a Scorpio takes their relationships very seriously. They put their heart and soul into each one, because otherwise they can't really see the point in having the relationship in the first place. Partners and friends will be left in no doubt about their importance in the Scorpio's life, even if the Scorpio never manages to say so in so many words. Their actions will speak louder than words anyway, as will their loyalty and steadfast affection. When a Scorpio is on your side, that's the way they'll stay unless something awful happens.

And sometimes awful things do happen to Scorpios. Their need for control can turn them into immensely powerful partners who are reluctant to back off and relax. If they've been badly hurt in the past (and many Scorpios have been through highly traumatic experiences in their time), they may be reluctant to let their partner out of their sight for long, in case they get up to something that the Scorpio will find threatening. In fact, some Scorpios ruin perfectly good relationships by being too controlling, possessive and jealous, purely because they remember how things went wrong with other people in the past. However, their need to exert an iron grip, call the shots and to know what their partner is doing every second of the day when they're out of sight, rarely goes down very well. Sometimes, it can even drive the partner into the arms of someone else, and that, of course, makes the Scorpio even more paranoid and controlling. The whole thing ends up being a vicious circle and it can make everyone concerned very unhappy.

Very often people who are highly jealous and possessive have double standards. They expect their partners to be completely loyal and faithful, but they won't play by the rules themselves and will have lots of secret affairs or one-night stands. Some Scorpios are like this, demanding obedience and trustworthiness from their partners while sleeping around themselves. They love the intrigue that comes from juggling a permanent partner with a lover, and adore coming up with excuses for one while they're with the other one. Some of them are really clever at this (maybe practice makes perfect?) and manage to get away with it. Others get caught.

However, this doesn't mean that every Scorpio is a love-rat. Far from it! Most of them are immensely loyal and loving, and will support their partner through thick and thin. If their beloved is in trouble, the Scorpio will do what they can to help.

There are two things that have the potential to cause more trouble in a Scorpio's relationship than any other – sex and money. Scorpios are renowned for their high sex drives, although that doesn't mean that every Scorpio on the planet is a walking sex machine. Some of them aren't very interested in it, while others can't get enough. It all depends on the particular Scorpio and their experiences but, even so, sex is usually a very important part of a relationship for members of this sign. That means that their partners must be able to respond enthusiastically and sensually. It will be a disaster if the Scorpio is highly-sexed and their partner would rather read a good book. Money can also drive a wedge between a Scorpio and their partner because the Scorpio can be very secretive about their own financial arrangements while wanting to know all about their partner's. There can also be resentment if one person in the relationship earns more than the other but they share the bills equally.

It's the same story with their friendships. Scorpios tend to keep their friends for years, staying in touch with people they met at school or college for the rest of their life. They can't see any reason not to. However, if anyone hurts the Scorpio badly or does something that they think is unforgivable, they may cut them out of their life completely in case they do it again. Once bitten, twice shy!

Family Relationships

As with every other area of a Scorpio's life, they take their relationships with their family very seriously. Even if a Scorpio isn't particularly enamoured of their family, they will still treat them with respect and consideration, hoping that no one will never guess how they really feel about their nearest and dearest. It's just one example of the Scorpio ability to hide behind a mask and not to give away any clues about how they feel.

However, the Scorpio will be ultra-loyal to the members of their family that they really care about, and will always be there for them. The family members will know that they can rely on the Scorpio completely when the chips are down. If there's a crisis, the Scorpio will be one of the first people to turn up and lend a hand, even if they do have a tendency to take charge and tell everyone what they should be doing. Mind you, they may be speaking from experience because Scorpios are no stranger to crises in their own lives, so it might be a wise move to listen to what they say.

When a Scorpio becomes a parent, their children will be incredibly precious to them. They'll be a doting mother or father, but they'll also be a very strict one who doesn't stand for any nonsense. This can make the atmosphere between parent and child rather tense and frigid at times, because the Scorpio parent will be determined not to budge and give in when they think their child has been naughty and must be punished. The result could be stalemate, especially if the child is another Scorpio or belongs to one of the other Fixed signs of Taurus, Leo or Aquarius. Repeated demonstrations of discipline from the Scorpio can make the child resentful and possibly even rather frightened of their parent. As a result, the Scorpio needs to temper all that strictness and discipline with plenty of light relief, such as lots of enjoyable outings, cosy bedtime stories and plenty of hugs. They should also ease up on nagging their child to do things the way the Scorpio wants, and allow the child to express themselves in their own way and, if necessary, to learn from their mistakes. Otherwise, the parent and child can have a rather uneasy relationship.

Something else that the Scorpio parent needs to watch out for is their sense of jealousy. It's never far away, and as a result they could feel envious if their child spends a lot of time with their siblings or friends rather than with their parent. The Scorpio will struggle to understand that the child has other interests besides the family. Yet, despite this, Scorpios can be very determined to send their children away to boarding school if they can afford it, and may even pack them off at a relatively early age. If the Scorpio feels broken-hearted at the departure of their child they'll do their best to hide it and will shrug off the whole experience. What they won't tell anyone is that they cry about it when they're alone or count the days until they can see their child again.

Education is certainly an important aspect of being a parent for a Scorpio. They expect their children to do well at school, and will move heaven and earth to make sure their children go to their chosen schools. When it comes to passing exams, the Scorpio will be very strict about making sure the children do their revision and may give them some sort of financial incentive to do well, such as promising to buy them something nice if they get good marks.

The Scorpio will certainly want their children to learn about the value of money from an early age. They'll give them pocket money so they can get used to having cash, even if it's only a tiny amount, and will encourage them to spend it sensibly while also allowing them to have some fun with it.

Creativity and Potential

Scorpios have a tremendous amount to offer the world. They often have dramatic experiences in life, the sort they can draw on for creative inspiration and which are often so difficult that they need to find a way to come to terms with them. It's therefore essential that Scorpios find creative and constructive outlets for their store of intense emotions.

When you talk to many Scorpios you discover that they really have seen life at its worst, so they have fascinating stories to tell. One obvious way for them to tell these stories is to write them down, whether they disguise them as fiction or present them as fact. They might also enjoy crafting detective stories, thanks to their enjoyment of puzzles and mysteries. And there's also the opportunity for them to write stories that truly make the flesh creep, such as horror or ghost stories. Bram Stoker, who created that world-famous vampire Dracula, could only have been a Scorpio, as the realm of the undead is governed by Pluto, which is the planetary ruler of this sign. Robert Louis Stevenson is another Scorpio who created one of the darkest characters in literature – the respectable Dr Jekyll who used to turn into the murderous Mr Hyde. So an imaginative Scorpio will be following in some very illustrious footsteps when they put pen to paper.

If the Scorpio thinks all that is rather ambitious, they could settle for writing down their thoughts in a diary that's intended for their eyes only. It will still give them a good emotional outlet and a chance to unburden themselves of whatever happens to be troubling them. Another option is for the Scorpio to get involved in performance poetry. They'll enjoy the drama of the experience and the chance to perform in front of poetry lovers.

Scorpios are naturally attuned to the areas in life that many of us shy away from, so a member of this sign could gain tremendous fulfilment from becoming a bereavement counsellor, working with people who have Aids or being a volunteer in a hospice. Alternatively, they could work on a crisis phone line, talking to the people who ring in. They would have the satisfaction of knowing they were doing something truly valuable. Chad Varah, who set up the crisis charity The Samaritans to help people on the verge of suicide, was a Scorpio.

If the Scorpio has a fairly sedentary life, they could change all that by becoming involved in an active sport. There are plenty to choose from but ideally the Scorpio will go for something that offers a thrill of danger, such as hang-gliding or bungee-jumping. They certainly won't be nearly so keen on something like tiddliwinks or Scrabble.

Many Scorpios have a keen interest in alcohol, so they might enjoy gradually building up a wine cellar. Mind you, they may drink the stuff almost as soon as they get it, but they would definitely enjoy tracking down elusive vintages and learning all about the different grapes and vineyards.

Something else that might appeal to a Scorpio is getting involved in topics such as astrology, tarot and palmistry. They will be fascinated by them and might love to learn more about them so they can practise them themselves. They could become so good that they start to give readings to their friends or even turn their hobby into a career.

Finally, with the Scorpio fascination for things that are out of the ordinary, they might enjoy delving into the world of the paranormal. For instance, they could join a ghost-hunting club and spend their nights listening out for strange noises, or they might simply be content to sit at home and read about things that go bump in the night. But they'll keep all the lights on, of course.

Holidays

Scorpios take such an intense approach to life that regular breaks are essential for them. They benefit from having a change of scene because it gives them the chance to gain a fresh perspective on their lives. Scorpios have a tendency to brood over problems, so holidays are a help because they give them something else to think about. Besides, holidays give Scorpios a chance to express the light, humorous and fun-loving side of their personalities.

When it comes to choosing which holiday or weekend break to take, Scorpios are prepared to spend quite a lot of money if necessary. They don't believe in stinting themselves, so they really aren't interested in bargain breaks unless they either have no choice or the bargains are too fantastic to miss. Scorpios are excellent at research, so they're good at tracking down the sort of offers that make the rest of us turn pea-green with envy. For instance, it will be a Scorpio who manages to find an expensive holiday that's being sold at a massive discount or who books a cruise with a company that's practically giving away the tickets. Naturally, if you decide to take a leaf out of their book and follow suit, you'll find the prices have risen dramatically. Scorpios have the sort of financial luck that enables them to grab bargains when they're on offer. It's most annoying for other signs!

If a Scorpio can only take a short break, whether because of lack of time or money, they adore the thought of staying in a fabulous country or city hotel, complete with spa, swimming pool, gardens and Michelin-starred dining room. Not to mention the occasional celebrity wafting in and out. So what if the bill makes the Scorpio's eyes water? They'll have had more than their money's worth in terms of enjoyment, both at the time and afterwards when they're regaling their friends with all the luxurious, sophisticated details.

Although Scorpio belongs to the Water element, members of this sign aren't very keen on spending two weeks grilling on a foreign beach. It's OK for a couple of days, but after that they can get very bored and will be looking for distractions. So ideally they need to stay in a resort where they can hire a car and go sight-seeing sometimes, or take off on organized trips that show them local places of interest.

Despite their love of luxury when they can get it, Scorpios

are surprisingly keen on camping holidays. They may take their own mobile home if they have one, but they're often just as keen on sleeping in a tent under the stars. However, they'll insist that everyone take his or her turn at doing the cooking and washing up, and may even set up a rota to make sure it happens. They'll love feeling closer to nature and might be inspired to keep a diary of their experiences and emotions.

An activity holiday is perfect for Scorpios, especially if it offers plenty of excitement. If they have children, the whole family will be able to get involved, provided that the activities aren't too dangerous. They could learn to scuba dive, improve their skiing, go pot-holing or practise body-surfing. Alternatively, they could stay in a family-orientated holiday centre where the children are supervised if the adults want to go off and do their own thing.

A less daredevil option for adult Scorpios is a wine-tasting holiday, which would fascinate them and allow them to increase their wine collection at the same time. Alternatively, if they enjoy unravelling puzzles they might love taking part in a murder-mystery weekend where they get the chance to play detective. If they feel like going on a cruise, they'll want to choose a destination that's unusual in some way, such as sailing through the icebergs of Antarctica.

Many Scorpios have a strong streak of spirituality running through them, so another consideration for them might be disappearing on retreat for a few days of rest and meditation. They could go on an organized, structured retreat, or they might prefer to book a room in a monastery or convent and soak up the atmosphere. Something like this will certainly give them a great opportunity to take a fresh look at their lives, especially if they happen to be facing upheaval or change.

Home

Privacy is essential for Scorpios, so their homes are very important to them. Many of them are very selective about who they invite back to their homes. It's as though people have to pass a test before they are allowed over the Scorpio threshold, but after that they're welcome visitors. However, even highly sociable Scorpios will struggle if they live with someone who doesn't mind if people drop in during the day or night. This goes against the Scorpio grain, as their need for privacy is violated and they won't be comfortable never knowing if someone is going to call unexpectedly when they're slopping about in their pyjamas or watching television while eating a whole tub of ice cream. Scorpios prefer to live rather more formally than this. They'll be delighted to see you if you want to visit them, but only if you give them some advance warning!

When a Scorpio lives with other people, even if they don't have an endless parade of visitors, ideally the Scorpio should have a room of their own that they can retreat to whenever they need to be alone. This might be their own bedroom, a study or sitting room, or even the greenhouse if that's their only option, but they will value having some sort of bolt-hole. The Scorpio certainly needs somewhere that they can go to get away from everyone else, even if that simply means locking the bathroom door while they luxuriate in the bath.

Scorpios have a healthy respect for money and the security that it can offer them, so they're very keen to buy their own homes as soon as possible. But it won't end there because they'll do their best to pay off the mortgage early, so as to reduce the amount of compound interest that accrues over the years. As a result, some Scorpios are happy to make do with second-hand furniture and items that have seen better days because they'd rather put their money to better use. Having said that, I've known other Scorpios who love being surrounded by expensive gadgetry and the latest technological equipment, and who obviously spend a great deal of money on their possessions.

Many Scorpios enjoy collecting antiques, especially if they're large and unusual. If they're valuable, then so much the better, although this doesn't always matter. Mind you, no self-respecting Scorpio will shell out a lot of money on a so-called antique that is actually worthless. Scorpios are also drawn to objects that have an interesting history, even if it only relates to their own family and wouldn't mean much to anyone else. They also love items that have a hint of mystery, such as antique silhouettes in which you can only see someone in profile. Who was this person, the Scorpio will wonder whenever they look at the picture.

Whether the Scorpio's furniture is old or contemporary, it will be extremely comfortable and there will be lots of it. This isn't a sign that enjoys the minimalist look, and instead Scorpios are like their Cancerian cousins in cramming their rooms full of furniture. Sometimes the effect can be rather claustrophobic for non-Scorpios, especially if the soft furnishings are dark and patterned. It can all be a bit much!

Scorpios love to create a particular effect, and very often their homes are decorated in a dramatic style, with plenty of velvet, silk and low lighting. This is the sign that's renowned for its sex appeal, so very often a Scorpio home will have a rather erotic and sexy atmosphere. The bedroom and bathroom will be especially intimate, as you'll discover if you're ever invited in there.

Clothes and Image
Think mysterious. Think sexy. Think inscrutable. Think black leather. These are all classic Scorpio images. No matter how well you think you know a Scorpio, you'll always get the impression that they've kept a little part of themselves hidden from view, away from prying eyes, and very often their clothes enhance this feeling. For instance, a Scorpio woman loves wearing filmy, semi-transparent fabrics such as chiffon (although it will probably be black or brown, not floral) and lace, so you get a glimpse of what she's wearing (or not wearing) underneath, but everything is unspoken and only hinted at. Goldie Hawn is a Scorpio who's very good at creating this discreetly sexy look.

Most Scorpio women love looking feminine, which you might think is a contrast to the rather abrasive and tough image that this sign is sometimes credited with. There are so many myths and clichés associated with Scorpios that they often get a very poor press. Perhaps it would be fairer to say that Scorpio women often look very cool and in control, while still leaving no one in any doubt of their femininity. Grace Kelly, Katharine Hepburn, Jodie Foster, Stephanie Powers, Meg Ryan, Joni Mitchell, Vivien Leigh, Bonnie Raitt and Winona Ryder are all Scorpio women who come into this category.

If Scorpio women are usually very feminine, Scorpio men are often very masculine and attractive. Burt Lancaster, Alain Delon, Kevin Kline, King Hussein of Jordan, Nigel Havers and Sam Waterston are all Scorpios who fit the bill. They also have an intensity and presence that makes them very powerful to be around.

When it comes to choosing clothes, both sexes like to look smart, and they often go for a slightly formal look. Scorpio women can look great in tailored trouser suits and Scorpio men also look good in suits and ties. As a rule, formal clothes suit both sexes better than anything very casual and sloppy.

Quality is important to Scorpios so they like to buy decent clothes that will last a long time. And they rarely have to worry about their clothes no longer fitting their new image because they rarely change it. These are people who find a look that suits them and then keep it for the rest of their lives. Scorpio is a Fixed sign, making it resistant to change, even when it comes to the style of clothes they buy. They can't understand people who switch their image from one year to the next. As a result, sometimes Scorpios can look slightly dated because they're still wearing massive padded shoulders or their hemlines never vary. Scorpio women can also get stuck in a rut when it comes to their make-up, choosing colours and styles that give away too many clues about their age.

If you want to spot a Scorpio in a crowd, look for the person wearing sunglasses. Scorpios can't resist them, especially when the sun isn't shining. Of course, sunglasses are always a big fashion accessory and they can look highly sexy, but that's not the main reason why Scorpios wear them. They love to look mysterious but they also like to hide their eyes from the world, so no one will know how they're really feeling. They can see out from behind their sunglasses but no one can see in, and that's exactly the way they like it. If they're short-sighted, they'll order prescription sunglasses so they can wear them all the time, even indoors. They're also keen on light-sensitive glasses that automatically turn dark in bright light. I've also known Scorpios who've worn coloured contact lenses, especially if these have formed a startling and unexpected contrast to the colour of their hair. It's another way of wearing a disguise.

Famous Scorpios

Pelé (23 October 1940); Kevin Kline (24 October 1947); Pablo Picasso (25 October 1881); Hillary Clinton (26 October 1947); Sylvia Plath (27 October 1932); Julia Roberts (28 October 1967); Winona Ryder (29 October 1971); Michael Winner (30 October 1935); Jan Vermeer (31 October 1632); L. S. Lowry (1 November 1887); Marie Antoinette (2 November 1755); Charles Bronson (3 November 1922); Loretta Swit (4 November 1944); Bryan Adams (5 November 1959); Sally Field (6 November 1946); Marie Curie (7 November 1867); Christiaan Barnard (8 November 1922); Katharine Hepburn (9 November 1909); Richard Burton (10 November 1925); Leonardo di Caprio (11 November 1974); Princess Grace of Monaco (12 November 1929); Whoopi Goldberg (13 November 1955); Claude Monet (14 November 1840); William Herschel (15 November 1738); Tiberius (16 November 42 BC); Martin Scorsese (17 November 1942); Alan Shepard (18 November 1923); Meg Ryan (19 November 1961); Robert Kennedy (20 November 1925); René Magritte (21 November 1898).

The Top Ten Scorpio Characteristics

Intense; Controlling; Passionate; Loyal; Resentful; Secretive; Strong-willed; Obstinate; Complicated; Jealous.

Are You A Typical Scorpio?

Try this quiz on the Scorpios you know to find out whether they're typical members of their sign.

1 Do you take life very seriously?
2 Do you bottle up your feelings?
3 Is it essential for you to have an emotional investment in what you're doing?
4 Are you very persistent?

5 Do you usually make a decision and then stick to it?
6 Do people accuse you of being secretive or uncommunicative?
7 Do you pride yourself on being strong-willed?
8 Are you superstitious?
9 Do you enjoy getting involved in intrigue?
10 Do you have a slightly obsessive streak?

Score

Score one point for every "no" and zero points for every "yes".

0–3   You couldn't be more Scorpio if you tried. You approach life with passion, intensity and determination, and you don't believe in doing things by halves. Although you give the impression of being in control, you don't allow anyone to see what's going on under your cool exterior.

4–6   You have a strong Scorpio streak but it's tempered by the influence of other signs. Read the Top Ten Characteristics of the other signs to see which ones ring a bell with you.

7–10   Although you were born under the sign of Scorpio you don't have many Scorpio characteristics. Look through the Top Ten Characteristics of Libra and Sagittarius to see if either of these sounds more like you.

Sagittarius

22 November–21 December

The Sagittarian Adult

A Sagittarian's optimism and positive attitude helps them to cope with any problems that life throws at them. Somehow they always manage to bounce back from even the most difficult situations, so they're able to survive them. What's more, Sagittarians are able to learn from the problems that life presents them with, and they do so quite willingly. They have a very philosophical attitude to life, so they often believe that they've been sent problems purely so they can learn from them and develop as people at the same time.

Some signs of the zodiac will watch the way Sagittarians appear to sail through life without a scratch and will feel very envious of them. They may even suspect that Sagittarians are unfeeling or inhuman because of the way they take disaster on the chin, but neither of those accusations are true. In fact, Sagittarians can suffer as much as everyone else but they're less likely to wallow in self-pity and more likely to do something constructive to solve the problems they're facing.

No wonder Sagittarians love a challenge. They'll always

pick up whatever gauntlet life throws at them, determined to do their best and, preferably, to enjoy themselves at the same time. And if it's the sort of situation that's difficult to enjoy, they'll use it as an opportunity to become wiser and more tolerant. Actually, Sagittarians set themselves little challenges every day, just to keep themselves up to the mark. They're always pushing themselves, not in a strict or moralistic way but simply to see what they can achieve when they put their minds to it. Sometimes, however, they can take on too much at once and end up having to admit defeat. They're so optimistic (sometimes blindly so) that they'll completely overestimate what they're capable of doing or the amount of time something will take. The result can be embarrassing climb-downs and fervent apologies, plus a string of projects that they started but never got round to finishing because they ran out of time, money or enthusiasm. This can be very disappointing for people who were counting on the Sagittarian, and they often feel let down as a result.

Sagittarians have their planetary ruler, Jupiter, to thank for this love of challenge and ability to bite off more than they can chew. And it's Jupiter that gives them their incredible optimism, as well, plus their broad-minded and magnanimous attitude to life. In fact, Jupiter helps them to expand their lives in many different ways, so they're always open to new experiences and adventures. This planet also gives them their infectious sense of humour and their jovial personalities. Sagittarius is a Fire sign, which gives members of this sign their enthusiasm, ebullience, affection and exuberance.

Knowledge is a source of endless fascination for Sagittarians. They're the eternal students of the zodiac and will cram information into their brains throughout their lives. They certainly don't believe that they stop learning when they leave school. In fact, some of them think that that's when their proper education starts. They're always fascinated by something or other, and will often study it in depth before moving on to the next interest that grabs them. Some Sagittarians can't stop themselves taking courses and classes, partly for the knowledge they'll gain and partly for the socializing they hope to do whenever the classes are over.

But don't get the impression that Sagittarians are completely extrovert and only interested in the things that go on around them. In fact, they have an introverted streak as well, so they like to spend time inside their heads, thinking things through. They often have a deeply religious or spiritual quality, even if they don't shout about it.

Although they're interested in almost anything, Sagittarians are particularly fascinated by philosophy, politics, conservation, philanthropy, the environment and anything else that can make the world a better place. They enjoy getting involved in debates and arguments, although sometimes they can be guilty of getting on their soap box and trying to convert everyone into seeing things from their point of view. They're also fierce and committed campaigners against injustice, and will dedicate a tremendous amount of time, vehemence and energy to any cause that they believe in.

Sagittarians are extremely honest, occasionally to the point of bluntness, so sometimes they can be incredibly tactless. They don't think before they speak, and they're so keen on being frank that they don't always realize the devastating impact their words will have on other people. They really can drop the most awful clangers sometimes, and you can't help wincing when you hear what they've said. Yet despite this love of honesty, Sagittarians can also be guilty of exaggeration, often because it makes a story sound better. They don't see this embroidering of the facts as having any connection with lying or not being truthful, even when more pedantic signs tick them off about it. The fisherman who talked in exaggerated fashion about the one that got away was definitely a Sagittarian!

The Sagittarian Child
Sagittarian children have a love of life that's very infectious. They want to cram as much experience into each day as possible, even if that means falling into bed each night in an

exhausted heap. They're fascinated by what life has to offer them, and it's a quality that they never grow out of.

One of the most noticeable characteristics of a Sagittarian child is their enthusiasm. They get really excited by things, and throw themselves into them with masses of energy. If they go out for a bike ride, they don't just peddle along. They'll rush along, do wheelies, practise riding without using their hands (which is never a good idea, given the Sagittarian clumsiness) and find out how fast they can go. Even if their parents frown at all these exploits, they should certainly encourage their Sagittarian child to be active whenever possible and to have fun in the process. After all, they'll be instilling some very healthy habits in their Sagittarian child, and will have hit on a great way for them to burn off any excess nervous energy. Sagittarian children particularly enjoy team games, such as football, hockey and cricket, because they like the camaraderie that develops as a result.

Sagittarian children are usually very popular at school because they're such good fun to have around. They're funny, they don't mind playing the fool and clowning around, and they're very generous towards their friends. They also enjoy taking part in lots of school activities, from plays to day trips, and they put a lot of effort and energy into everything they do.

Children born under this sign aren't only active physically – their brains are usually whirring away as well. They're intrigued by life and want to know as much about it as possible. They'll ask their parents a string of questions so it's important that they get some helpful and patient answers even if they do go through a stage of asking the same questions over and over again. These children should also be taught how to look up information for themselves by consulting books, going to libraries and surfing the internet. Ideally, their parents should make all this as much fun as possible, rather than turning it into a dreary lesson or a boring chore.

It's no surprise, therefore, that a Sagittarian child should have plenty of bookshelves in their bedroom. They'll soon fill them up! They should also have access to a computer, even if they don't have one of their own. They also need a desk at which they can study, preferably equipped with a good lamp and plenty of pens and pencils. They'll love having their own study area and will spend a lot of time there. If they have their own bedroom, it will usually be a complete tip. Adult Sagittarians are very untidy and they were equally messy when they were children. Their parents will probably go blue in the face trying to encourage them to be more ordered and tidy, but their words will inevitably fall on deaf ears.

Because they belong to such a gregarious, affectionate and expansive sign, a Sagittarian child should ideally have some siblings to play with. Failing that, they need some friends or cousins who live nearby, so they've always got someone to chat to when they feel in need of company. An older Sagittarian child will enjoy looking after their younger siblings, especially when it comes to teaching them important facts about the world. For instance, a Sagittarian child might love taking their younger brother off on a fishing trip and showing them exactly what to do, or explaining the rules of a board game to their sister on a rainy afternoon before beating her hollow. If the Sagittarian is the youngest child, they'll really look up to their older siblings, even to the point of hero-worshipping them.

School is an important experience for every child but it's especially important for Sagittarian children because they have such a capacity to learn and acquire knowledge. In fact, with the right school a Sagittarian child will develop a passion for knowledge and information that stays with them throughout their life and will lead them in some very satisfying and creative directions. A poor school, however, will discourage or stifle the classic Sagittarian thirst for knowledge, sometimes with disastrous results.

Speaking of creativity, this is something else that should be developed in Sagittarians from a young age. They have so much to offer the world that they need plenty of opportunities to explore their creativity in all its forms, even if some of their experiments aren't successful. They're bound to find some activities that they really love and which help them to express themselves. Ideally, though, they should be encouraged to stick with projects and to persevere with them when they're going wrong, to avoid the typical Sagittarian habit of leaving a trail of half-finished projects behind them.

Health

If you read some astrology books it sounds as though Sagittarians can never sit down for more than two minutes at a time because they have such a strong need to be on the go from dawn till dusk. If they aren't working up a sweat in the gym they're cycling to and from work or jogging ten miles before breakfast. But this doesn't apply to all Sagittarians by any means, even if they wish it did. For a start, many Sagittarians don't have the time to be this active because they've got to fit their exercise periods around their working and family lives. And secondly, many Sagittarians become much less physically active as they get older and switch to being more mentally active instead.

Even so, this is a very active and energetic sign. Sagittarius is a Fire sign, and a Mutable one at that, which means that members of this sign love having plenty of changes of scene. Just like Geminis, their opposite numbers in the zodiac, Sagittarians thrive on variety. They feel jaded, bored and sometimes even ill when life becomes too predictable for them. They also have lots of nervous and physical energy that needs plenty of positive outlets, such as brisk walking, a regular exercise routine, swimming, hiking, dancing and playing tennis. Another option might be archery, because this is the sign of the Archer. Horse-riding is also a classic Sagittarian sport, because horses are ruled by this sign. Because they're fascinated by spirituality and philosophy, many Sagittarians are also attracted to forms of exercise that involve more than just getting puffed and burning up calories. For instance, they might love yoga or Tai Chi because they both have a thoughtful, spiritual quality.

The natural Sagittarian body shape is long and lean. A typical member of this sign is tall and skinny, with long arms and legs. And some Sagittarians are positively lanky. However, time can take its toll on the Sagittarian silhouette, as can too much good living (something that they can't resist, in common with their fellow Fire signs of Aries and Leo). Sagittarians have a healthy appreciation of good food and drink, with big appetites. There's nothing wrong with that, especially if they're always on the move. But problems can arise as they get older and become less active, with more money to spend on enjoying themselves. That's when excess weight can start to creep up on them. It's stealthy at first, so they barely notice it, then one day they realize there's much more of them to love than there used to be, and they wonder what on earth has happened.

Sagittarius rules the hips, so that's one place where members of this sign can expect to put on weight. Unfortunately, older Sagittarians can also experience problems with their hip joints, such as aches and pains, so they should take plenty of gentle exercise to keep these in good working order. They can also have problems with sciatica, as the sciatic nerve (which is the longest nerve in the body) is ruled by Sagittarius. This sign also rules the liver, through its association with Jupiter, which means that Sagittarians have to be careful not to eat too much rich food because it can make them feel quite liverish and sluggish if they overdo it. So they need to go carefully when eating anything very fatty or creamy. They may love it at the time but they can bet that it'll wreak its revenge later on! It's far better for them to replace all that fat and cream with fresh fruit and vegetables, even if that seems like a boring option at first. But they'll be very encouraged when their clothes start to fit them better and they begin to have more energy. That's when they'll become really enthusiastic about their new diet and will want to discover other foods that can help them to stay fit, well and lithe. Before they know where they are, they'll be a complete convert to healthy living and will be telling all their friends about it. So if you know a Sagittarian who suddenly switches from drinking wine to swilling water, and who spurns crisps in favour of seeds and nuts, you'll know what's happened!

Money

Money and Sagittarians don't always go together. Unfortunately for them. Often, it's not acquiring money that's the problem. After all, some incredibly rich people have been born under this sign, including Christina Onassis, J. Paul Getty and Kerry Packer. It's keeping money that can be so difficult for members of this sign. That's because most Sagittarians have plenty of interests, which are bound to leave them out of pocket every now and then. They seem to have high-maintenance lifestyles. I used to have a Sagittarian friend who spent all her spare money on oil paints, canvases, photographic equipment and travel. As a result, she was always broke.

So what do most Sagittarians like to spend their money on? Books are one of their greatest extravagances, although any self-respecting Sagittarian will say that books are actually a necessity. They may try borrowing books from the library whenever they're on an economy drive, but this disciplined way of living won't last long. Like a drug addict being coaxed back into having one last fix, a Sagittarian has only got to walk into a bookshop to start scanning the shelves for that must-have purchase. And, unless they're paying cash, they'll tell themselves that if they're going to be paying by credit or bank card they might as well make it worth their while. Which means that, before they know it, they'll be back to square one, with a huge book-buying habit to support.

Travel is something else that can take huge bites out of a Sagittarian's bank balance. They adore visiting different countries, especially if these are far away from the usual tourist areas, and once they develop the taste for exotic travel it's very hard for them to restrict themselves to a fortnight on a familiar beach once a year. And there are all those weekend breaks to pay for as well, whether they spend them in a modest bed and breakfast or a five-star hotel.

If a Sagittarian can't travel physically, they'll want to take off on some mental journeys instead. Many Sagittarians have a wide range of interests that is always expanding, rather like the universe (and yes, they can be fascinated by astronomy), so there's always something that they want to spend their money on. This is the sign of the eternal student, so evening classes and correspondence courses are often full of Sagittarians eager to learn something new. You only have to look at their bookshelves to chart the number of enthusiasms they've had.

It's true that a Sagittarian and their money are soon parted. But at least they have lots of fun in the process! They are also very generous when it comes to spending their money on other people. When they can afford it, and sometimes even when they can't, they like taking friends out to restaurants and bars. They also enjoy buying presents for their loved ones, even when it isn't a special occasion. And on top of all this, many Sagittarians have a social conscience that makes them want to donate money to their favourite charities or the beggar they walk past in the street.

All this can mean that Sagittarians aren't very good at saving money. If they can't make themselves put aside some cash every now and then, ideally they should arrange for a set amount to be debited from their bank account each month and put into a special savings account that they can't get their hands on. Then they'll build up a nice rainy day fund that they can feel proud of.

One thing that Sagittarians aren't keen on is keeping track of where the money goes. They have a rather hit and miss attitude to such things, usually veering between carefully checking bank and credit card statements, and then going for months without bothering to even look at them. They hope that the good fortune that protects them from so many disasters will also prevent any financial mishaps.

Career

As with so many other areas of a Sagittarian's life, they need a career that offers them a challenge and gives their brain plenty of scope. They will soon get bored if they have to do the same things over and over again, and even if it's a well-paid job it will soon pall if it doesn't stretch them intellectually. Anything that's a doddle will soon lose its appeal for a Sagittarian, purely because it's too easy. They will also struggle to concentrate if their work is very sedentary, because that will only make them feel sluggish, and might even send them to sleep on really bad days.

When it comes to choosing the right sort of career, almost anything will suit a Sagittarian. This is a Mutable sign, which means Sagittarians are very flexible and adaptable so they can turn their hands to almost anything. But having said that, there are definitely some   careers and professions that suit them much better than others.

Take travel, for instance. This is the sign of travel, so it's bound to appeal to many Sagittarians. They might enjoy working in a travel agency selling holidays to the public, so they can do lots of travelling vicariously. Alternatively, they might prefer to go travelling themselves through their work for an airline, railway or cruise ship. You'll also find lots of Sagittarians working as tour guides, especially in far-flung corners of the world.

Education is another big interest for Sagittarians. They are firm believers in the value of knowledge, so you'll find lots of Sagittarians working as teachers, lecturers and professors. Even if they don't teach full-time, many Sagittarians find themselves teaching part-time courses, running workshops or doing something else that involves spreading their knowledge to other people. Very often, they seem to fall into this, so it happens without being planned. It's simply because Sagittarians are born teachers.

Most Sagittarians are confirmed book-lovers, so they're often attracted to publishing, book-selling, printing and working in libraries. It's a marriage made in heaven for them because they're working with something they love. And, of course, there are lots of Sagittarian writers who have helped to produce all those books, including Gustave Flaubert, Rebecca West, Anthony Powell, C. S. Lewis, George Eliot, Jane Austen and Joseph Conrad. Their work is often very humorous or satirical, and Jonathan Swift, Mark Twain, Noel Coward, James Thurber, Woody Allen and Bill Bryson are six shining examples of this.

Philosophy and religion also have a big appeal for Sagittarians. They enjoy wrestling with huge questions such as the meaning of life and have a deep need to connect with the spiritual part of themselves. Many Sagittarians are on a life-long spiritual quest, and choose jobs that reflect this in some way.

Whatever a Sagittarian does for a living, ideally they should do it with other people nearby. They aren't very good when left on their own for long periods of time. They'll enjoy it at first, and will relish the chance to think in silence without lots of distractions. But after a while they'll miss those distractions and will create some of their own, such as ringing up friends, staring out of the window, seeing how many paperclips they can link together without the chain breaking or suddenly feeling the urge to write emails to all their friends.

Some signs are much better suited to being employed than to working for themselves, but Sagittarians thrive on being their own bosses. Even when work is thin on the ground, their innate optimism will help them to stay positive and to trust that everything will turn out all right in the end. And being self-employed has other big benefits, because they definitely appreciate being able to organize their day in a way that suits them. They also like not having a boss breathing down their neck whenever they want to take the afternoon off!

Love and Friendships

It's a rare Sagittarian who isn't extremely popular. People enjoy being around them, and it's hardly surprising. After all, Sagittarians have a great sense of humour, an infectious enthusiasm for life (thanks to their Fire element), a big streak of generosity and they're not exactly stupid, either. They have the happy knack of being able to make friends – and to influence people as well, probably!

However, there's one thing that they really don't like, and that's being tied down. Sagittarians have an instinctive need for freedom and independence, even when they're in a committed relationship, which can lead to clashes if their partner isn't wild about the idea. But don't get me wrong. This doesn't mean that Sagittarians are faithless heartbreakers who will trample all over your feelings and then laugh at you when you start to cry. They're usually very loyal and affectionate, but they simply hate to feel as though they've lost their independence as well as the right to do things on their own. Some signs like to be joined to their partners at the hip, but the very thought of this gives Sagittarians the shudders. Yes, they like to be part of a couple but not to such an extent that they can't even go shopping by themselves because that's seen as some sort of betrayal.

For a Sagittarian, the ideal relationship consists of being with someone who's witty, intelligent and great company. They must be the Sagittarian's intellectual equal because the relationship won't last long if their partner wasn't around when the brains were being handed out. Even if they're stunning to look at, that's absolutely no consolation if they can't string a sentence together or they think Albert Einstein was a Hollywood film star. What's more, this partner mustn't have a possessive bone in their body, because that's something the Sagittarian will really, really hate. Questions like "What time will you be home?", "If you're going out can I come too?" and "Why didn't you phone to say you'd be so late?" will have the Sagittarian gritting their teeth so hard that they'll need a crowbar to prise their jaw open again. It's not that the Sagittarian will necessarily want to disappear on their own for hours at a time or go everywhere without their partner. It's simply that they need to know they can do it if they want to.

It's also important for Sagittarians to have friends of their own, so they can maintain some sort of independent social life from the one they share with their partner. They might want to go out for a drink with a chum every now and then, or join an evening class so they can make some new friends. Their partner must understand that it doesn't mean they want to run off with someone else, but simply that they need to do things on their own once in a while. Otherwise that marriage vow or emotional commitment will start to feel like a ball and chain.

But it can sometimes take a while before a Sagittarian is ready to settle down. They love a challenge, so sometimes they may be more interested in the thrill of the romantic chase than in enjoying the winner's spoils. Occasionally, a Sagittarian will want to chalk up their conquests like notches on their bedpost, but will never hang around for long enough to get emotionally entangled. They're the original love 'em and leave 'em types, but they're definitely not in the majority. Most Sagittarians are looking for loving relationships rather than anything based solely on sex.

Because Sagittarians belong to the Fire element, they're demonstrative and affectionate. However, they can become embarrassed at anything that strikes them as being sentimental or slushy. Yuck!

Sagittarians make great friends because they're such good fun. They're always eager to do something on the spur of the moment, and they love taking off on adventures, too. But just as they don't want possessive lovers, they don't want possessive friends, either, so they'll keep their distance from anyone who tries to restrict them in any way or who seems to think that the Sagittarian is their personal property. When that happens, you won't see the Sagittarian for dust.

Family Relationships
When it comes to family connections, Sagittarians are remarkably unsentimental. If they like someone, they'll want to see them. If they don't, they won't. It's as simple as that. They certainly won't feel duty-bound to spend every weekend with all their relatives unless that's their idea of fun. But if they do like one of their relatives, they won't care how young or old this person is, even if there's a vast difference between their ages. The Sagittarian will manage to cross any generation gap with no trouble at all, and won't even notice it. Having said that, they'll be particularly keen on spending time with younger members of the family, such as nieces and nephews, and will always try to keep them amused. Even when the Sagittarian is ancient, they'll still retain their wonderful sense of fun and will

enjoy making the younger members of their family laugh. They'll be especially keen on telling the sort of corny jokes that have children rolling around the floor while the other adults simply roll their eyes. Not that the Sagittarian will care.

When the Sagittarian becomes a parent, their whole world changes in a split second. Suddenly, they feel much more responsible and they also start to worry about all sorts of things that have never occurred to them before. But they'll also be fascinated by the entire process of pregnancy, childbirth and child-rearing, and of course it will be a fabulous excuse for them to acquire a whole new set of books or to spend hours researching useful information on the internet.

Sagittarians make fantastic parents. Their ruler, Jupiter, and their Fire element combine to make them expansive, affectionate, fun-loving, warm and open-hearted, leaving their children in no doubt about how much they're adored. They'll also do their best to make their children fall in love with all the opportunities that the world has to offer them, so they'll take them off on all sorts of jaunts and outings even when they aren't really old enough to know what's going on. When they do this, they'll be subtly ensuring that their children are learning more about the world, because education is such an important part of life for Sagittarians.

However, just like their Gemini counterparts, Sagittarians can find their children's babyhood rather limiting because of the difficulties in communicating with them. They can also get rather fed up with toddlers' restricted vocabularies, so ideally they need to be able to escape for a couple of hours every now and then. It's important for Sagittarian parents to keep up their social lives so they can have intelligent, adult conversations every once in a while. It stops them feeling that their brains have turned to mush.

Once their children have learned to communicate and talk, the Sagittarian will be completely enchanted with them. They'll want to chat to their children and find out what they think, so will encourage their children to voice their opinions and use their brains in the process. Family meal times will involve lively conversations in which everyone is encouraged to have their say, and there will also be plenty of good-humoured laughter.

The Sagittarian parent will want to encourage their children to read from an early age, and will have fun wandering around the children's section of bookshops looking for suitable purchases for them. They might even be inspired to write their own stories for their children, or to make up a long-running saga that they can tell their children each night when they're tucking them up in bed.

Above all, the Sagittarian parent will want their children to have happy, enjoyable childhoods. As far as they're concerned, a happy childhood is the best start in life, and they'll be much more interested in making their children feel safe and loved than in instilling lots of discipline in them. Other parents may even think that the Sagittarian is rather lax, but they won't take any notice of that. They'll also encourage their children to bring their friends home so they can meet them, and will really enjoy having an open house, so everyone comes and goes as they wish. It will be one big happy family, preferably with friends from all walks of life hanging around so the Sagittarian's children grow up to be open-minded, liberal and aware that there's much more to people than the way they speak or dress, their religion and the colour of their skin. If the Sagittarian can achieve all that, they'll have good reason to feel proud of themselves.

Creativity and Potential
Where do I start? Sagittarians have so much to offer the world that it's difficult to know where to begin. They're capable of achieving almost anything they set their minds to, thanks to their positive approach to life, their intellect, their enthusiasm and their determination to give virtually anything a try. After all, they reason, how do they know what they want to do until they've given it a go? They could be in for a big surprise.

Sagittarians have such open minds that they're always inter-ested in finding new ways to express themselves. One of their most endearing qualities is their habit of falling in love with new interests throughout their lives. They're always getting excited about a new enthusiasm, often to the point where they have to buy lots of books or videos on the subject, take evening classes in it or join a club or organization that caters for it. They'll completely immerse themselves in it until they either become world experts on the subject or start to get interested in something completely different, when the whole process will repeat itself all over again. As a result, Sagittarians have a tremendous amount of knowledge about all sorts of things that you would never have expected.

The Sagittarians you know have probably already worked their way through a string of different interests, and they know there are plenty more where those came from. If they're ever stuck for ideas, they could develop something that's already a theme in their life. For instance, if they enjoy travel they might decide to learn a foreign language. It will give them a big kick to go abroad and chat away to the locals in their own tongue. They might also have fun combining their holidays with the chance to learn something new, such as staying on a beautiful Mediterranean island while studying yoga or oil-painting.

If they're interested in history (and many of them are absolutely fascinated by it), a Sagittarian might decide to study a particular period in great detail, or collect items that date from that period. They might decide to start their own archae-ological dig in their back garden or research the history of their house.

It's important for Sagittarians to get plenty of fresh air, so they might enjoy joining a walking club. If they don't want to do anything that sounds as organized as that, they might prefer to spend their spare time hiking up mountains or walking around their country's coastline, especially if they can take a tent and rucksack with them. The thought of being completely free for a short while, with nothing to do but walk and take in the scenery, gives them a sense of rejuvenation and independ-ence that helps them to reconnect with their true selves. At its best, it can be a spiritual journey for them.

Activities that improve the environment may also appeal to them, whether that means walking around country lanes picking up rubbish or lobbying governments about climate change. Sagittarians love getting involved in causes that they believe in, so they might devote lots of their spare time to projects that mean a lot to them. It's only a short step from this to becoming involved in politics. They won't do this for the power that it can bring (well, not usually, anyway) but because they truly have a burning desire to change the world even if it's in a very small way. And with the Sagittarian love of challenge, they'll never give something up as a lost cause but will keep on fighting for it.

Finally, Sagittarius is a Fire sign and it's ruled by expansive Jupiter, which means that members of this sign love getting involved in projects that allow them to grow. One way of doing this is to join an amateur drama group, because they'll have a lot of fun whether they land the starring role or are helping to sell programmes. And they'll be treading in some illustrious footsteps, because Sagittarian actors include Kenneth Branagh, Brad Pitt, Boris Karloff, Jane Fonda, Jenny Agutter, Kim Basinger, Kiefer Sutherland and John Malkovich. A pretty impressive line-up!

Holidays

Show a Sagittarian a holiday brochure or an atlas and watch their face light up. And then watch them grab the brochure or atlas out of your hands and start to pore over it. Oh yes, Sagittarians love holidays. In fact, they enjoy almost any sort of travel, so they're always keen to up sticks and visit somewhere new. Travel is in their blood and they love exploring the world.

Dyed-in-the-wool Sagittarians have probably already chosen the destinations of their next ten holidays. They'll have a wish list of dream destinations and a more practical list of places that they can actually afford to visit. And if they're really lucky, sometimes the two will overlap.

Unless somewhere has very special meaning for a Sagittarian, they won't want to visit it more than once or twice.

The idea of buying a time-share holiday and going there every year for the rest of their lives is enough to make them run off shrieking in the opposite direction. They don't understand why anyone would want to do anything like that because it's such a dull and unimaginative option. Why, when there's a whole world out there waiting to be explored, would they want to concentrate on one place and ignore everywhere else? Sagittarians are equally bewildered by someone wanting to stay at the same hotel each year, especially for sentimental reasons. It will be a real source of friction if they live with someone who's much less adventurous in their choice of holiday destinations, and they may even find that the only way to resolve the problem is to take separate holidays, although that probably won't be a very popular option with the Sagittarian's partner, either, unless they happen to be an Aquarian. Not that the Sagittarian will mind going off by themselves, because it will be a chance to pretend that they're fancy-free again, even if they don't act on it.

As you might have guessed by now, Sagittarians like to choose holidays that will provide them with some sort of adventure and plenty of intellectual stimulation. Any sort of trip is better than none, so they'll go on a package holiday if that's all they can afford or if it keeps the rest of the family happy, but they'd much rather do something more challenging. For instance, they'd love a fly-drive holiday that allows them to explore another country and they'd also enjoy a trip to somewhere that's off the beaten track or is still a well-kept secret. They might also fall in love with a particular country and enjoy visiting different parts of it over the years. In the end, they'll be quite an expert on the subject.

Wherever they go, a Sagittarian's ideal holiday offers a combination of delicious food and drink, breathtaking scenery, comfortable sleeping arrangements, plenty of history, loads of culture and lots to look at. Being roasted on a beach for two weeks, looking only at the sand, is not their idea of fun, although they'll enjoy having a few days in which they can catch up on their reading. They'd much rather jump on a local bus and see where it takes them, laze the afternoon away in a restaurant, explore the local museum or put their guide book through its paces. And they enjoy both heat and cold, which means they can be happy almost anywhere in the world.

When it comes to sending postcards, it depends on what sort of mood the Sagittarian is in at the time. It also depends on what sort of holiday they're having. If it's a disaster, they may not bother to send any cards because they won't want to admit that the holiday has turned out to be such a disappointment. But if they're having a whale of a time they'll manage to send lots of cards saying as much. They'll do their best to find some interesting souvenirs to take back home, whether for themselves or their loved ones. Although kitsch items will make them laugh, the Sagittarian will probably decide to leave them on the shelf and go for things that have a more enduring appeal, especially if they also reflect the culture of the country they're visiting. Very often, they buy their best souvenirs from museums and art galleries. Sagittarians are such culture vultures!

Home

It won't take much detective work to tell you that you're in a Sagittarian's home. The shelves and shelves of books will give you a big clue, especially as they'll be arranged in no particular order and some of them may even be upside down. You'll also notice the countless objects that the Sagittarian has brought back from their travels all over the world, ranging from the sublime to the ridiculous. And the chronic untidiness will be another major clue. In common with their opposite sign of Gemini, Sagittarians have problems in keeping their belongings under control. Like the prisoners of Colditz castle, a Sagittarian's possessions always seem to be breaking free of their restrictions and spreading themselves all over the place. Sometimes, this can lead to quite a mess! The Sagittarian may even wonder how on earth everything got into such a higgledy-piggledy state, but won't be able to work up the enthusiasm to do anything about it. After all, they have so many more important things to do with their time than to tidy up after themselves. Instead, they'll stare in bemused fashion at the piles of books, magazines, newspapers, bags and empty envelopes strewn all over their side of the sofa and then dump them on the floor. That's a Sagittarian's idea of making the place neat and tidy. Any more than that is excessive, as far as they're concerned.

Something else that will tell you you're in a Sagittarian's home is its eclectic atmosphere. They enjoy collecting objects that catch their eye, trusting that everything will go together when they get them home. Sagittarians love mixing old and new, Eastern and Western objects, and they often do it very well. For instance, they might match Indian silks with Chinese plates and Dutch tiles. They especially like items that have a spiritual or religious quality, so it's quite likely that they'll have a Buddhist thang-ka next to a Greek Orthodox icon or a carving of Ganesha, the Hindu elephant god. Sagittarians see nothing wrong in this, no matter what their religious beliefs happen to be.

It's the same story with the Sagittarian's furniture. They love mixing contemporary pieces with antiques, which gives their home a timeless quality that won't date. But there are two items that they must have. One is a desk or table at which they can study or write, and it will probably have a computer on it. The other is a big television set. Sagittarians adore watching television, and especially news and documentaries, because it's their window on the world whenever they aren't off on their travels. And with their tendency to keep learning new subjects throughout their lives, they also watch television to increase their knowledge. They'll need a comfortable sofa to slump on while they're watching, of course, preferably with plenty of space so the rest of the family can join them on it, including some boisterous dogs and lively cats.

There is almost bound to be some sort of pet in the Sagittarian household because this is a sign that loves animals. If the Sagittarian lives in the countryside, there may even be some chickens scratching around in the garden, partly to provide eggs and partly because of their beautiful plumage. And there will be a row of muddy boots by the back door, ready for when the Sagittarian wants to take a long country walk.

Sagittarius is one of the most sociable and gregarious signs of the zodiac, so it will be very important for the Sagittarian to have plenty of space in which they can entertain their friends and neighbours. Ideally, they should have a big kitchen that everyone can eat in, because Sagittarians prefer to entertain informally rather than to stand on ceremony. Besides, they can be so clumsy that they're bound to break any very expensive china or precious glass, so they're much better off with simple things that can easily be replaced. They'll need lots of chairs in the sitting room, too, or will make sure the carpet is soft so everyone can lie around on that.

Some signs like to know when their guests are coming so they can be fully prepared but Sagittarians are perfectly happy for people to drop in unannounced. They love the spontaneity of it, provided that their visitors don't mind taking the Sagittarian household exactly as they find it. Which might easily mean finding the Sagittarian still in their dressing gown at three in the afternoon, glued to the pages of a book. That's life in a Sagittarian home for you.

Clothes and Image

Sagittarians like to feel free, so they hate wearing clothes that restrict their movements in any way. Tight waistbands, collars that choke them, sleeves that stop them waving their arms around and shoes that prevent them striding along are all big no-nos for Sagittarians. Even when they're in the city, they want to feel deep down that they're on a beach or hillside, with the wind blowing through their hair. So they go for casual, relaxed and informal clothes whenever possible. If they have to spend their working days looking smart, as soon as they get home they'll start taking off their clothes when they're still only halfway through their front door and will quickly change into something much more relaxing, such as an old T-shirt and a pair of sweatpants. If they're feeling very organized they'll hang up their work clothes ready for the next day. If they aren't, or can't be bothered, they'll leave them draped in a heap on a chair. If it's been a very bad day, they'll leave them on the bedroom floor, where they'll provide a nice comfortable bed for the Sagittarian's dog or cat. Which will probably be moulting. And do they have a clothes brush? What do you think?

By now you should have got the picture. Sagittarians have many sterling qualities but looking neat and tidy isn't one of them. And they're glad about it, because it makes them feel uncomfortable when they're in their very best outfits. Besides, there's always the danger that they might spill something on them and ruin them, whereas it would be difficult to ruin a pair of old jeans that are already in holes and covered in ink stains.

When they do want to look good, Sagittarians like fairly loose, relaxed clothes. Many Sagittarian men seem to have been born in jeans, although they can also look very good in velvet trousers. They like open-necked shirts and some Sagittarian men only own one tie, which they unearth on very special occasions (assuming that they can remember where they've put it). If they have to wear a suit, they'll make sure it's trendy and flattering. Sagittarian women are also keen on wearing jeans and trousers, rather than anything very girlie and ultra-feminine which often doesn't suit them. Both sexes enjoy wearing suede, especially jackets. Very often, they like to look as though they've just stepped off a ranch, complete with checked shirts and riding boots. It's an image that really suits them, especially if they've got the money to buy at the top end of the market. Famous Sagittarians with the classic carefree Sagittarian image, which each of them interprets in their own way, include Jeff Bridges, Keith Richards, Jimi Hendrix, Jasper Conran, Jane Fonda, Tina Turner, Judi Dench and Paula Radcliffe.

Sagittarians can't resist lots of accessories, either. Belts, bangles, beads, rings, scarves, bags . . . they love them all. Sometimes they get the combination just right and look fantastic, but at other times they can take things to extremes and look completely weighed down by their accessories. Both sexes enjoy carrying large bags, which usually weigh a ton and are crammed full of all sorts of essentials, from indigestion pills to a couple of books.

Hair can sometimes be a problem for Sagittarians. It's usually very thick and lustrous, and can need quite a lot of careful management. Even when they haven't been out in the open air it can look as though they have, with their hair standing up on end or blown into a bird's nest. No wonder they often like jamming hats down on their heads, because a good hat can hide a multitude of sins. Shoes are another difficulty for Sagittarians. Ideally, they wouldn't wear them at all and, like Pisceans, would prefer to walk barefoot whenever possible. Sagittarians really enjoy walking, so they prefer footwear that will let them stride off into the distance without having to worry about scuffing the heels of their shoes, wearing out the leather soles or getting covered in blisters. Sagittarian women may like wearing sexy high heels sometimes (Betty Grable, she of the fabulous legs, was a Sagittarian) but they can struggle to walk in them, especially if they're more used to wearing their Nike trainers or Birkenstock sandals. Besides, with their tendency to trip over, high heels can be a rather dangerous option sometimes.

Famous Sagittarians

Thomas Cook (22 November 1808); Boris Karloff (23 November 1887); Scott Joplin (24 November 1868); Andrew Carnegie (25 November 1835); Tina Turner (26 November 1939); Jimi Hendrix (27 November 1942); William Blake (28 November 1757); Louisa Mae Alcott (29 November 1832); Mark Twain (30 November 1835); Woody Allen (1 December 1935); Maria Callas (2 December 1923); Jean-Luc Godard (3 December 1930); General Franco (4 December 1892); Jeff Bridges (5 December 1949); Dave Brubeck (6 December 1920); Hermann Maier (7 December 1972); Mary Queen of Scots (8 December 1542); John Malkovich (9 December 1953); Kenneth Branagh (10 December 1960); Alexander Solzhenitsyn (11 December 1918); Frank Sinatra (12 December 1915); Laurens van der Post (13 December 1906); Nostradamus (14 December 1503); Don Johnson (15 December 1950); Jane Austen (16 December 1775); Kerry Packer (17 December 1937); Brad

Pitt (18 December 1963); Edith Piaf (19 December 1915); Jenny Agutter (20 December 1952); Jane Fonda – 21 December 1937).

The Top Ten Sagittarian Characteristics

Optimistic; Enthusiastic; Expansive; Magnanimous; Need for challenge; Honest; Tactless; Freedom-loving; Love of knowledge; Philosophical.

Are You A Typical Sagittarian?

Try this quiz on the Sagittarians you know to find out whether they're typical members of their sign.

1 Do you wish you were less clumsy and cack-handed?

2 Do you sometimes confuse frankness with tactlessness?

3 Have you ever exaggerated a story to make it sound better?

4 Are you looking for more meaning in your life?

5 Do you enjoy being active?

6 Are you adaptable?

7 Do you try to be philosophical when things go wrong?

8 Are you always looking to the future?

9 Are you always keen to learn something new?

10 Do you have good judgement?

Score

Score one point for every "no" and zero points for every "yes".

0-3   You couldn't be more Sagittarian if you tried. Your glass is always half-full, never half-empty, and you do your best to take life in your stride even when things go wrong. You have an endless curiosity about the world and you want to live your life to the full.

4-6   You have a strong Sagittarian streak but it's tempered by the influence of other signs. Read the Top Ten Characteristics of the other signs to see which ones ring a bell with you.

7-10   Although you were born under the sign of Sagittarius you don't have many Sagittarian characteristics. Look through the Top Ten Characteristics of Scorpio and Capricorn to see if either of these sounds more like you.

Capricorn

22 December–20 January

The Capricorn Adult

Capricorns belong to one of the most serious signs in the
zodiac. But don't get the impression that Capricorns are
dreary or boring because they aren't at all. In fact, they have a
fantastic sense of humour, and are particularly good at making
dry, deadpan comments. I've had more laughs with my
Capricorn friends than with any other sign. These people are
life-enhancing!

Perhaps they have such a great sense of the ridiculous
because life has usually delivered them several kicks on the
shins by the time they're in their twenties. Capricorns go
through the mill, and in common with Scorpios often have to
endure experiences that would demolish some of the other
signs. It's as though they've seen the worst that life can offer
them and they know they can cope with it.

The good news for Capricorns is that their lives often
improve dramatically once they reach thirty. The lack of
confidence that plagued them when they were younger, and
the chronic shyness that used to leave them virtually tongue-
tied, start to disappear, and are replaced by a dawning self-

esteem and self-reliance. They begin to feel good about themselves, although it's a rare Capricorn who develops a massive ego and wants to throw their weight around. They simply feel more comfortable with who they are, and therefore find it easier to connect with other people.

The most notable Capricorn characteristic is that they don't age in the same way as the rest of us. Their ageing process works in reverse, so you find young Capricorns with old heads on their shoulders. As they get older, they start to lighten up and relax, until they're positively skittish by the time they enter middle age. While everyone else is turning old and grey, they seem to have captured the secret of eternal youth and look better than ever.

Of course, Capricorns still have to battle with the doom-laden side of their personalities. They can't help taking a rather dour view of life, and their realistic and practical approach often borders on pessimism, especially if life has treated them badly in the past. They know that one of life's banana skins is waiting round the corner for them and that it will make them trip up sooner or later. At their worst, they can be dreadfully gloomy and negative, and terrible wet blankets. It's as though they're being followed everywhere by their own personal rain cloud, and if you spend too much time with them you get soaked as well. Eeyore, the donkey in the *Winnie the Pooh* stories, is a classic Capricorn. He's got a heart of gold underneath all that grumbling but he's a terrible moaner. His gloomy comment about birthdays being 'Here today and gone tomorrow' is typically Capricorn.

Capricorns are ruled by Saturn, which is the planet of restrictions and foundations. He's also the planet of hard knocks, and he can dole out some pretty tough lessons. As a result, many Capricorns have to endure a lot of adversity in their lives, or they may have to work very hard for their success. Unfortunately, wonderful things rarely drop into a Capricorn's lap without any effort on their part. Nevertheless, Saturn gives them tremendous sticking power and a determination to succeed despite the odds. It also gives them backbone as they get older and an ability to weather life's storms. Something else that Saturn confers on them is a very strong sense of responsibility (which admittedly can sometimes be too strong, so they take on more obligations than are strictly necessary) and great reliability.

The combination of Saturn as their ruling planet and Capricorn belonging to the Earth element means that members of this sign are very down-to-earth – sometimes literally, as they often have a complete passion for gardening. They're also very prudent and disciplined, with a lot of control over their emotions. Sometimes you can't help wishing they could open up a bit more and be less rigidly composed.

Saturn is the planet that rules time, and as a result Capricorns have a great respect for what time has taught us. This means they're often very conservative and traditional, with a dislike of anything too modern, unorthodox or iconoclastic. They believe in doing things a particular way, often because that's simply how they've always been done. And Capricorns have a particular respect for the blessings and structure of family life, even if they don't always get on well with their own nearest and dearest.

Capricorn is symbolized by the mountain goat. If you think about one of these creatures, you'll picture it leaping up rocky slopes and surviving in inhospitable surroundings. Capricorns are the same, with an ability to cope in difficult circumstances but to keep on plodding away until, if they're lucky, they reach the top of wherever they want to go. They're helped in this by their Cardinal quality, which gives them a huge dose of ambition and persistence. Some Capricorns don't achieve everything they set out to do, but others do reach the dizzy heights of success.

One of the greatest Capricorn bugbears is their tendency to overwork. They have such an over-developed sense of responsibility, and such a powerful need to win the respect of the people around them, that they often work themselves into the ground. If they aren't doing it through their job, they're helping any relatives who are going through a hard time, working their fingers to the bone in the garden or helping out as a volunteer for lots of committees and organizations. They rarely get a moment to themselves, and when they do they can spend it telling themselves how much better they should be doing everything. Yet what they don't realize is how steadfast and reliable they really are, and how much everyone depends on them. Their innate modesty and self-deprecation stops them seeing themselves as they really are, which is their curse but also one of the reasons they're so endearing.

The Capricorn Child

With most children you have to encourage them to be more responsible. With Capricorn children, you have to encourage them to relax and not to be so caught up in duty, responsibility and good behaviour. These children are much older than their years would suggest, and even if they enjoy racing around having fun they also have a serious streak that will emerge many times each day. My Capricorn niece demonstrates her serious streak by never having to be told to put her toys away, by keeping a watchful eye over her younger brother and sister, and by often looking rather anxious when she thinks no one is watching.

All children need love but little Capricorns are particularly in need of it. The world can be a rather unsafe place to them, and they need to know that they've got plenty of emotional security. They also need to know that the love they get from their parents and the rest of their family is unconditional. However, very often Capricorn children get the impression that they'll only be loved if they're good. If they're bad, they'll be punished by not being loved any more. This means they can try to repress their perfectly natural childish exuberance in case it gets them into trouble and casts them into what feels like a loveless wilderness. It isn't a recipe for a happy childhood and their parents must do their best to reassure them that they'll always be loved.

As you will have gathered by now, Capricorn children have already got worrying down to a fine art. They're anxious about so many things, and often stew quietly about whatever happens to be bothering them. Ideally, they should have someone to confide in, whether it's a parent, grandparent, sibling or best friend. And sometimes they'll tell their teddy bear or doll all their troubles. It doesn't really matter who they talk to, as long as they talk to someone.

Capricorn children do best when they have brothers and sisters to play with. These siblings will help the Capricorn child to relax and will probably tease them when they become too serious or studious. They will also teach the little Capricorn to laugh at themselves, which is a very valuable Capricorn trait. Capricorns who are only children can become rather serious and often slightly isolated unless they have lots of neighbouring children to play with. It will also help if they've got pets to look after and play with. Ideally, these should be the sort of pets that can give and receive love, such as cats and dogs, rather than the less affectionate variety, such as stick insects and goldfish.

When a Capricorn child goes to school they'll do really well. They'll work hard to win their teacher's approval, and they'll also enjoy exercising their very capable brains. They'll enjoy having to do homework at first (until the excitement wears off and it becomes a chore) because it will make them feel so grown-up, especially if they have older siblings that they admire. Incidentally, Capricorn children often prefer to have friends who are older than they are, because they find that children their own age can be rather silly or immature. Perhaps that's why Capricorn children often get on so well with their grandparents. They don't notice the generation gap and are only aware of how much fun they have when they're with their grandparents, especially if they're given the sort of treats they don't get at home.

Although the Capricorn child will enjoy doing well at school, their parents should ensure that they don't turn into a little swot. They must have some fun as well as all that education, otherwise they'll become very bogged down and possibly even depressed. I used to know a Capricorn who would read maths books for pleasure and send postcards written in Latin. And, no, I'm not making this up! Not surprisingly, it was difficult for this little Capricorn to fit in with their schoolmates because they had so little in common with them. So Capricorn children really must be encouraged to take life less seriously, to abandon their schoolbooks at some point every day and to be less obsessed with their academic achievements. They also need plenty of fresh air and exercise so they can run around and let off steam to their heart's content. And they need lots of outside interests, too, such as dancing, swimming, music lessons, acting and anything else that they'll enjoy. They should be prepared to experiment until they find various activities that they absolutely love.

Finally, all Capricorn children should be given piggy banks, money boxes or savings accounts. They love saving up their pocket money and spare cash, and in fact by doing so they'll be starting a life-long habit of valuing their money and conserving it. They shouldn't be encouraged to be mean or miserly, of course, but they'll certainly be interested in making their money work for them, even at an early age. They'll also be keen on doing odd jobs to make extra money, such as being paid to help Daddy dig the vegetable patch, and will be proud of having part-time jobs like paper-rounds when they're old enough. And then they'll never look back.

Health

Not surprisingly for people who take life so seriously, Capricorns have a tremendous ability to worry. They tend to think that if something can go wrong, it will, which means they often walk around in a state of mild anxiety, rising to outright panic at times of crisis. Their innate streak of pessimism rears its ugly head, tormenting them with all sorts of doom-laden thoughts and fears until they feel utterly miserable. Of course, this doesn't do their health much good, because this endless worrying puts a tremendous strain on their bodies. It's therefore extremely important for Capricorns to learn how to relax and put their worries to one side, so they can keep them in proportion. Otherwise, they can have sleepless nights when things are difficult for them, leaving them tired and fretful. They may also find that they have no reserves of energy to draw on when they're faced with a tough situation because they're already mentally and physically exhausted.

It's also very important for Capricorns to find time in their lives for play as well as work. For many of them, their work spills over into the rest of their lives so in the end it dominates everything, even if they have a family. They're real workaholics, and can get addicted to working overtime and at weekends even when it isn't strictly necessary. They may also end up only socializing with their colleagues, so they can talk shop and keep up with all the office gossip. When this happens to a Capricorn it means they can never get away completely from their job, so they never get a chance to relax. One answer for them is to widen their social circle so they start to mix with people from different walks of life. Otherwise, they're never really off-duty and that can eventually take its toll on them. They can also be very reluctant to take holidays, which means they work virtually all-year round. Such an emphasis on work can then have bad repercussions on the Capricorn's relationships and family life, which will worry them. And so it goes on!

Capricorn rules three areas of the body – the skin, teeth and bones. The skin is the largest organ in the human body but it's often taken for granted. So Capricorns should make sure they keep their skin moisturized and cared for. I've noticed that Capricorns often suffer from a variety of skin complaints, such as contact dermatitis and psoriasis, especially when they're agitated and anxious about something. So they should take note of whether any fabrics, metals, foods, detergents or cosmetics irritate their skin, and make sure they avoid them in the future. And it would help if they learned to relax more as well, although that's sometimes as easy as making water flow uphill. Many Capricorns seem to think they were programmed from birth to be tense!

One good way for them to relax is to get out into the fresh air whenever possible. Gardening is especially good for them because it brings them in contact with the earth, so they're literally in their element. I have a couple of Capricorn friends who grow a formidable array of fruit and vegetables and who feel much better for it. It's good for a Capricorn to be doing something productive and it's even better if it isn't always work-related.

This sign is governed by Saturn, the planet of structure, so it makes sense that the skeleton is ruled by Capricorn. After all, without that skeletal framework we'd all collapse in a heap. As a result, Capricorns need to take extra care of their bones. They must do their best to prevent bone-related problems such as rheumatism, arthritis and osteoporosis, preferably by taking plenty of exercise, keeping warm and eating the right foods. Their knees are often particularly sensitive, so Capricorns should take care of them throughout their lives and only practise sports such as skiing, which places a lot of strain on the knees, in moderation.

And as for their teeth, Capricorns need to make friends with their dentists and to visit them regularly, even if the very thought makes them go weak in their sensitive knees.

Money
This is where Capricorns really come into their own! Money is a subject they understand inside out and they may even earn their living by being involved in some form of finance.

True to their practical Earth element, Capricorns have a great appreciation for the power of money. They may agree with the song that money can't buy them love, but they also recognize all the things that it can buy – such as physical security, comfort, warmth and respect. Now, respect is something that's dear to every Capricorn's heart. They need the approval of their family, and one way of achieving that is to prove that they can provide for their material needs. They also value the respect of their friends and colleagues, and they believe that one of the easiest ways to get this is to be well-off.

Capricorns aren't noted for their unthinking generosity, which is a polite way of saying that they can be rather stingy at times, and some of them are downright mean. Ebenezer Scrooge was undoubtedly a Capricorn, with his dislike of spending money unless it was absolutely necessary, at which point he still begrudged parting with a penny (until his transformation, that is). Capricorns are far too cautious to flash their cash around in all directions, even if they're in the happy position of having a lot of it. For a start, they don't want to advertise their financial status in case someone takes advantage of it, and they're also worried about squandering their money in case they run out of it. Howard Hughes, the eccentric millionaire, was a classic example of this Capricorn miserliness.

Yet Capricorns can certainly be generous in the right situations, although they like to keep quiet about this in order to preserve their modesty. For instance, they may make regular donations to their favourite charities but they don't tell their friends about it because they don't like to brag.

Some signs of the zodiac like to live for today and don't worry much about tomorrow, but that isn't the Capricorn style at all. Capricorns are always concerned about what the future will hold, even to the extent of ignoring their current needs, so they rarely have to be told to put some money aside for a rainy day. Most Capricorns have been good at saving money from an early age, and like to know that they've got some savings to fall back on in a crisis. They might tell themselves that they could always spend some of the money if the crisis doesn't happen, but they won't do it. This is one of those signs that can live very frugally even when there's a massive amount of money in the bank. I've known wealthy Capricorns who've lived with threadbare carpets and holes in their sofas rather than fork out the money to replace them.

When it comes to managing their money and making it work well for them, a Capricorn has usually got it taped. They're very disciplined about keeping track of their bank statements and making sure that they don't contain any mistakes. They'll also keep an eye on the best deals for banks and credit cards, in case they aren't getting the most favourable rate of return on their money. They may also be a canny investor on the stock market, although they'll be very careful about which companies they invest in and they most definitely won't want to take any risks. A Capricorn would much rather have a slow and steady return on their money than make a quick fortune while also running the risk of losing the lot. It may not be a very exciting financial attitude but it's one that suits them down to the ground.

Career

Let's get one thing straight right from the start. Capricorns only want to move in one direction in their careers, and that's upwards. They are fiercely ambitious and powerfully driven, and they have some big goals to meet. Some of them will achieve what they set out to do and others won't manage it but they'll all give it a try, even at considerable personal sacrifice.

Capricorns pay a lot of attention to their work. Whatever they do for a living, they'll want to do it to the best of their ability, and if that means putting in overtime then so be it. It's a rare Capricorn who isn't ambitious and who doesn't want to be a success at their job. Like the mountain goat that represents their sign, a Capricorn wants to climb to ever higher levels, no matter how long it takes. Bosses and superiors are usually very happy to let them do this because they like the Capricorn's sense of responsibility and their belief in the importance of fulfilling their duties and obligations. In other words, you can always count on a Capricorn to get the job done. This means they can sometimes be taken for granted or turned into a willing workhorse, partly because they have such a strong sense of responsibility and partly because they don't want to show themselves in a bad light by not pulling their weight.

This sense of responsibility usually starts at an early age. Many Capricorns held some position of power or authority when they were at school, such as being the class monitor or the head girl or boy, and have continued like that ever since. They tend to rise to the top quite naturally, powered by their tremendous ambition and drive.

Just as Capricorns need to be respected for the work they do, they also need to respect their bosses and superiors. They won't be happy if they think their boss isn't any good at their job, because they won't be able to respect them. And the boss will feel uncomfortable because they'll know that the Capricorn is nipping at their ankles, with one eye on their job!

So what sort of jobs suit Capricorns? They're excellent at anything involving finance, such as accountancy, banking, economics and the Civil Service. These may not be fascinating topics to anyone else but Capricorns find them very inspiring and can make a lot of money out of them. Aristotle Onassis, the Greek shipping magnate, was a Capricorn who started with virtually nothing and ended up as one of the richest men in the world. Capricorn is ruled by Saturn, the planet of structure, so they can enjoy working as architects, structural engineers and builders. They'll soon gain a well-deserved reputation for being ultra-reliable, which is bound to ensure their success. You'll also find Capricorns working as osteopaths, orthopaedic surgeons, chiropractors and dentists. And lots of Capricorns have been attracted to politics and public office, including Richard Nixon, Woodrow Wilson, Helmut Schmidt, J. Edgar Hoover, William Gladstone, David Lloyd George and Martin Luther King, Jr. Science is another fascination for Capricorns, and many of the great scientific names have been born under this sign, including Sir Isaac Newton, Tycho Brahe, Louis Pasteur, Johannes Kepler and Stephen Hawking.

Whatever a Capricorn does for a living, they'll be assiduous and hard-working. Very often, they don't know when to switch off so they end up being workaholics whose entire identities are tied up with what they do for a living. It can be almost impossible for them to leave their work behind when they go home at night, so they take it with them either mentally or physically. This doesn't always go down very well with their family, especially if their job commitments interfere with family life or mean the Capricorn is rarely available for fun. Their workaholic tendencies can also mean that they're the first person to arrive at work and the last person to leave.

Capricorns are good colleagues if they can allow themselves to show the light-hearted side of their characters, but often they become so serious about their work that they make heavy weather out of it. It's almost as though they don't think they're working hard unless they're suffering in some way. They really need to lighten up!

Love and Friendships

Although they may give the impression of being self-sufficient, Capricorns need happy and fulfilling relationships just as much as anyone else. In fact, maybe they need them more than other people because it does them good to know there's someone they can talk to and with whom they can unburden themselves. Otherwise, they can become rather shut off from the world, separated from the rest of humanity by an invisible protective barrier. They need plenty of friends to help them to relax, unwind and talk about some of their inner fears. However, it can take a long while for a Capricorn to be able to unburden themselves to a friend, so it's a terrific compliment when they do finally open up. Capricorns are loving, loyal and firm friends, and they enjoy mixing with people from all walks of life and all ages. Very often, there will be big age differences between a Capricorn and their friends, especially if the Capricorn is the younger one in the partnership. I've known some Capricorns with friends who are forty years older than them, and who haven't given it a moment's thought.

One of the big problems for Capricorns in relationships is their innate shyness. It can give entirely the wrong impression at times. People may think that the Capricorn isn't really interested in them, when in fact the poor Capricorn is trying to find something to say but rejecting everything that springs to mind because it sounds too trite or boring. This hesitancy and timidity can make the Capricorn seem slightly imposing or stand-offish at first, although once people get to know them they discover there's a very different person lurking underneath such a reserved exterior. Some Capricorns really know how to let their hair down, and turn out to be the life and soul of the party. They aren't nearly as strait-laced as they seem, and some become incredibly raunchy in the right company. They can certainly have very strong sex drives, and their Earth element gives them a huge streak of sensuality. The powerful contrast between their reserved public self and their uninhibited sexual self can be quite startling!

One of a Capricorn's biggest emotional fears is rejection. This is a sign that's terrified of being rejected and ignored, and often Capricorns cope with these fears by pretending that they don't care. They can be cool and reserved with their partners, as though they can take them or leave them, and can turn up their noses at romance or anything else that they consider to be soppy or embarrassing. Yet they're always thrilled when their partner does something romantic or affectionate, even if they do their best not to show it. When the Capricorn is in the early stages of a relationship and perhaps hasn't yet made their feelings clear, they can be so reserved and will take things so slowly for fear of being rejected that the other person may doubt whether anything is ever going to happen between them. No wonder Capricorns can be so misunderstood.

Sometimes, a Capricorn's ambitions get the better of them, and they can't resist getting involved with someone because of who that person is rather than what they are. So you'll occasionally meet a Capricorn who got married for entirely mercenary reasons, perhaps because their other half is absolutely loaded, has very good social or professional connections or is related to the Capricorn's boss. Alternatively, they may choose friends because of what they can get out of the relationship.

However, once a Capricorn has found a partner they love, they'll hope to stay with them for life. Saturn, their ruling planet, provides the grit and glue in relationships, so Capricorns are prepared for the long haul and to stick by their partners through thick and thin. They are very loyal, even when times are hard. It takes a lot for them to walk away from a committed relationship, especially if children are involved, because they have such a deep sense of responsibility. They also don't like to admit defeat, and having what they see as a failed relationship definitely comes into that category.

One of the biggest potential downfalls for Capricorns is the clash between their work commitments and their domestic responsibilities. Many Capricorns are workaholics who think about their work even when they aren't doing it, and who often take refuge in working round the clock. Such a strong involvement in their work, with all that it entails including a restricted social life and a Capricorn who's rarely able to spend much time with the rest of the family, can cause all sorts of emotional problems. Being so busy at work all the time can also drive a wedge between the Capricorn and their partner unless they're able to find a happy medium in which play and relaxation are given the same importance as the daily grind.

Family Relationships

Blood ties mean a lot to most Capricorns. They have such a powerful sense of tradition, and such a strong connection with their roots, that it will be a source of great sadness if they aren't as close to their family as they would like. Even so, they will do their best to keep in touch with everyone (even if they don't really like them) because, deep down, they believe that stable families are the bedrock of society. This means that there are plenty of Capricorns who grit their teeth and make themselves visit their parents or get together with other members of their families, mostly out of a sense of duty and guilt.

When bringing up their own family, a Capricorn will be happiest with a traditional family unit of two parents, preferably with their extended family in the background. However, they have such a well-developed sense of responsibility that they'll do a good job of bringing up their children on their own if needs be, and will do their utmost to fulfil the role of both parents.

When a Capricorn first becomes a parent they'll be gripped by fear of what they've taken on. Of course, most parents experience something similar but Capricorns have such strong inferiority complexes that they feel genuine anxiety about letting down their child. Being such bookworms, they will buy every child-rearing manual they can track down and then read the lot. They'll be deluged with all sorts of information but will instinctively veer towards a disciplined, structured and traditional way of bringing up their child. They'll want to do the whole thing properly, and will place a heavy emphasis on discipline and good behaviour. They'll also want their child to respect their elders and will be very annoyed if they think that isn't happening.

Unfortunately, sometimes a Capricorn parent can be so strict that they inadvertently take a lot of the fun out of their children's lives. They place the accent on duty, responsibility, homework, shiny shoes, clean hair, tidy bedrooms, bedtime prayers, being punctual and the need for their child to eat up everything on their plate. They emphasize the importance of getting good grades in exams and being polite to adults. They can even turn family outings into educational experiences, so no one has any fun because they're too busy trying to take in what they're looking at or remembering important facts for when they're grilled about them later by the Capricorn. What the Capricorn parent forgets about is enjoyment, laughter, being silly, doing nothing, relaxing, playing with toys and being a child. With luck, they will have a partner who believes that childhood should be fun and who will encourage the Capricorn to lighten up and be less of a hard taskmaster.

Another potential difficulty for a Capricorn parent is their inability to show their emotions and be demonstrative. Even if they cherish and adore their children they may have difficulties in showing it, and as a result can come across as stuffy, withdrawn and unemotional. Both Capricorn mothers and fathers can fall into this trap. It can make their children equally reticent about expressing their emotions, and they may also get the impression that their Capricorn parent isn't very bothered about them, even though that isn't true.

Creativity and Potential

Capricorns have a tremendous amount to offer the world and they usually have lots more creativity inside them than they've given themselves credit for. After all, most Capricorns have some form of low self-esteem, so they often tell themselves that they aren't able to do things that would actually come quite easily to them. When I used to go to a weekly art class, the two Capricorns in the group frequently produced the best work even though they didn't think so. They used to dismiss any praise they received as though the rest of us, including our teacher, didn't know what we were talking about.

Capricorns are much more versatile than they give themselves credit for, but they're frightened to try anything new in case it turns out to be a disaster and makes them feel embarrassed. And there's another reason why they don't experiment with their potential as much as they should – they simply don't have the time because they've got so many other commitments. It can be almost impossible to prise a Capricorn away from their job or from all the other duties they have to attend to, so they have very little spare time. I have a Capricorn friend who's an opera singer, and he's always very busy helping with the church choir, the local Christmas show and goodness knows what else. He does all these things out of the goodness of his heart and he certainly isn't paid for them.

If a Capricorn can perform a miracle and magic up some spare time, there are plenty of things for them to do. It will help, of course, if they choose occupations and hobbies that help them to relax, especially if their life is one long round of duties and obligations. Because they belong to an Earth sign they benefit tremendously from being out of doors, so they might enjoy going for long walks, and can either meander along by themselves or join a walking club. Capricorns are also good at gardening, whether they're producing flowers or growing their own vegetables. It will give them a huge sense of achievement, and also help to relax them.

Something else that might appeal to more adventurous Capricorns is rock climbing. After all, they do belong to the sign of the Mountain Goat! Even if they can't bear the thought of dangling off a cliff face, they might like the idea of doing some hill walking or attempting some gentle mountain slopes. Alternatively, if the Capricorn is looking for an unusual pet, how about keeping a goat or some chickens? I have a Capricorn friend who dreams of keeping both in his back garden.

Music is another great way for Capricorns to relax. This is a sign with important links to music through its ruler, Saturn, which governs time. They might simply enjoy listening to their favourite music or they might want to learn how to sing properly. Some very famous singers were born under this sign, including Elvis Presley, David Bowie, Shirley Bassey, Joan Baez, Annie Lennox, Donna Summer, John Denver and Janis Joplin, so they'd be in excellent company.

Capricorns often bottle up their feelings so it can help them to have spare-time interests that allow them to release all that pent-up emotion. One option is for them to start writing, whether that simply means keeping a daily diary or trying something much more ambitious. They're particularly good at writing about mysteries and other spine-chilling topics, as proven by Charles Addams, William Peter Blatty (who wrote *The Exorcist*), Wilkie Collins, Edgar Allen Poe, Jacob Grimm, Dennis Wheatley and Patricia Highsmith. Capricorns can be very good at making the flesh creep!

Finally, because Capricorns take life so seriously they are often attracted to a spiritual quest. In typical Capricorn fashion they usually do this in a quiet and modest way, although not always – Joan of Arc was a Capricorn on a noisy mission. Other Capricorns whose lives took them on a spiritual journey include St Bernadette, Kahlil Gibran, Paramahansa Yogananda, Swami Vivekananda, Maharishi Mahesh Yogi, Dr Albert Schweitzer and St Ignatius Loyola.

Holidays

Very often, the question isn't where a Capricorn should go on holiday but whether they want to take one at all. Although a

Capricorn may enjoy being on holiday when they finally get there, they aren't always convinced of the need to take time off and do nothing. In fact, the very description of it goes completely against the Capricorn attitude to life, which is that they should make the most of every moment and do as much as possible. So the thought of spending a fortnight relaxing by a pool or having nothing more strenuous to do than write some postcards is so weird that most Capricorns can't cope at all. They'd rather stay at home, thanks. They could always finish work a little earlier each day for a fortnight if they absolutely must, but that's as far as they're prepared to go.

Of course, this means that if any sign of the zodiac deserves a holiday it's a Capricorn. Often, holidays are their only chance to spend time with their family or loved ones, and the only opportunity they get all year to relax. Assuming that you're able to persuade the Capricorn in your life to actually take a holiday, of course. So why is this?

Well, a Capricorn isn't entirely convinced by the need for holidays because they can seem like such an unnecessary extravagance. When they leaf through holiday brochures they can't help blanching at the prices. How much? Deep down, the Capricorn would much rather stay at home and feel good about the money they've saved. This has the added bonus of them not having to cope with strange food and unfamiliar surroundings, both of which they find very unsettling. If a Capricorn is persuaded to go away, they won't want to throw their cash around willy-nilly and will choose somewhere that doesn't cost the earth. Nevertheless, they aren't keen on places that are too cheap and cheerful, and they're quite choosy about the company they keep. Scratch a Capricorn and you'll uncover a snob, so it's important that they choose a holiday destination they're happy with and where they can mix with people who are on the same social level as them.

A Capricorn might enjoy a skiing holiday, rock-climbing or simply relaxing high in the mountains somewhere. However, don't forget that they're lousy at sitting around doing nothing, so for 'relaxing' you must translate that as taking walks, visiting local sites of interest, catching up on their reading and making big plans for the future (which they'll do mentally, so no one can see what they're doing and accuse them of not unwinding).

If a Capricorn has plenty of money they'll enjoy staying in an expensive hotel, but even then they may have a few pangs of guilt about how much it costs. They'll ask themselves why they didn't choose somewhere cheaper, and the ensuing guilt and angst might even take the edge off their holiday. I know several Capricorns who usually stay in self-catering apartments or cottages, and who like to go back to the same place year after year. If they're lucky it becomes a home from home for them, and they appreciate its familiarity.

Capricorns are very practical, so might like a holiday in which they learn a new skill or craft. They have a powerfully conservative streak, so will avoid anywhere that's too exotic, strange or dangerous. They're also reluctant to go too far afield, which means that long-haul flights might be out of the question for them. Instead, they choose places that feel familiar, and preferably where there's no language barrier.

By the way, don't waste time hanging around waiting for a postcard to arrive from a Capricorn on holiday. You'll wait an awfully long time because they probably won't bother. For a start, they'll tell you they wouldn't know what to write even if they did decide to send you a postcard. Besides, none of the postcards were all that nice. And anyway, do you know how much stamps cost in that part of the world? Get real!

Home

Tradition is very important to a Capricorn, and this is usually obvious the moment you walk into their home. It's unlikely to be filled with the latest fashions in furniture and décor. You're far more likely to find lots of antiques and old pieces of furniture, especially if they belonged to other members of the family before they reached the Capricorn's home. They love the sense of continuity that comes from filling their home with family heirlooms and objects that they grew up with. Anything very modern or contemporary seems soulless to them by comparison. It's just not the same. If the Capricorn is very lucky, this means they have some beautiful china and lovely glasses, as well as glorious old furniture and interesting pictures.

Capricorns love wandering around antique shops, as well as going to jumble sales, thrift shops and other happy hunting grounds. They pick up all sorts of interesting objects as a result, especially if they can see beyond their current state to how they could be when they've been renovated or restored. One of my Capricorn friends is brilliant at this, buying all sorts of objects that look like rubbish to everyone else and then lovingly restoring them to their former glory for a fraction of what they're worth. So, next time you're in a Capricorn's home you should have a closer look at what's on show. Some of it may have an interesting story attached to it.

When a Capricorn does buy anything modern, you wouldn't know it. It will already look old, perhaps because it's a very traditional design or because it's a copy of something from the past. Capricorns particularly enjoy Victorian pieces, although too much of them can make a room seem too dark and claustrophobic. When looking for new furniture, they're attracted to items that will last – and last, and last. They hate the thought of spending money on anything that will soon date or fall apart, because that seems such a waste. However, they can't see the value of false economies, either, so would rather spend a decent amount of money on a piece of furniture that will wear well than buy something that's much cheaper but which will have to be replaced in a few years. They go for large, study items rather than anything very delicate or flimsy, and everything must be comfortable. As a result, a Capricorn's sitting room often seems to be full of furniture, because everything is so big. They also like to have lots of side tables and footstools, which can increase the cluttered feeling and make guests worried about knocking things over.

If you're visiting a Capricorn for the first time, wear plenty of warm clothes. Many Capricorns don't seem to feel the cold at all, and are apparently quite happy in temperatures that seem close to freezing to the rest of us. I know one Capricorn whose house is chilly even in the summer, although I haven't a clue why. Being such strong traditionalists, Capricorn like nothing better than a log fire or wood-burning stove to keep them warm. Unfortunately, though, they often turn off the central heating when the fire is lit so you have to sit very close to the flames to avoid the danger of congealing into a frozen lump.

You can usually expect to find a few pets when you visit a Capricorn. They're especially fond of dogs but are very strict with them, and certainly won't allow them to misbehave.

In common with their fellow Earth signs of Taurus and Virgo, Capricorns like to buy their homes as soon as possible. They think that home ownership is a great way to make money, so they're likely to have a mortgage from an early age. If they can possibly afford it, they'll own more than one property so they can live in one home and let out the others as a profitable sideline.

Clothes and Image
No matter how hard a Capricorn tries to look relaxed, they'll still look slightly formal. It must be in their blood, because there isn't much they can do about it. This isn't a sign that's happy to slop around in old jeans, tatty jumpers and T-shirts full of holes, even when they're on their own. It doesn't seem right, somehow, and they'll worry that someone will call unexpectedly and find them looking a mess. No, strangely enough Capricorns are much more relaxed when they're looking smart. At least they know that they're at their best and aren't letting the side down, so they're prepared for all eventualities. Their choice of smart clothes also says something about their need to impress people and be respected, even when they're in relaxed surroundings with old friends.

I've had many Capricorn friends over the years but I've never seen any of them wearing bright colours. Deep purple or bottle green is about the brightest they can manage, but anything more than that is completely out of the question. In fact, the classic Capricorn colours are black, charcoal grey and brown. Hardly a riot of colour, yet their sombre tones suit members of this sign. Having said that, Capricorns must be careful not to shroud themselves completely in funeral shades. Only ever wearing dark colours, and especially black, can have a very bad impact on a Capricorn's mood, making them feel miserable, lonely and lethargic. They need to find some way to relieve such a monochrome palette, even if they can only do so by wearing brightly coloured socks or underwear, or a bright tie or scarf. For many Capricorns, wearing such dark colours is a great way to blend into the woodwork and avoid standing out from the crowd. Dark clothes are their camouflage and their way of protecting themselves from too much public scrutiny.

The classic Capricorn outfit is the pinstriped suit. It encapsulates the Capricorn need for formality and tradition. And classic Capricorn fabrics are natural, such as wool, cotton and silk. This isn't a sign that's comfortable with modern synthetics because they feel so alien.

When it comes to choosing clothes, Capricorns like to go for conventional styles. Just as they don't want to wear bright colours, they aren't keen on very flamboyant or unusual designs either, and they usually steer clear of anything that's ultra fashionable because they know it will date in no time at all. Capricorns aren't interested in being slaves to fashion because it's such a fickle master. Instead, they need to create their own highly personal sense of style that escapes the vagaries of fashion but stops them looking dowdy or dull. Capricorn women who have managed to do this effortlessly include Marlene Dietrich, Faye Dunaway, Ava Gardner and Joan Baez, all of whom are also blessed with the classic high cheekbones and timeless beauty that are so typical of female members of this sign. As for Capricorn men, they are typically equally good-looking, and are usually tall, dark and handsome. Mel Gibson, Denzel Washington, Kevin Costner, Freddy Rodriguez, Elvis Presley, Muhammad Ali, Cary Grant and Jim Carrey all fit effortlessly into the classic Capricorn mould.

When choosing accessories, Capricorns will once again go for items that won't date easily. Both sexes like to look businesslike, so they need to carry their belongings around in smart bags and briefcases. They can spend a lot of money on these because they've got to last a long time and still look in good shape. However, I've noticed that Capricorns often don't pay nearly so much attention to their shoes, and sometimes these spoil the effect of an outfit because they're old, tatty or unpolished. When getting dressed, Capricorns need to look down as well as up.

Famous Capricorns

Robin and Maurice Gibb (22 December 1949); Helmut Schmidt (23 December 1918); Ava Gardner (24 December 1922); Sir Isaac Newton (25 December 1642); Mao Tse-tung (26 December 1893); Gérard Depardieu (27 December 1948); Denzel Washington (28 December 1954); Marianne Faithfull (29 December 1946); Rudyard Kipling (30 December 1865); Henri Matisse (31 December 1869); Joe Orton (1 January 1933); Christie Turlington (2 January 1969); Mel Gibson (3 January 1956); Louis Braille (4 January 1809); Diane Keeton (5 January 1946); St Joan of Arc (6 January 1412); St Bernadette of Lourdes (7 January 1844); David Bowie (8 January 1947); Simone de Beauvoir (9 January 1908); Rod Stewart (10 January 1945); Joely Richardson (11 January 1965); Jack London (12 January 1876); Sophie Tucker (13 January 1884); Dr Albert Schweitzer (14 January 1875); Martin Luther King, Jr (15 January 1929); Dian Fossey (16 January 1932); Al Capone (17 January 1899); Cary Grant (18 January 1904); Dolly Parton (19 January 1946); Buzz Aldrin (20 January 1930).

The Top Ten Capricorn Characteristics

Responsible; Practical; Self-effacing; Shy; Pessimistic; Conventional; Taciturn; Undemonstrative; Loyal; Great sense of humour.

Are You A Typical Capricorn?

Try this quiz on the Capricorns you know to find out whether they're typical members of their sign.

1 Are you very careful with your money?
2 Do your joints get stiff, especially in cold, wet weather?
3 Do people accuse you of being sceptical?
4 Are you an inveterate worrier?
5 Is your cup always half-empty rather than half-full?
6 Are you easily embarrassed by emotional displays?
7 Do you pride yourself on being logical and practical?

8 Do you always think you could do better?

9 Do you believe we should all take responsibility for ourselves?

10 Were you very serious as a child?

Score

Score one point for every "no" and zero points for every "yes".

0–3 You couldn't be more Capricorn if you tried. Life can be tough for you, although you pride yourself on being used to adversity. You have a practical attitude but can be very hard on yourself. You'd love to be more relaxed but it's not the way you're made.

4–6 You have a strong Capricorn streak but it's tempered by the influence of other signs. Read the Top Ten Characteristics of the other signs to see which ones ring a bell with you.

7–10 Although you were born under the sign of Capricorn you don't have many Capricorn characteristics. Look through the Top Ten Characteristics of Sagittarius and Aquarius to see if either of these sounds more like you.

Aquarius

21 January–19 February

The Aquarian Adult

Idiosyncratic. Iconoclastic. Eccentric. Original. Unconventional. These are only a few of the words that describe Aquarians. These aren't people who like to play by other people's rules. They have their own set of rules to follow, and these are often very different from everyone else's.

A typical Aquarian is a law unto themselves. They like to do their own thing, and if other people don't understand then it's just too bad. Sometimes they will adapt to fit in with everyone else but very often they won't compromise and will continue to do what they think is best. What else would you expect from one of the Fixed signs? This very sure and rather dogmatic approach to life means an Aquarian can come across as extremely uncompromising at times, even if they think they're behaving perfectly rationally and that everyone else is over-reacting or being foolish. Actually, an Aquarian often gets the distinct impression that they're the only one who's talking any sense and that the rest of the world has lost its reason. And who's to say that they're wrong? Very often an Aquarian is able to zero in on the truth, even if it's uncomfortable or

236

unpleasant, and to deal with the facts instead of emotional impressions, theories or wishful thinking. It can sometimes make them unpopular, because they highlight what needs to be looked at and talked about, especially if everyone else wants to sweep it under the carpet.

One reason for this typical Aquarian behaviour is that this sign is ruled by Uranus, the planet of radical views and extremes. He encourages Aquarians to be true to themselves, no matter whether it makes them unpopular or people think they're odd. Most Aquarians have probably spent all their lives knowing that other people don't understand them, so it's nothing new! The simple fact is that they have a different way of looking at the world and not everyone appreciates it. It's a threat for some people if they don't like the Aquarian brand of honesty and uncompromising directness. Some famous Aquarians have made themselves very unpopular in some circles by saying exactly what they think, and they include Germaine Greer, Angela Davis, Abraham Lincoln, Charles Darwin, Thomas Paine, John McEnroe and Toni Morrison. However, some Aquarians are more like Capricorns because they respond to their traditional ruler, Saturn. They blanch at the idea of being typically outspoken and unconventional. If you know an Aquarian who sounds like this you might learn more about them from reading the Capricorn chapter than this one. Or you could find that they're an intriguing mixture of both signs.

Aquarius belongs to the Air element, making members of this sign extremely intelligent and clever. They often have a powerful intellectual streak and love getting involved in thought-provoking discussions. Aquarians have a natural tendency to disappear into their thoughts, and sometimes they retreat into intellectual arguments when they feel at a disadvantage. Talking about ideas, and dealing with the realm of solid facts, can be reassuring for them. They aren't nearly so comfortable when talking about their emotions and other messy things that can't be quantified or proved.

Aquarians have a burning desire for freedom in all its forms.

They want the freedom to be whoever they really are, without feeling the need for any window dressing or pretence. They will adapt their behaviour to fit in with other people up to a point, but they won't change their beliefs to please anyone. Some of them become tactful over the years and change the subject when the conversation strays into controversial territory, but others never learn how to do this and spend their entire lives ruffling other people's feathers by saying what they think without checking it first for its potential to cause offence. The Aquarian motto is definitely "Dare to be different".

Aquarians express their need for freedom in other ways, too. For some of them this can mean never getting involved in a long-term relationship in case it clips their wings. For others it can mean lending their support to a campaign that promotes human rights, such as Amnesty International, or they might become a vociferous champion of animal rights and complain about animal slavery.

Because Aquarius belongs to the Fixed element, Aquarians can sometimes be highly resistant to the idea of change. They dig in their heels and stubbornly refuse to budge. However, they always have a good reason for doing so, as they'll tell you. But they can't see any point in sticking to tradition purely for the sake of it. They can have very iconoclastic views, wanting to wipe out all sorts of rules and conventions that they think have outlived their usefulness or have caused more harm than good. For instance, many Aquarians can be very trenchant on topics such as politics and religion and they aren't afraid to say what they think. And yes, sometimes they can be quite extremist and eccentric. Not that they care. In fact, for some of them such words are a compliment! Sometimes, an Aquarian can be years ahead of their time, so they're a lone voice crying in the wilderness. It may take years before everyone else agrees with them, but it's amazing how often society eventually comes round to the Aquarian view of the world.

If you have an Aquarian in your life one of the first things you'll notice about them is their unpredictability. They'll like their coffee made a certain way on Monday and will want it to taste totally different on Wednesday. They'll tell you one week how much they enjoyed a television programme but will refuse to watch it the following week, complaining that they don't want to keep doing the same things all the time. They need plenty of scope for spontaneity in their lives, otherwise they feel they're suffocating. So they need to be able to do things on the spur of the moment, rather than have everything planned out for weeks in advance with no possibility of varying their schedule.

Something else you'll notice about Aquarians is their absent-mindedness. Such forgetfulness is hardly surprising when someone's head is so full of ideas, opinions and plans for making the world a better place that they can't remember where they put their glasses or it's only when they reach the supermarket check-out that they realize they left their wallet at home.

Another major feature of Aquarians is their kindness and compassion. This can come as a surprise when you've heard an Aquarian banging on about how all politicians should be sacked, or whatever else they happen to believe, but it's absolutely true. When you need a friend (and that's something that Aquarians are very good at) or you're in trouble, ask an Aquarian for help. They'll do whatever they can, whether that means driving you to hospital at some unearthly hour in the morning, doing your shopping in their lunch-hour or sticking by you when your world is falling apart. Aquarians are the great humanitarians of the zodiac, and we all need them in our lives.

The Aquarian Child

Before we go any further, here's a very important fact. It's perfectly normal for an Aquarian child to feel that they don't fit in with their family. Some of them nurse secret fantasies about being changelings or having been adopted, because they can't believe that they've got anything in common with their parents and siblings. And very often you can't help agreeing with them. I've known lots of Aquarians who, even as adults, don't seem to have anything in common with their families. And sometimes it's as though they've come from another planet because they're so extraordinarily different to everyone else, from their beliefs and opinions to the way they earn a living.

The Aquarian need to be different kicks in at an early age. An Aquarian child may want to wear different clothes from their siblings or read different books, but very often they express these differences subconsciously at first. Later on, when they're more aware of their motives and behaviour, they may deliberately make choices that set them apart from their family and friends. For instance, if they decide to learn a musical instrument they might choose something that no one else is interested in, such as the cello if all their friends are learning the recorder or piano. And they won't want to jump on the bandwagon of being a fan of a particular pop star or television programme. They might even announce loudly that they hate whoever or whatever it is. And they'll mean it! It isn't just an act.

With their very smart brains, Aquarian children need to be given plenty of intellectual stimulation from an early age or they'll get bored and get into trouble. If they don't pay attention at school it's often because they're way ahead of the rest of the class and have already grasped what the teacher is telling them. They will also lose interest in what they're being taught if they sense they're being patronized or talked down to. They won't like that at all, and it will be the same when they're with their parents.

In fact, an Aquarian child's parents will be surprised at how adult their child is in many ways. They'll discover this when they're asked awkward questions about religion or morals by their Aquarian child who makes it plain that they don't want to be fobbed off with easy answers or be told that they shouldn't bother their little head about such things. One of the best things the parents can do for their child is encourage them to talk and to voice their opinions. Ideally, family meal times should become debating sessions in which the Aquarian child can discuss whatever happens to be on their mind. After all, this is an Air sign, so the little Aquarian needs to communicate their thoughts. The child's reading habits may also indicate that they're mature for their age. They won't want to read anything that they consider to be soppy or childish, and will be fascinated by encyclopaedias and science books.

Every parent needs to impose discipline on their children, and Aquarian children are perfectly happy to obey the rules if they understand them and they make sense. But they'll react badly to any rules or judgements that they think are arbitrary, unnecessary or unfair, and when they ask for an explanation they won't consider "Because I say so" to be a satisfactory parental answer in the slightest.

Something that should be encouraged from an early age is the Aquarian capacity for friendship. An Aquarian child will make friends with whoever they happen to like, whether it's the elderly couple who live next door, the milkman or their school friends. They're instinctively friendly and open, which is a fabulous gift that needs to be nurtured. Of course, their parents should teach them how to safeguard themselves against potential dangers, such as not getting into cars with strangers, but they certainly shouldn't tell them that evil people are lurking on every corner or make them wary of people they don't know.

With their instinctive love of animals, Aquarian children enjoy having pets to look after. Even when they're very young they'll worry about the ethics of keeping goldfish in tiny bowls and mice in cages, so they might be much happier if they have their own dog or cat, provided that they're allowed outside. And they'll also enjoy getting involved with some sort of charity or good cause at an early age, even if it's simply helping Grandma with the household chores or donating the toys they no longer want to their local hospital. It's never too soon for an Aquarian to develop their humanitarian instincts, and if they begin as a child these will soon become second nature to them.

Health

Most Aquarians are bursting with health. Visiting the doctor is a rare occurrence for them because it's not often that they have anything wrong with them. They get coughs and colds just like the rest of us, of course, but usually they stoically carry on regardless, dismissing them as just a minor inconvenience. Even when there is something more seriously wrong, an Aquarian may be more inclined to consult a complementary health practitioner than their doctor. They're especially interested in holistic and integrative medicine because it makes complete sense to them. Depending on what's wrong with them, they may respond particularly well to acupuncture, homeopathy, cranial osteopathy, chiropractic and healing. They like the idea of the body's healing mechanisms being gently nudged into action by a complementary therapy rather than being blasted by an allopathic medicine. However, anything that strikes them as being too wacky or New Age will probably send them into fits of laughter! They also have a good nose for anyone who's trying to rip them off, so they'll be very wary about forking out a lot of money for something that seems bogus or too ludicrous for words.

It's very important for Aquarians to keep on the move but without doing anything that's so strenuous or jarring that it will eventually damage their joints. Steady walking is good for them, especially if they can vary the scenery from day to day, and so is cycling and swimming. Like Capricorns, Aquarians have a tendency to develop aches and stiffness in their joints if they spend too much time being sedentary, so it's important for them to stay active. This will also help them to combat any weight gain as they get older. However, weight gain is rarely a problem for them when they're younger because the classic Aquarian shape is tall, lean and muscular.

Yoga, Pilates, Tai Chi and similar exercise techniques appeal to Aquarians. They like the fact that these techniques are slightly unusual and they also like the fact that they work, because they enable the Aquarian to keep supple and healthy in ways that they enjoy. The idea of kicking a ball around a muddy field, for instance, may strike a typical Aquarian as bizarre, and they may also wonder why anyone in their right mind would want to go jogging. So it's important for them to find a form of exercise that they enjoy and which they can develop. They certainly won't want to do something in which they can't progress and grow.

The parts of the body ruled by Aquarius are the ankles and the circulatory system. Many Aquarians have problems with their ankles, such as twisting them or breaking them. They need to choose shoes that will support their feet and vulnerable ankles. And as for their circulation, it's important for them to keep active so they can keep their blood flowing properly. They can have problems with varicose veins, too. Some Aquarians may also experience back pain, which they get from their opposite sign of the zodiac, Leo. Even if they haven't yet had any twinges they should take care of their backs and be particularly careful when bending or lifting heavy objects. Leo also rules the heart, so that's another area of the body that Aquarians need to look after.

Money

Money and Aquarius is a strange combination. It's not that Aquarians don't need money, because of course they do. But they have a different attitude towards it than the rest of us, and they can be very ambivalent towards it. Some of them even seem to go out of their way to avoid having to deal with it.

Aquarians know that they need money in order to live, but they certainly don't want it for its own sake. The idea of accumulating vast reserves of wealth that they keep to themselves is abhorrent to most of them, because it goes against their strong humanitarian principles. If they are ever in the happy position of having more money than they know what to do with, they do their best to use it to help others. Aquarians believe that money is energy, and that it should be used to do good. So they get involved in charities and other good causes so their generous donations of money will help others as well as themselves. Paul Newman is a great example of an Aquarian who has used his wealth and connections to help others. In his case, he started a string of camps for ill children and their families, and pours all the profits ($175 million at the last count) from his range of foods into them as well as into thousands of other educational and charitable projects.

Although Aquarians like the idea of giving to charity, they're very choosy about who they donate their money to. They certainly won't shell it out willy-nilly, with no thought about where that money might be going. Some Aquarians have very strong opinions about what governments should pay for, and wouldn't dream of letting those governments off the hook by helping them with their financial responsibilities in looking after their deprived citizens. They would much rather get involved in a charity or voluntary scheme themselves, so they can see exactly where the money is going and make sure that it isn't being squandered on unnecessary expenses.

For a sign that doesn't place a lot of importance on money, Aquarians are surprisingly well organized about it. They keep up to date with what's going on in their bank accounts and credit cards, and have no compunctions about switching accounts in order to get better rates of interest. They can develop quite an interest in the activities of the stock market, although they'll avoid any shares in companies that they consider to be unethical or exploitative. This can cover a wide range of investments, including pharmaceuticals, oil companies, arms manufacturers and massive conglomerates. An Aquarian is quite prepared to put their money where their mouth is, and will stand by their beliefs. They certainly won't do any secret U-turns or make any hypocritical decisions even when they'd benefit from them financially.

When looking into financial arrangements and deciding which ones are right for them, Aquarians are very forthright and have no qualms about asking people questions or asking for what they want. My Aquarian husband taught himself an enormous amount about finance and has used the information to get us some great mortgage deals. But he has absolutely no interest in acquiring money simply so he can gloat over it or stash it away in the bank.

When looking for things to spend their money on, Aquarians can't see the point in making false economies. They would rather stump up a fortune on something that's top of the range and will last for years, than spend half that amount on something that isn't very good and will probably conk out in a few months. This can cause friction with their partner if there isn't a lot of money to go round and they would rather spend it on other things, such as the groceries. And, even then, an Aquarian can't see the point of saving money on cheap brands of food when they could buy something that would be so much better. So if your housekeeping budget is already stretched to breaking point, you'd better accompany your Aquarian on their shopping trips!

Career

Whatever an Aquarian does for a living, it's essential that it allows them to use their highly capable brain. They need plenty of intellectual stimulation and will soon become fed up if they're doing something mindless or so predictable that it makes them want to scream. They also need to be allowed to think for themselves, rather than always having to take orders from someone else (which is something they really struggle with). Ideally, an Aquarian needs a little variety in each day if they're to operate at their best. Although they belong to a Fixed sign that likes a certain amount of stability, they also need spontaneity and change, thanks to their planetary ruler, Uranus. If life at work becomes too predictable and dreary for them, they're quite likely to down tools and walk out, even if that's the last thing they can afford to do. They believe that life is too short for them to put up with situations that make them bored or unhappy, regardless of what everyone else might tell them.

Another important Aquarian requirement concerns their colleagues. Aquarians need to work with people who are bright, clever and interesting to talk to, otherwise they will quickly become dispirited and withdrawn. They have no desire to spend time with people whose brains appear to have been replaced with old potato peelings. Aquarians will also struggle if they work with people whose political, spiritual or moral beliefs are completely at odds with their own, because their differing opinions will eventually drive a wedge between them.

Among the careers that would suit an Aquarian are anything connected with science, technology and engineering. Many Aquarians have an instinctive understanding of such subjects and really enjoy playing around with the latest technological equipment. An Aquarian might make a good electrician, too, because Uranus is the ruler of electricity. Uranus also governs innovative thinking, and Aquarians are traditionally the inventors of the zodiac. Thomas Edison, whose inventions helped to develop the electric light, the phonograph and the typewriter, was an Aquarian. What else could he have been? Charles Darwin, whose belief in the evolution of mankind are still the source of considerable controversy in some quarters, was a typical Aquarian who wasn't afraid to voice opinions that flew in the face of accepted religious thinking. Astronomy is another classic Aquarian interest, so it's no surprise that Nicolaus Copernicus and Galileo Galilei, two of the world's greatest and most revolutionary astronomers, were both Aquarians.

New Age techniques and philosophies can appeal to Aquarians, although they will stop short of believing in anything that they consider to be totally barmy or illogical. Television and radio also have a big attraction for many Aquarians, whichever side of the microphone they happen to be. And you'll find many Aquarian actors. They get their love of drama from their opposite sign of Leo, although they combine that with a typically quirky and individual quality. Big Aquarian stars include Telly Savalas, Geena Davis, John Hurt, Bridget Fonda, Patricia Routledge, Alan Bates, Jack Lemmon, Gene Hackman, Oliver Reed, John Travolta, Jennifer Jason Leigh and Mickey Rourke.

Aquarius rules hobbies and pastimes, so some members of

this sign might be able to turn a leisure interest into a full-time job. Alternatively, they could run a business that supplies the equipment for people's hobbies.

Some signs aren't cut out for self-employment but it often suits Aquarians much better than being another person's employee. They like being able to have some say over their own working hours, rather than having to conform to what someone else wants them to do, and they enjoy being their own bosses. Aquarians aren't good at being told what to do because they have a natural antipathy to taking orders from other people. If anyone's going to give the orders, they are!

Love and Friendships

Friendship is one of an Aquarian's greatest gifts. These people excel at making friends and they attract people from all walks of life and all ages. They can see nothing odd about a thirty-year age gap between friends, nor are they interested in choosing influential or wealthy friends because of what they might be able to do for the Aquarian. If an Aquarian likes someone, they like them, and that's all there is to it. They don't have any ulterior motives, other than wanting to spend time with their friends for the sheer pleasure of their company. They're very loyal and reliable, and will gladly come to the rescue if one of their friends is in trouble or is going through a hard time. My Aquarian husband once gave away all our spare kitchenware to a friend in need. That's the sort of thing Aquarians do.

This Aquarian emphasis on friendship means that an Aquarian needs a partner who understands them. Very often, the partner started off as one of the Aquarian's friends and gradually became a lover. It makes sense, because it's essential for an Aquarian to be good friends with their long-term partner. Yes, they can get carried away by careless rapture sometimes and start a red-hot relationship with someone who wasn't a friend to begin with, but the love affair usually burns itself out sooner or later. And Aquarians believe that there's a lot more to a long-standing relationship than sex. They've got to like their partner and be able to talk to them, otherwise they can't see any point in continuing the relationship. Actually, many Aquarians eventually lose most of their interest in sex. They're much keener on having an intellectual relationship with their partner than a sexual one, especially as they get older. This means there can be problems if a low-sexed Aquarian pairs up with a highly-sexed member of another sign. Both partners will have to compromise if they want their relationship to last.

Aquarians are very loyal, devoted and loving partners, but they're an Air sign which means they can find it difficult to show or talk about their feelings. These certainly aren't lovey-dovey people who will deluge you with romantic notes, gifts and who'll remember every anniversary. It's simply not their style. (They're far more likely to forget every anniversary unless that will mean their life isn't worth living.) However, when they do bring you a special gift or they tell you they love you, the gesture has extra value because you know they really mean it. They aren't doing it because you expect it. They're doing it because they want to.

So when you pair up with an Aquarian you get a friend as well as a lover. And you'll get someone who supports you in everything you do and who actively encourages you to bring out the best in yourself. If there's something you've always wanted to do, your Aquarian will cheer you along and give you masses of encouragement. They'll commiserate when things go wrong and buy champagne when they go well. And they'll hope that you'll do the same in return. Which is where some Aquarian alliances can come unstuck.

Aquarians are highly original, don't forget, with a string of different interests and lots of friends. So when they want to pursue a dream or achieve an ambition, it may not include their partner. It may even mean that their partner is left by themselves for long periods while the Aquarian goes off and does their own thing. And that could be anything from taking off on a month-long meditation retreat to taking a part-time university course in psychology or locking themselves away in the garden shed every weekend while they write a film script.

Something else that is very important for an Aquarian is their independence. They'll want to go off and see their own friends without their partner tagging along and they certainly won't want to be joined to them at the hip. Of course they'll do things with their other half and they'll enjoy having friends in common, but they'll also want to keep part of their life completely separate. Now, this really can cause problems in a relationship if the partner is jealous or threatened by their Aquarian's behaviour. There has to be some give and take, but it doesn't always come from the Aquarian. So, if you pair up with an Aquarian, be prepared to make lots of compromises!

Family Relationships

Aquarians aren't always very family-minded. They enjoy seeing their relatives every now and then, but they don't feel a burning need to spend lots of their spare time with them purely because they're related. Mind you, it's a different story if they really enjoy a relative's company because then they'll become more like a friend. And friends, as we know, are very important to Aquarians. Of course, it's also a different story if one of the family goes through a crisis. The Aquarian will be one of the first people to rally round and offer their help, even if they don't really like the person who's in trouble. It's one of the many examples of their instinctive kindness and humanitarianism. Sometimes an Aquarian will help their nearest and dearest even if it causes them severe inconvenience. My Aquarian father-in-law once gave his three-piece suite to his younger daughter because she needed some furniture, leaving he and his wife with nothing to sit on until the replacement furniture arrived.

When an Aquarian has their own family, they'll be a proud and doting parent even if they don't always show it. Big demonstrations of affection don't necessarily come easily to an Aquarian, which means they can sometimes be a rather remote and chilly parent who's more interested in finding out what their children think about world events than in giving them a hug or playing games with them. This can create an aura of reserve between them unless they all work hard to be more affectionate.

Aquarians are particularly flummoxed by babies, partly because of their inability to communicate in words. In true Air sign style, they get much more interested in their children when they start to speak and develop their own distinct personalities, because then they become people in their own right.

Throughout a child's upbringing, the Aquarian will be very concerned about respecting that child's rights. For instance, the Aquarian will believe that babies shouldn't be petted or held all the time because that might be intrusive and upsetting for them. They'll want each of their children to have their own rooms if possible, so they don't have the embarrassment or inconvenience of sharing. And they'll make it plain that everyone should respect everyone else's property and not use it without asking.

An Aquarian parent will also be looking keenly at their children for signs of their originality, and they'll actively encourage every spark of individuality that they see. Aquarians want their children to be different in some way, even if that doesn't suit the children. Actually, when an Aquarian does this they're projecting their own need to be different on to their children, especially if they were expected to conform to family values or tradition during their own childhood. But they must move beyond this and realize that they've got to treat each child in the way they suits them, regardless of whether that fits the Aquarian's needs. For instance, many Aquarians would much prefer to teach their children at home than send them to school, especially if they hated school themselves. But their children might love the thought of going to school where they can mix with lots of friends, and could become very isolated if they're taught at home and rarely have the chance to get together with other children of their own age.

Something else that means a lot to an Aquarian parent is family discussions. They'll do their best to encourage their children to form their own opinions, and discuss them, about all sorts of local, national and world events. If their children ask them difficult questions, the Aquarian will always answer them honestly and directly, rather than beating about the bush or making up fairy stories. For instance, if the pet rabbit dies and the children ask where it's gone, the Aquarian is much more likely to say in a matter-of-fact fashion that it's died and been buried in the garden than to say it's run away to heaven or is being looked after by bunny angels. The words would stick in any self-respecting Aquarian's throat!

Creativity and Potential

There's a huge spark of originality inside every Aquarian, and it's just waiting to be fanned into a massive fire of creativity. If an Aquarian's job doesn't give them enough scope to express their inner self, they need to find hobbies and spare-time interests that will give them the creative satisfaction they crave. And if these don't fit into other people's ideas of what's suitable or so-called normal, then it's too bad!

Aquarians are the eccentrics of the zodiac. They do things differently from the rest of us, and that's simply how they're made. They certainly don't go out of their way to be unusual, contrary or unconventional. Other signs may try hard to be wacky or quirky but these traits come completely naturally for Aquarians. So, when an Aquarian is casting around for ways to express their potential, the last thing they should worry about is what other people will think. Instead, they should concentrate on finding ways of letting their innovative, inspired and brilliant personality find its wings and take flight. That might mean going out on a limb, but so be it.

Astrology is a very Aquarian pursuit, so an Aquarian might enjoy learning about it in a lot of detail. They could teach if they want to go beyond simple Sun sign astrology. Alternatively, something like the tarot or numerology could appeal, especially if the Aquarian can find rational explanations for why they work.

Many Aquarians are on a quest to find more meaning in

their lives, and they're especially open to Far Eastern religions and philosophies. Buddhism is particularly attractive to Aquarians, who like its pacifist, non-judgemental approach. They're also interested in forms of exercise with a spiritual dimension, such as yoga, which can help them to relax and keep fit at the same time.

They could also consider doing something that brings out their humanitarian streak. For instance, they might decide to work as a volunteer who helps people, or they could lend a hand in a charity shop or get involved in a fund-raising campaign for a cause they really care about. Anything like this will make them feel they're contributing to society and doing their bit to make the world a better place. Aquarians are also great animal lovers, so they might find it very rewarding to work as a volunteer in an animal rescue centre.

Alternatively, an Aquarian could get involved in politics, even if only at a very modest local level. This is an especially good outlet for Aquarians who usually shout at the television when they hear things they don't agree with. They could soon be shouting at their fellow councillors or politicians!

This is such an intellectual sign that many Aquarians enjoy writing. There are lots of famous Aquarian writers, including Virginia Woolf, Edith Wharton, Bertolt Brecht, Georges Simenon, Colette, Susan Hill, Toni Morrison, Carson McCullers, Ruth Rendell and Jules Verne. Aquarians are a pretty versatile lot, so each one is bound to find a style of writing that will suit them.

Something else that appeals to Aquarians is painting and drawing. But don't expect them to conform to everyone else's standards, or even to paint things that you'll recognize. Most Aquarians aren't interested in producing the sort of chocolate-box images that might appeal to less adventurous signs. Aquarians want to make a big, bold statement, and they don't care if it takes several tubes of paint and a canvas that's too big to get through the door. Jackson Pollock was a typical Aquarian artist who developed a very idiosyncratic style of painting that caused a huge fuss when it was first seen.

Finally, if the Aquarian is fascinated by outer space, they could buy themselves a pair of binoculars and a star map, and then move on to a proper telescope when they're totally hooked. Watching a science fiction film will never be the same again!

Holidays

The last thing an Aquarian wants to do on holiday is be surrounded by crowds and feel that they're part of a gigantic marketing machine. Quite honestly, they'd rather stay at home than be subjected to something like that. Instead, they're drawn to places that are off the beaten track, unfashionable (so they don't have to rub shoulders with every Tom, Dick and Harry) or which are yet to be discovered by most people. They most certainly don't want to be anywhere really fashionable, with plenty of celebrity-spotting and paparazzi hanging around. It doesn't appeal to them in the slightest and they'll complain like mad if they find themselves anywhere even remotely like this.

Aquarians have no interest in simple beach holidays, unless they can alternate sun-bathing with plenty of sight-seeing. If they do find themselves stuck on a beach for a long time, perhaps with a sun-worshipping partner, they'll soon get bored and wander off on their own. This will cause huge ructions, unless their partner doesn't mind and is quite used to the Aquarian pleasing themselves. But usually, it's very important for the Aquarian to negotiate with their partner, or with the rest of the family, so they can settle on a holiday that they'll all enjoy even if they have to compromise on some of the things they want.

Destinations steeped in history and culture are ideal for Aquarians, because they love tuning into the atmosphere and learning more about the country they're visiting. However, they won't be happy in a place that has a bad record on things that mean a lot to them, such as animal welfare or human rights. Aquarians truly don't want to visit anywhere that they disapprove of, because they consider that to be hypocritical.

It's also essential that an Aquarian's holiday destination offers peace and quiet so they can read all those books they've brought with them. And if it gives them the chance to spend some time by themselves, then so much the better. But they won't want to spend all their time on their own, because for them part of the pleasure of going on holiday is meeting the locals, so it's important that they visit somewhere friendly and welcoming. It helps if they can speak the language, but if not the Aquarian will do their best to communicate through a mixture of smiles, sign language and stammered words taken from their phrase book.

For a sign with so many wide-ranging interests, holidays can be an opportunity for an Aquarian to learn something new. They might enjoy an activity holiday set in lovely surroundings, such as a painting or walking holiday, or something with a more contemplative theme, such as meditation or healing.

Wherever an Aquarian goes on holiday they'll want to take as little luggage with them as possible. I've known Aquarians who've gone away for six weeks with little more than a large knapsack full of clothes. They quickly work out a system in which they take two of everything, so one is on their back and the other is in the wash. They certainly can't see the point of trailing masses of luggage around with them so they ruthlessly pare down what they're taking to the bare essentials. And sometimes, given most Aquarians' tendency to be forgetful, "bare" is the operative word because they leave something essential, such as their underwear, at home.

Will you get a postcard from your Aquarian friend when they're on holiday? Yes, you will, but don't be surprised if it carries the same message as all the other cards they send. They don't have the time or patience to think up different messages for each person they write to, unless they're feeling particularly inspired or they know that everyone will be comparing notes and they don't want to be caught out.

Home

Unpredictable as always, an Aquarian's home could be a showcase of the latest contemporary styles or a homage to a bygone era. For instance, this could be the sort of person who buys a Victorian house and decides to live in a Victorian manner, complete with coal fires, oil lamps and button-back chairs, or they might go for a 1950s extravaganza and even dress the part.

When an Aquarian goes for a contemporary look, they like to keep things sleek and streamlined. They love the idea of having a very minimalist home, even if it doesn't suit the rest of the family. All that space! All that room to breathe! Other people might find it rather soulless and antiseptic, but the Aquarian will revel in the clean, functional atmosphere. But they're just as likely to suddenly go off the whole thing, rip it all out and opt for cluttered cosiness instead. You can never tell with an Aquarian, and half the time they don't even know themselves what they're going to do next. At least it helps to make life interesting for anyone who lives with them.

The state of an Aquarian's home depends on how they're feeling at the time, who they live with and how big their budget is. This means they will sometimes put up with rather strange furniture or colour combinations, and will tolerate decorative schemes that would drive a Libran crazy. It's not that they don't care about their surroundings but they usually have their minds on more important topics than what colour curtains to have or whether the carpet picks up the pink in the sofa. Having said that, they often have what you might politely call unusual taste. Sometimes, Aquarians seem to like things that don't necessarily appeal to anyone else. I can only imagine that they were designed by Aquarians for Aquarians.

What you will find, no matter what sort of home the Aquarian has, are books. Aquarians are fascinated by knowledge and love books, which they keep in neat, tidy rows. They may even categorize their books so they know exactly where to find whatever they're looking for. They own books on a variety of subjects, some of which are quite esoteric. Very often, the more unusual the book, the more an Aquarian loves it!

Aquarians adore modern technology, so you can expect to find an impressive array of electrical equipment, including state-of-the-art television sets, DVD players and sound systems. And, if money and space permit, the Aquarian will have a special room fitted out as a home cinema. But they won't keep it to themselves – they'll enjoy entertaining their friends in there, too.

Some signs seem to leave a trail of mess behind them wherever they go, but not Aquarians. They're extraordinarily tidy, and expect everyone else around them to be equally neat. Their clothes are arranged in orderly piles in their drawers, and the hooks of all the coathangers will be facing the same way in their wardrobes. They take comfort from all this order, especially if it's at odds with the way the rest of the household lives.

Aquarians love animals so you will often find a few pets milling around somewhere in their homes. They have a deep respect for all living creatures but aren't happy about keeping any pets that are very exotic or whose living conditions are a world away from their natural habitat. The sight of birds in cages upsets them, and they think it's cruel to keep reptiles in tanks. They're much more comfortable with domestic animals such as dogs, cats and horses, but will only have them if they can look after them properly and the animals have plenty of space to roam around freely. But whichever animal an Aquarian has, it will be treated like one of the family.

Clothes and Image

Aquarians like to look different. They hate the thought of conforming to everyone else's tastes and ideas of what looks good. They certainly don't want to look like one of the crowd or to blend into the background, and they have absolutely no desire to fit in. They want to go their own way and wear clothes in the styles they like. And that's the end of that! Sometimes they take this to extremes (surely not!) and create a very eccentric image. They can put together clothes in combinations that they like but which look weird to the rest of us. Sometimes their clothes themselves are strange, with peculiar decorative features or unusual patterns and shapes.

As a result of all this, it's difficult to describe the Aquarian image because it's so diverse. Some Aquarians like to look ultra-fashionable, especially when they're young, and will keep switching their image according to their whim. They'll even change their hair colour on a regular basis whenever they start to get bored with whatever shade it happens to be at the time. And you'll find plenty of Aquarians who don't follow fashion but who set it. Mary Quant, the designer whose clothes sparked off a fashion revolution in the 1960s, is an Aquarian. What else could she be?

Aquarius can be a very glamorous sign and some Aquarians absolutely exude glamour. Christian Dior is an Aquarian fashion designer who also caused a revolution, but in a different way from Mary Quant. In the late 1940s he created a style called the "New Look" (which is a very Aquarian title, by the way) that was a world away from the austerity that had been so prevalent during the Second World War. His clothes typify the sophisticated, look-but-don't-touch side of Aquarius. Incidentally, Aquarian men can look really attractive in dinner jackets and black ties, and the women can look stunning in evening dresses.

And then there are the Aquarians who haven't got a clue what's in fashion and wouldn't care about it even if they did know. They prefer to stick to a look that they've perfected over the years and which is their signature. They might wear the same clothes for years on end as well, having taken care not to buy anything too fashionable in the first place so it won't date. This is a strategy that obviously works best if they're prepared to buy well-made clothes of good quality. Aquarians who've created a particular image and kept it, each in their own way, include Alice Cooper, Zsa Zsa Gabor and Yoko Ono.

Aquarius is a Fixed sign, so many members of this sign can get set in their ways as they get older. Even if they chopped and changed their look on an almost weekly basis when they were young, they become much more resistant to this as the years go by. So sometimes you can meet Aquarians who have got stuck in a slight time-warp, and whose clothes and make-up (which is not necessarily only worn by Aquarian women!) date from the happiest period in their lives.

When it comes to choosing colours, most Aquarians look fantastic in blues and turquoises. They look better in shiny fabrics, such as silks, satins and some cottons, than in anything very tweedy and rough which can be too heavy for them.

The typical Aquarian build is tall and slim but slightly muscular. They are often very slender when they're in their teens and twenties, sometimes to the point of being almost scrawny, but they usually put on weight as they get older. And unless they put on masses amount of weight, it normally suits them. Both sexes are often extremely attractive, with traffic-stopping good looks. And many of them have piercing eyes and high cheekbones, just to add to their charisma. However, they can have problems with their hair, which is often fine and thin, making it difficult for them to do much with it. One answer is to hide it all underneath a hat, and some of them will do this whether or not it suits them. That's Aquarius for you!

Famous Aquarians

Placido Domingo (21 January 1941); Lord Byron (22 January 1788); Humphrey Bogart (23 January 1899); Natassya Kinski (24 January 1961); Virginia Woolf (25 January 1882); Paul Newman (26 January 1925); Wolfgang Amadeus Mozart (27 January 1756); Mikhail Baryshnikov (28 January 1948); Oprah Winfrey (29 January 1954); Vanessa Redgrave (30 January 1937); Anna Pavlova (31 January 1882); Clark Gable (1 February 1901); Holly Hunter (2 February 1958); Gertrude Stein (3 February 1874); Charles Lindbergh (4 February 1902); Charlotte Rampling (5 February 1946); François Truffaut (6 February 1932); Charles Dickens (7 February 1812); James Dean (8 February 1931); Mia Farrow (9 February 1945); Greg Norman (10 February 1955); Jennifer Aniston (11 February 1969); Abraham Lincoln (12 February 1809); Robbie Williams (13 February 1974); Jack Benny (14 February 1894); Galileo Galilei (15 February 1564); John McEnroe (16 February 1959); Barry Humphries (17 February 1934); Toni Morrison (18 February 1931); Nicolaus Copernicus (19 February 1473).

The Top Ten Aquarian Characteristics

Honest; Humanitarian; Independent; Eccentric; Stubborn; Opinionated; Unpredictable; Sociable; Intelligent; Rational.

Are You A Typical Aquarian?

Try this quiz on the Aquarians you know to find out whether they're typical members of their sign.

1 Do you have a fear of being one of the crowd?
2 Would you break a rule or a law if you didn't agree with it?
3 Is it sometimes difficult to fit in with other people?
4 Have you ever been told you're contrary or an extremist?
5 Do you have set beliefs and opinions?
6 Do your opinions sometimes provoke controversy with others?
7 Do you consider yourself to be independent?
8 Do you sometimes wish you weren't so tactless?
9 Do you need plenty of time to yourself?
10 Do you pride yourself on being rational and logical?

Score

Score one point for every "no" and zero points for every "yes".

0–3   You couldn't be more Aquarian if you tried. You march to the beat of a different drummer, and you're proud of it. People can find you unorthodox and eccentric, but you can't help being yourself. If other people don't like it, that's their problem.

4–6   You have a strong Aquarian streak but it's tempered by the influence of other signs. Read the Top Ten Characteristics of the other signs to see which ones ring a bell with you.

7–10   Although you were born under the sign of Aquarius you don't have many Aquarian characteristics. Look through the Top Ten Characteristics of Capricorn and Pisces to see if either of these sounds more like you.

Pisces

20 February–20 March

The Piscean Adult

Pisces is the last sign of the zodiac, and one astrological theory maintains that Pisces contains a little of each of the other eleven signs. Some people even believe that being born with the Sun in Pisces means that they won't have to be reincarnated again on earth. But Pisces is a much more complicated sign than this theory suggests.

Pisces is the sign of the saint and the sinner. There are some Pisceans who have so much compassion, benevolence and empathy for their fellow creatures that they don't seem human at all, while other members of this sign don't seem human for very different and extremely sinister reasons. No wonder this sign's symbol is two fish swimming in opposite directions, because Pisces can hit the heights or plumb the depths. And often they'll do both in the same lifetime.

Pisces is ruled by Neptune, the planet of dreams, imagination and confusion, which immediately tells you a great deal about members of this sign. Neptune can give them tremendous sympathy for other people but he can also give them a lack of self-esteem and self-confidence. They can have a very low opinion of themselves and their abilities, so they never achieve their tremendous potential. Many Pisceans say they drift through life, not knowing what they are meant to be doing and without any distinct goals. They can be very passive, allowing themselves to be influenced by other people and reacting to situations, rather than making autonomous decisions and creating favourable circumstances and opportunities. When they do decide to take risks or try new ventures, they can be easily discouraged at the first sign of trouble.

Neptune can also cloud their judgement, in extreme cases even to the point where they're unable to stop themselves doing something wrong. For some Pisceans, lying and telling fibs comes very easily, and sometimes they will even manage to convince themselves that what they're saying is the gospel truth. Occasionally you'll find a Piscean who has woven a complex web of deceit around themselves, and which will ruin their reputation if it's discovered.

Something that Pisceans will even admit themselves is that they often take the line of least resistance when faced with a problem. And sometimes this means pretending that nothing's wrong and hoping that the whole thing will go away. Sometimes it does and sometimes it gets worse until they're forced to take action. It's very difficult for them to summon up the courage to face trouble head-on, because the very thought of such a brave move makes them go weak at the knees. However, they can surprise themselves when the chips are down, discovering inner qualities of steel and resilience that they never knew they had. I've known Pisceans to face major crises with great fortitude once they've got over the initial shock.

Neptune makes Pisceans very idealistic. They look up to other people and admire them tremendously, and seem to forget that these people are just as human as everyone else. When coupled with their Water element, this means they're extremely sensitive and can easily be hurt by others. They're also sensitive in other ways because they quickly absorb the atmosphere around them, whether it's positive or negative. It may help them to take protective measures if they have to be with people who really disturb them. For instance, they might carry a crystal that they think protects them, or mentally wrap themselves in a cloud of white light.

Many Pisceans have psychic powers or highly developed extra sensory perception. They may experience these abilities through hunches and gut feelings, or they might have prophetic dreams. Some of them are even well-qualified mediums, healers and psychics. As with any other gift, the more they use these talents the better developed they will become. However, sometimes Pisceans can confuse reality with wishful thinking, and they're able to deceive themselves into believing almost anything if they really want to. So they might convince themselves that they have a psychic gift when they don't really, or tell themselves that the nocturnal creakings of their house are noises caused by ghosts and spirits. They must be very careful not to kid themselves, although that's far easier said than done.

Because they belong to the Water element, a Piscean's feelings are never far from the surface. They can be very emotional and often get het-up, leading to tears and depression. Many Pisceans are easily upset, often by things that other people manage to shrug off or distance themselves from. For instance, a Piscean may have to walk out of the room if a very distressing item appears on the television news. They certainly won't be able to look at the pictures and they may not even be able to bear listening to the voice-over. They find it particularly upsetting to hear about cruelty to children and animals.

Pisces is a Mutable sign, which means that members of this sign like change. And, in common with Gemini and Sagittarius, Pisces is a dual sign, which means that Pisceans can be very versatile and flexible. They might always have two books on the go at any one time, have two part-time jobs or even two lovers.

This duality, and the symbol of the fish swimming in

opposite directions, means that Pisceans can be incredibly indecisive. Listen to them weigh up the pros and cons of a problem (assuming that they can bear to even think about it), and you'll hear them switch from one decision to the other and then back again. Even when they're about to take the decision and act on it, they're likely to waver and wonder if they're doing the right thing. They really need someone to talk to, who is practical and matter-of-fact, and who can guide the Piscean in whichever direction is right for them. But they must also be completely trustworthy because sometimes Pisceans can be rather gullible and easily deceived.

So life isn't exactly a bed of roses for Pisceans, but what they lose on the swings they gain on the roundabouts. They may be indecisive and easily led, but they have tremendous reserves of kindness, charity and empathy that they shower on the people they love. And they can also share these with the wider world through their involvement in charities and good works. The world would be a much poorer place without Pisceans and their particular brand of loving kindness.

The Piscean Child

The most important thing to remember with a Piscean child is how sensitive and emotionally fragile they are. It's as though there are no boundaries between them and the rest of the world, so they soak up atmospheres and experiences through the ether. If there's trouble between their parents or some other family problem, the Piscean child will probably react by becoming ill. This won't be a deliberate action but will be a subconscious reaction to what's going on.

Even as a child, a Piscean will have a very powerful imagination that sometimes works overtime, conjuring up all sorts of ghouls and fears. This is the child who may have to be reassured several times each night that the dark shape in their bedroom is only their dressing gown hanging on the back of the door and that there isn't really a werewolf hiding under their bed. Their parents should be sympathetic when comforting their little Piscean, who will be genuinely terrified.

That Piscean imagination can sometimes prompt the child to embellish what they say so it will sound better, and that can often lead to lots of little white lies about what's happened and what they've been up to. The Piscean's parents should try to discourage their child from telling fibs and making up stories in this way, and channel their rich imagination into creative activities instead, such as writing stories, painting pictures and playing imaginative games with their toys. Small Pisceans also learn from an early age to tell fibs in order to get themselves out of tight corners and not be told off. They may also say what they think their parents want to hear rather than tell the truth and risk upsetting them. However, if their parents don't teach the Piscean the difference between fact and fiction, they may be laying the foundations for bigger problems in the future.

Most parents want to believe that their child is extraordinarily gifted in some way or other, and will encourage them to explore and develop their talents. This is especially important for the parents of a Pisces child, because they should encourage their little one's natural gifts without turning them into a chore or a duty. Pisceans, even as children, have a tendency to put themselves down and not believe in themselves, so they need loving parents who will bolster their egos and tell them when they're doing well. They certainly won't flourish if they have a parent or teacher who is always cracking the whip or for whom nothing is ever good enough. This tactic might work for some children (although I've yet to meet one who isn't crushed by it) but it will be a disaster for a sensitive Piscean, who's far more likely to rush to their bedroom and cry their eyes out.

Although Piscean children can be very bright, you might not know it from looking at their school reports. Pisces is the sign of the daydreamer, and if a Piscean child isn't interested in what they're being taught they'll soon tune out and disappear into their own little world. This may be good for their imagination but it won't do much for their academic progress. Thanks to their ruler, Neptune, Pisceans can struggle to concentrate on what they're doing, especially if they're rapidly losing interest in it. This means that Pisceans often leave school as soon as they can purely because they've got so bored and have lost track of what they're being taught. It may not have anything to do with their intellectual or academic abilities, which they may rediscover later in life.

With their kind hearts, Pisceans like having people and animals to look after. So a Piscean child will lavish tremendous amounts of love and tenderness on their pets, with whom they'll have a special affinity. Of course, there will be terrible tears and upsets when the pets die, because the Piscean will be completely distraught, but usually the happy experience of loving the pet will outshine the pain. Pisceans will also adore having some siblings to play with and look after. They'll look up to their older brothers and sisters, and be very protective towards their younger siblings. And if they don't have any brothers or sisters, the Piscean will take great care of their toys. They must have something to love!

Health

Pisceans need to look after themselves. They belong to such a sensitive sign that they're very susceptible to all sorts of ailments and strange complaints. Very often, it's their emotions that can make them ill, rather than specific viruses and bugs that they've been exposed to. For instance, if they get upset or worried about something or someone (and this is a very common occurrence for Pisceans, who usually have some reason for feeling het up), it can soon have a detrimental effect on their health, perhaps triggering a cold or simply making them feel off-colour. And it's the same story if they spend too much time in an unpleasant atmosphere, such as being with people who are very angry or malevolent. The Piscean will end up feeling ill and won't know why.

As I said earlier, Pisceans are very prone to worry. They get this partly from belonging to the Water element and partly from their modern ruler, Neptune. And it doesn't help that they have such active (and sometimes overactive) imaginations, because these make them fantasize about all the terrible things that might happen, which makes them feel worse than ever. "What if . . . ?" is a typical Piscean question, usually uttered in anxious tones. Worry never helped anyone, of course, and it has certainly never solved any problems, but it's particularly problematic for Pisceans who can literally make themselves sick with it.

When a Piscean is ill, they should be very careful about how they treat themselves. Some signs reach for over-the-counter medicines at almost every opportunity, swallowing aspirins as though they were sweets. But that isn't always wise for a Piscean. They have such a sensitive body and such a finely-tuned nervous system that they often react badly to pharmaceutical drugs, even when they're prescribed by their doctor. Allopathic medicines are frequently too strong for a Piscean, with too many side effects. So a Piscean may find that they get on much better with complementary therapies, once they've consulted their doctor to discover what's wrong with them. Homeopathy and healing are especially effective for Pisceans, probably because they both work at an energetic level.

Pisces rules the feet, so it's no surprise that a great many Pisceans have problems finding comfortable shoes. That might be because their feet are an odd shape, such as very long and narrow, or very wide. They may also suffer from physical problems with their feet, such as hammer toes or bunions, which can make it difficult to find shoes that fit. But regardless of whether their feet are beautiful, ugly or problematic, Pisceans need to take care of them. They enjoy regular visits to a good chiropodist or podiatrist, and consider pedicures in beauty salons to be the height of luxury. If they're interested in complementary therapies they could get a lot from reflexology because it's practised on the feet.

It can be hard for a Piscean to unwind at times, especially when they're worried about something, so a relaxation technique will be very valuable. They might like to try yoga, meditation or creative visualization. They can also benefit from working with crystals or essential oils. Something else that is very therapeutic for a Piscean is being in or near water. That can mean anything from relaxing in a warm, scented bath to walking by a river or swimming in the sea. Walking barefoot along the seashore is also excellent for a Piscean, especially if they can take their time and amble along.

A Piscean doesn't always have as much stamina as they'd like, and they certainly need to make sure they get plenty of rest. They also appreciate having time to themselves because it enables them to recuperate and recharge their batteries. Ideally, they should set aside at least a few minutes every day when they're left completely undisturbed.

With such a delicate metabolism, it's important that a Piscean chooses their food and drink carefully. Organic food, if they can afford it, may make quite a difference to their general health and they may also benefit from a vegetarian or semi-vegetarian diet. They could easily be allergic to certain foods or find that too much alcohol makes them feel lousy. Cigarettes don't do them much good, either. Incidentally, it's very easy for Pisceans to get addicted to something, whether it's relatively harmless or highly dangerous, so they must be very wary of getting hooked on something that they then can't give up. Even being addicted to chocolate biscuits will eventually cause them health problems.

Money

Money and Pisceans don't always go together. It isn't that Pisceans don't need money, because of course they do. And it isn't that they hate it, either. It's simply that they aren't always very good at handling it, and nor are they interested in acquiring it for its own sake. Mind you, some Pisceans end up being incredibly rich, such as Rupert Murdoch and Meyer Amschel Rothschild, who founded the banking dynasty that bears his name. Others never seem to have two pennies to rub together.

One reason why many Pisceans never seem to have much money is because they're so good at giving it away. Their innate generosity, kind hearts, compassion and tendency to accumulate lame ducks means they often dip into their bank accounts to help people out. Some of them believe that charity begins at home and always bail out their nearest and dearest when times are hard. Others prefer to donate to local, national or international good causes, usually without making a big song and dance about it. They also find it very difficult to pass someone in the street who's holding a collecting tin without putting some money in it. It seems so rude to ignore them, somehow!

Another reason for the Piscean lack of money is that they sometimes aren't very good at managing it effectively. Some of them have to nerve themselves to open their bank statements, and have a similar aversion to credit card statements. They just hope for the best and trust that everything will be all right. This ostrich-like tendency to stick their head in the sand is even more pronounced when they know they're broke because then they really dislike dealing with harsh reality. Sometimes, this can get them into real financial trouble if they choose to ignore the facts or refuse to open warning letters from their bank or credit card company.

It's a rare Piscean who values money for its own sake. They can't see the point in being like Scrooge and hoarding their cash in a miserly fashion. They find something distasteful in the very idea, especially when they only need to switch on the television news to hear about people who are struggling to survive. However, this doesn't mean that Pisceans don't like shopping and spending money! They enjoy looking good and they have a weakness for beautiful objects.

When a Piscean has some spare money and is looking around for ways to invest it, they should be very careful. For a start, they might leave themselves open to someone who wants to take advantage of them, perhaps by persuading them to hand over all their money which this person can then invest on their behalf (or so they say). A Piscean can be equally vulnerable when dealing with a professional financial adviser or bank, because they have a tendency to believe what they're told without checking the facts themselves and they're far too polite to ask awkward questions. So they may take advice that turns out to be wrong for their particular situation, and they'll only find out when it's too late. They should also be careful of any complicated financial arrangements that leave plenty of scope for mistakes, oversights and misunderstandings.

When a Piscean does want to invest their money, they should keep it simple. Ideally, they should look for solid savings schemes that offer them security, even if they don't have massive rates of interest. They will also want to think carefully about which stocks and shares they buy because, like Aquarians, they will have ethical considerations and won't want to put their money into anything they disapprove of. They wouldn't be able to live with themselves if they did.

Career

A Piscean should forget about getting involved in any dog-eat-dog profession. They're unlikely to enjoy it because it simply isn't in their nature to be ruthlessly ambitious. They'll feel like a fish out of water if they're thrown into a cut-throat profession or job, which is bad news because they belong to the sign of the Fish! However, whichever way they choose to earn their living, they will need plenty of encouragement and praise from the people around them. Most Pisceans have very low self-esteem and don't believe they're capable of half the things they could do if they tried. As a result, many members of this sign never reach their full potential because they hold themselves back through their lack of confidence and tendency to think that everyone else is so much more talented than they are. For instance, they may have a lot more artistic ability than they ever give themselves credit for.

Ideally, a Piscean needs a career that enables them to express their tremendous compassion and ability to care for other people. They may think of it more as a vocation than a career. Anything that puts them in touch with the public is good, and it's even better if they're working in the medical profession or in an institution. For instance, a Piscean would make a wonderful nurse or doctor, full of compassion and empathy for their patients. They would also enjoy being of service to others, which is a characteristic they get through their opposite sign of Virgo. But no matter how long the Piscean works in medicine, they will never stop being affected by the sad cases they come across. As well as hospitals, you will also find plenty of Pisceans working in prisons, care homes and other institutions. They can also be attracted to work that is carried on behind the scenes or which is secret in some way.

Pisceans can also be drawn to complementary therapies, especially the ones that are generally considered to be rather wacky by people who don't know about them. For instance, a Piscean might enjoy working with crystals, colour therapy, sound healing or auras.

Both Jupiter, which is Pisces' traditional planetary ruler, and Neptune, which is the sign's modern ruler, have strong connections with religion and spirituality, so it's no surprise that many Pisceans are drawn to them in their careers. They might enter the Church and work as a minister or priest, and some of them may prefer to withdraw from the world and live as a nun or monk in an enclosed order. Charity or voluntary work can also appeal.

Jupiter can inspire Pisceans to make a career in the travel business. My Piscean mother used to work for a shipping line (very Piscean!) before she was married and had the enviable task of being sent on cruises to make sure they were up to scratch. Other Pisceans might work in travel agencies or become travel guides in holiday destinations.

Neptune, on the other hand, gives Pisceans a longing for glamour and sophistication. One way for them to get this, at least in theory, is to work in the film business. Cameras are also ruled by Neptune, so they might enjoy working as cinematographers. Alternatively, they could become film directors, in common with their fellow Pisceans Vincente Minnelli, Robert Altman, Ron Howard, Victor Fleming, Spike Lee and Bernardo Bertolucci. Or perhaps they'd prefer to appear in front of the camera, like Elizabeth Taylor, Bruce

Willis, Sharon Stone, Glenn Close, Rob Lowe, Joanne Woodward, Miranda Richardson and Billy Crystal.

Other Neptune-related professions that might appeal to a Piscean include fashion (Joseph Ettedgui, Gloria Vanderbilt and André Courrèges are all Pisceans), perfumes and the beauty business in general.

Whatever job a Piscean has, it's important that they work with people they like and admire. They'll be very unhappy if they work with people who are unpleasant or unsympathetic, or who dump most of their work load on the Piscean's shoulders. They really need to feel that they belong to one big, happy family.

Love and Friendships
Pisceans are the great romantics of the zodiac. Even the men. They can't help it, they were just made that way. They have huge hearts and a tremendous capacity for love, which really does make their world go round. However, love doesn't always work out well for them.

The trouble is that Pisceans are highly idealistic. If they love someone they think the very best of them and turn a blind eye to their faults and flaws. For the Piscean, it's as though their beloved is perfect and they don't want to know anything to the contrary. But, of course, no one is perfect, which means the Piscean is letting themselves in for a major disappointment when they finally realize that their beloved isn't a saint in human form after all. And their loved one's fall from grace will seem like a huge betrayal because the Piscean has invested so much energy and effort in putting them on a pedestal for so long. This tendency to ignore the facts also means that the Piscean may refuse to notice any warning signs which are telling them that their relationship is in trouble. Finally, when it's too late to save the relationship, they'll wake up to the fact that something is wrong. And once again, the whole experience will feel like a terrible betrayal.

But don't get the impressions that Pisceans are always the wronged party when a relationship turns sour. Sometimes, they're the reason for the problems, even if they refuse to admit it. That might be because they will never accept that there's anything wrong, or that they've done something to annoy their partner. But it can be a lot more involved than that. With their love of fantasy, some Pisceans enjoy leading double lives, so they might be involved in a committed relationship yet be conducting another liaison on the side. And I'm not just talking about the odd fling, either. Some Pisceans get heavily embroiled in their clandestine relationship, even to the point of running two households, with neither of them knowing about the other. They thrive on the duplicity and the secrecy involved.

It's very important for a Piscean to be choosy about who they spend their time with because they're so easily influenced by other people. Pisceans are like psychic sponges so they can feel quite ill if they have to spend too long with people they don't like or whose attitude to life is in sharp contrast to their own. This is because the Piscean will have absorbed part of the other person's energy and it may not do them much good!

Even so, Pisceans always like to think the best of people until proved wrong. Even then, they'll give them the benefit of the doubt for as long as possible. Pisceans believe that finding fault with others somehow diminishes themselves in the process. Besides, they much prefer to tell themselves that everything in the garden is lovely, even when it's not.

Pisceans enjoy having a partner around, and they'll do whatever they can to make their other half happy and contented. Sometimes, this means putting their own needs second. The Piscean won't mind doing this, although in the end it may lead to resentment in them and an ingrained selfishness in the other person. Pisceans really should avoid situations in which they feel martyred and misunderstood, whether or not such emotions are justified.

When it comes to friendships, Pisceans make good friends. Just as they do with their partners, they'll often put their friends on lofty pedestals and expect the very best of them. Pisceans definitely have a tendency to hero-worship their friends, which is very nice if you happen to be the lucky recipient of their adoration. However, Pisceans can irritate their friends because of their reluctance to say what they think, their dithering and lack of organization, and their habit of cancelling arrangements at the last moment. Yet the rewards of friendship with a Piscean definitely outweigh the disadvantages.

Family Relationships

Family is very important to Pisceans. They are usually close to their families, and especially to their siblings. They find it very comforting to be with people that they've known for most, if not all, of their lives. It gives them a strong sense of belonging, too, especially if they can all talk about the past and share some cherished memories.

A Piscean would be very lucky if all their relatives were loveable and likeable, but they'll do their best to tolerate the ones they don't much care for. Quite apart from not wanting to rock the boat, they will feel sorry for these unpopular members of the family, especially if they suspect that no one gets on particularly well with them. But the Piscean will lavish a lot of love on their favourite members of the family and will find many ways to let them know that the Piscean thinks they're special. And, in true Piscean style, they'll idealize these people and only see their good points.

When a Piscean becomes a parent, their first reaction will be fear. How can they possibly look after such a vulnerable little baby? They haven't a clue what to do! No one told them it was going to be like this! They will happily listen to any advice they're given, even if they don't take it, but will soon feel slightly resentful if any doting grandparents start to muscle in and take charge. Although the Piscean will be grateful in some ways, they'll be angry and jealous in others, and then will feel wretchedly guilty about what they see as their unkind reaction.

As parents, Pisceans learn to rely on their instincts. These tell them when their children need help, are in trouble or are ill, often before the children themselves say a word. They'll do anything in their power to protect and care for their children, but often they're so worried about being unfair or horrid that they'll find it almost impossible to administer any discipline. They might tell their children off about something one day, but they'll let them do the same thing without comment the next, so in the end the children don't know where they stand. The Piscean parent will also go to great lengths to protect their children from harsh reality, little realizing that their children might appreciate being given the facts rather than a sanitized or highly sentimental version of what's happening.

Piscean parents tend to project their own needs and emotions on to their children, so they treat their offspring as though they're miniature versions of themselves. But, of course, they aren't, which can be irritating for the children who feel their individuality is being taken away from them. The Piscean will look back to their own childhood and try to reproduce it if it was happy (and even if it wasn't, they won't dare to admit it to themselves), and avoid any factors that caused them problems. So if they loved having piano lessons as a child, they'll insist that their child should learn to play the piano too, even if they'd much rather be part of their school's cricket team. And if they hated sports as a child, they'll convince themselves that their child hates them too, even when they don't. All this can be very annoying for a Piscean's children.

But a Piscean parent has a great deal to offer, too, including an all-encompassing love and compassion that makes their children feel safe and cherished. For instance, they'll keep all the presents that their children give them, as well as all the cards and letters they write, and will fill their home with pictures of their beloved offspring. They also have a marvellous imagination, which really comes to life whenever they tell their children bedtime stories or play games with them.

Creativity and Potential

Any Piscean who is looking for new ways to express their talents should have plenty of scope. That's because Pisceans have a great many gifts and abilities, even if they aren't aware of them. With Pisceans, it's a case of them not knowing what they can do until they try, and then being pleasantly surprised.

If the Piscean is searching for a new hobby or form of exercise, swimming is something that might appeal. Even though this is the sign of the Fish, I've known Pisceans who can barely keep afloat in water, let alone swim, so regular swimming lessons would be a good way for them to learn and also give them an efficient way of keeping fit.

Dance is another Piscean activity, whether they're doing the dancing or watching someone else. Pisces rules the feet, so it makes sense that members of this sign should enjoy dancing. Some famous dancers have been born under this sign, including Rudolf Nureyev and Nijinsky.

It's certainly very important for a Piscean to do something that allows them to express themselves, especially if their job doesn't offer them any creative outlet, otherwise they'll feel stifled and unfulfilled. They might be interested in picking up a paintbrush or pencil and seeing how artistic they are, even if they only ever do it as a hobby. However, they will need a good teacher who can encourage them and stop them telling themselves that they're hopeless even before they've started.

Something else that appeals to many Pisceans is poetry. In fact, this is the sign of poetry, and famous Piscean poets include W. H. Auden, Elizabeth Barrett Browning, Edna St Vincent Millay, Henry Longfellow and Vita Sackville-West. Or perhaps they would prefer to write prose, whether it's in the form of a diary, articles for their local paper or a novel. If so, they'll be following in some notable footsteps, including those of Jack Kerouac, Henrik Ibsen, Mickey Spillane, Cyrano de Bergerac, Samuel Pepys, Stephen Spender and Anthony Burgess.

Music is also strongly Piscean, thanks to Neptune. If the Piscean doesn't think they can write music (although they won't know until they've given it a try), they could learn to play a musical instrument instead, especially if they're picking up the rudimentary skills they learned at school. Or they could learn to sing. They have many options and many talented Pisceans to inspire them, including George Harrison, Lou

Reed, Dame Kiri Te Kanawa, Harry Belafonte, Frederic Chopin, Wilson Pickett, Brian Jones and Antonio Vivaldi.

Alternatively, the Piscean could connect with the mystical and spiritual part of their soul. They might do this by developing their psychic abilities, perhaps by teaching themselves how to read the runes, the tarot or any other form of divination that appeals to them. Something else that could appeal is learning to heal people, whether they do it simply with their hands or with the help of something like crystals, acupuncture or aromatherapy. Their powerful intuition will stand them in good stead and they might have some strange experiences that can't be dismissed as coincidence. In fact, they might discover a fantastic new talent that could earn them some pin money or might even become their new career.

Many Pisceans experience a powerful need for more spirituality or religion in their lives, whether they find it through a recognized authority or as a result of their own research and contemplation. There are plenty of Piscean spiritual teachers whose insights might help them, including Meher Baba, Edgar Cayce and Rudolf Steiner. And they may also enjoy going on spiritual retreats where the emphasis is on silence and meditation. The Piscean will get a tremendous amount from activities like these but will quickly become disillusioned if politics, rivalry, jealousies or other ordinary human frailties upset the atmosphere or reveal that their revered teacher or spiritual leader has feet of clay after all.

Holidays
Pisceans are so sensitive to atmospheres that they need to choose their holiday destinations very carefully. They should try to avoid political trouble spots or places that are heaving with fellow holiday-makers because their delicate nerves will soon become jangled and they'll start longing to go home again. They may also be unhappy in places that have a history of violence or bloodshed, because they'll pick up the vibrations and could feel quite unsettled as a result.

Pisceans adore being near water, whether it's a lake or

ocean, and find it very relaxing just to listen to the sound of the waves while gazing into space. The clear blue waters of a tropical island would be paradise for them, because they would enjoy swimming and also lying on the beach relaxing. However, Pisceans should avoid anywhere that's too hot and humid because they'll find it hard to cope and will soon start to wilt. Although they enjoy being in the sunshine, there's only so much of it that they can take before they start to feel ill. Something else they'll enjoy is going on a cruise, provided that the water isn't too choppy because some Pisceans aren't good sailors. They'll especially enjoy going on up-market cruises that give lectures about the history and culture of the ports they'll be visiting. Pisceans love soaking up the local atmosphere and their romantic souls thrill when they visit ancient civilizations and places that have played a huge role in world culture.

This is a very sophisticated sign and Pisceans like to continue to be sophisticated when they're on holiday. This means they aren't comfortable if they've got to rough it. The idea of a camping holiday is enough to make them break out in a rash, unless they're staying in a very superior tent with all mod cons. They certainly don't like the idea of washing in a bucket and having to disappear behind the nearest (or perhaps furthest) tree when they need to go to the loo. They'd rather stay at home! So they're happiest when they're staying somewhere that offers plenty of luxury, especially if it has a distinctive atmosphere as well, such as a beautiful old manor house, a castle (although they'll worry about being visited by ghosts in the middle of the night), a pretty country cottage or a sumptuous Art Deco hotel. However, the Piscean will be very disturbed if there's a marked contrast between their level of comfort and that of the locals. It will really upset them and might even ruin their holiday if the difference between the haves and the have-nots is too pronounced.

Pisceans are quite happy to go far afield, thanks to the influence of their traditional ruler, Jupiter. In fact, several explorers and intrepid travellers have been born under this sign, including Matthew Flinders, Robin Knox-Johnstone, Sir

Richard Burton, Sir Ranulph Fiennes and Yuri Gagarin. They particularly enjoy visiting countries with a spiritual, religious or mystical atmosphere or connection. Something else that might appeal nearer to home is a meditation or spiritual retreat, in which they can catch their breath, get in touch with their inner selves and let the rest of the world carry on without them for a short while.

Wherever a Piscean goes on holiday they need to take care with the food they eat and the liquids they drink. Many Pisceans have rather sensitive stomachs, thanks to the influence of their opposite sign of Virgo, so they benefit from taking a mini first aid kit with them whenever they go away. Rich foods and drink don't suit them, so they must restrict their intake of these even when they're sorely tempted to over-indulge. Otherwise, they know what the result will be!

Pisceans are very kind-hearted so they will always send postcards home to their loved ones. They wouldn't be happy if they didn't because the resulting guilt would cast a dampener over their holiday. They also enjoy looking for souvenirs to take home to their favourite people, although these are often slightly sentimental or kitsch. But at least they prove once again (as if it were needed) that the Piscean's heart is in the right place.

Home

Pisces is one of the most gentle signs of the zodiac and a Piscean's home always reflects this. It's comfortable, relaxing and peaceful, with soothing colours, attractive fabrics and thick carpets. Above all, it has a welcoming, inclusive atmosphere that quickly makes everyone feel at home even if they've never been there before. In fact, a Piscean home feels like a refuge from a more jangled world, a place where you can heave a sigh of relief, sit back and take things easy.

If the Piscean has a garden it will feel like an oasis, with shady nooks and fragrant flowers. There will be plenty of edible plants, too, such as fruit trees, vegetables and herbs, and since many Pisceans are in favour of the organic movement they won't use any pesticides in their gardens so the air will be full of the buzzing of bees and the singing of birds. Very often, the Piscean will have a pond as well, which they'll make as decorative and attractive as possible. It will be full of wildlife, including frogs and fish, and will be the Piscean's pride and joy.

Don't be surprised if you're asked to remove your shoes when you visit a Piscean's home. It may be for religious reasons, because they've got expensive, pale carpets that could get dirty or simply because they prefer their visitors to leave their shoes at the door. Many Pisceans walk around their homes barefoot, even in winter, because they hate to feel that their feet are being restricted.

Very often a pet is a cherished member of the household. Pisceans have a particularly soft spot for dogs, and will probably spoil their own dogs rotten, but they also like having cats around. The pet will be treated like royalty and indulged at every opportunity. And it's highly likely that it will be a rescue animal, whether it's come from a shelter or it's a stray that has cleverly adopted the Piscean. When I was growing up we had a dog and later a cat, both of which had been rescued by my Piscean mother who couldn't bear to think of them being without a home.

If you visit the Piscean's bathroom you may be struck by the number of different lotions, potions, oils, soaps, shampoos, scents and creams they manage to cram in there. It will be like a miniature beauty salon, whether it belongs to a man or a woman.

Wherever you look in a Piscean's house there will be something interesting on show. They might have lots of beautiful paintings and sculptures (although they'll be too modest to display any of their own work), and there are bound to be plenty of photographs too of family and friends. Very often a Piscean will make an informal display of their photos, perhaps by pinning them on a board, so they can change them around at will. Close members of the family will probably be embarrassed to see pictures of themselves at the age of two, or wearing peculiar outfits in their teens.

There could be a musical instrument on display as well, and very often it's a piano. The Piscean will also have a good collection of CDs or records that they'll enjoy listening to, often through headphones so they don't annoy the neighbours. (Pisceans can be very considerate.) There will be plenty of videos and DVDs too, especially of sentimental and weepie old films that the Piscean loves. And you might also see various objects with religious or spiritual connections, such as a Buddha sitting on a shelf or the statue of a Hindu god on the landing.

Look out for lots of books in the house, too, although they'll be arranged in a rather higgledy-piggledy manner. In fact, the entire Piscean home may look as though a bomb has hit it, with every available surface covered with papers, magazines, books, vases, ornaments and pairs of spectacles that the Piscean frequently mislays. They don't have the need for clutter in the same way as Cancerians, it's simply that they aren't very good at tidying up after themselves. Whenever they do have a blitz on the mess, they'll spend the next few weeks trying to remember where they put everything.

Clothes and Image

Pisceans like to look good whenever they get the chance. This is the sign of fashion, after all, so most Pisceans are fascinated by clothes. Both sexes enjoy looking at the latest fashions in glossy magazines. And even if they don't completely emulate the style they see there they will still want to look vaguely fashionable.

As well as being the sign of fashion, Pisces is also the sign of romance, and many Pisceans like to create a romantic look for themselves. Piscean women look fantastic in floaty, feminine dresses and skirts, especially if they're made from filmy fabrics such as chiffon and georgette. Piscean men enjoy looking like soulful, romantic poets, in floppy shirts and velvet trousers. The colours that suit them best are sea greens, mauves and purples.

Many Pisceans are drawn to the hippie or boho look,

whether it's in fashion or not. They love looking ethnic and draping themselves in vintage clothes, but they should be careful about this because sometimes it can be rather ageing, especially if they are old enough to have worn hippie clothes when they first became fashionable in the 1960s.

Both sexes are very particular about the types of fabric they wear. Pisceans don't like to wear many synthetic fabrics, unless they're really beautiful and look like the real thing, because they don't feel right. Instead, they prefer silks, satins, cottons, linens, wool, velvet and cashmere. One thing they will draw the line at is real fur. The very thought of it makes them feel sick, and they may even be unhappy about wearing fake fur because they don't want anyone to think that they might be wearing the real thing. If a Piscean woman has inherited a fur coat from her mother or some other relative, she'll fret about what to do with it because she certainly won't want it in the house. The very idea!

Pisceans really come into their own when they get dressed up for an evening out. Piscean women look absolutely fantastic in sophisticated evening dresses and the men look great in dinner jackets. They also love the sense of occasion that comes from getting all glammed up, and will spend hours getting ready and having their hair done. However, they must make sure that all the little details have been taken care of ahead of time, otherwise they may ruin the whole look by wearing the wrong shoes, and the Piscean woman may discover she doesn't have a suitable evening bag or dressy coat.

Actually, even when they aren't going out for a night on the tiles it can be horribly easy for a Piscean to spoil the image they've worked so hard to create by getting something wrong. A Piscean man might have spilled something on his tie, only noticing when it's too late to do anything about it, and a Piscean woman could wear the wrong coloured tights or not notice that there's a button missing from her blouse.

One thing that Pisceans always pay a lot of attention to is their shoes. Some of them have no problems in buying shoes that fit them, so can indulge their love of footwear to the hilt.

They'll have an enviable collection of shoes, boots and sandals, and will always be acquiring new ones because they simply can't resist them. But other Pisceans have tremendous difficulty in buying shoes that fit, so they will have an almost equally big collection of footwear that they've bought in the vain hope that it will end up being comfortable. As a result, they'll leave all those expensive shoes in the wardrobe and have to rely on a couple of pairs of trusty shoes that do fit, regardless of what they look like. Ill-fitting shoes have even been known to cause accidents. I know a Piscean woman who fell over in the street and broke her upper arm because her shoes were too loose and she tripped over them. So next time you see a Piscean wearing a pair of trainers with a smart outfit, you'll realize that they either forget to change out of them or they're the only thing the Piscean can comfortably wear.

Famous Pisceans
Sidney Poitier (20 February 1927); Jilly Cooper (21 February 1937); George Washington (22 February 1732); Samuel Pepys (23 February 1633); Alain Prost (24 February 1955); George Harrison (25 February 1943); Johnny Cash (26 February 1932); Elizabeth Taylor (27 February 1932); Stephen Spender (28 February 1909); Gioacchino Rossini (29 February 1792); David Niven (1 March 1910); Mikhail Gorbachev (2 March 1931); Alexander Graham Bell (3 March 1847); Antonio Vivaldi (4 March 1678); Rex Harrison (5 March 1908); Dame Kiri Te Kanawa (6 March 1944); Piet Mondrian (7 March 1872); Cyd Charisse (8 March 1921); Yuri Gagarin (9 March 1934); Sharon Stone (10 March 1958); Rupert Murdoch (11 March 1931); Liza Minnelli (12 March 1946); Neil Sedaka (13 March 1939); Albert Einstein (14 March 1879); Ry Cooder (15 March 1947); Bernardo Bertolucci (16 March 1941); Nat King Cole (17 March 1919); Edgar Cayce (18 March 1877); Glenn Close (19 March 1947); Henrik Ibsen (20 March 1828).

The Top Ten Piscean Characteristics
Compassionate; Kind; Loving; Sensitive; Easily discouraged; Deceptive; Intuitive; Imaginative; Indecisive; Artistic.

Are You A Typical Piscean?
Try this quiz on the Pisceans you know to find out whether they're typical members of their sign.

   1 Do you struggle to reach decisions?

2 Does your imagination ever run riot?

3 Do you wish you could be more tidy and organized?

4 Do you worry about your loved ones?

5 Are you sensitive to difficult atmospheres?

6 Do you have a low opinion of yourself?

7 Do you sometimes wish you could run away from everything?

8 Are you anguished when you think you've hurt someone's feelings?

9 Do you associate certain pieces of music or smells with certain people or events in your life?

10 Do you procrastinate over things that scare you?

Score

Score one point for every "no" and zero points for every "yes".

0–3 You couldn't be more Piscean if you tried. Sensitive, highly-strung and emotional, sometimes the world seems too harsh for you. You aren't as confident as you pretend and often doubt your abilities even when other people have faith in you.

4–6 You have a strong Piscean streak but it's tempered by the influence of other signs. Read the Top Ten Characteristics of the other signs to see which ones ring a bell with you.

7–10 Although you were born under the sign of Pisces you don't have many Piscean characteristics. Look through the Top Ten Characteristics of Aquarius and Aries to see if either of these sounds more like you.